MAKING HISTORY

MAKING HISTORY

A PERSONAL APPROACH TO MODERN AMERICAN HISTORY

Revised Second Edition

By BRUCE OLAV SOLHEIM
CITRUS COLLEGE
ILLUSTRATIONS BY GARY DUMM

cognella® | ACADEMIC PUBLISHING

Bassim Hamadeh, CEO and Publisher
Kassie Graves, Director of Acquisitions and Sales
Jamie Giganti, Senior Managing Editor
Miguel Macias, Senior Graphic Designer
David Miano, Acquisitions Editor
Alexa Lucido, Licensing Associate
Abbey Hastings, Associate Production Editor

Cover image copyright © Depositphotos/maxximmm1.

Printed in the United States of America.

ISBN: 978-1-5165-2918-6 (pbk) / 978-1-5165-2919-3 (br)

CONTENTS

PREFACE

I am a frustrated comic book artist at heart. I have collected, read, and admired comics since I was a young boy. Comic books helped me learn to read and got me through my lonely and awkward teen years, and the artwork fueled my imagination. I created a few self-made comic books in the 1970s, and then in 1982, I created a sci-fi comedy comic strip called *Snark*. It was published in *The Technocrat*, the school newspaper at Montana Tech in Butte, Montana. For this second edition of *Making History*, I returned to my comic book roots. This book was inspired by and is dedicated to comic book legend, Harvey Pekar. Harvey published and wrote *American Splendor* and established a new genre of adult comic books—autobiographical, literary, down to earth, and quotidian in their sensibilities. As Harvey wrote: "Ordinary life is pretty complex stuff."

In addition to adding a new first chapter on Reconstruction and updating the final chapter to include recent American history, I decided to add comic book pages for each chapter based on my personal history. As I was looking through old issues of *American Splendor* gaining inspiration, I noticed the high quality of the artwork. There was Robert Crumb, of course, probably the most celebrated underground comic book artist, but there was another remarkable artist whose work caught my eye—Gary Dumm. I contacted Gary, and after he had a chance to read the first edition of *Making History*, he agreed to illustrate the second edition.

So, dear reader, what you have before you is a modern American history anti-textbook with high-quality comic book illustrations from a well-known, respected, and talented artist who has been drawing comics since the 1960s and was Harvey Pekar's friend and key collaborator on the iconic *American Splendor* comic book. Gary and I have created comic book pages for each chapter because I believe these comic book words and pictures better convey the personal side of history, which, in my opinion, is where history is made. It is my hope that this collaborative effort will spawn a new genre of history anti-textbooks that will help young students understand the journey of the American people, contemplate and visualize their own journey, and inspire them to make history themselves.

PROLOGUE

HISTORY IS NOT JUST SOMETHING THAT HAPPENS, it is something that you make happen. History begins and ends with the individual. When our standard history books tell us that America went to war, America did not go to war—it was individual Americans who went to war. When these same sacred tomes tell us that the United States suffered through an economic depression, the United States did not suffer—individual American citizens suffered. We pride ourselves on being rugged individualists, people who are not afraid to take chances, to be bold in their actions, thoughts, and deeds, yet we write history as if it was a dry, lifeless corporate report.

I have read that we have been looking for consensus in telling the American story. We used to have a national perspective that focused on the nation-state and the presidents and the most prominent American figures in history. Ethnic minorities were excluded, as well as workers, women, gays, lesbians, teachers, immigrants, among many others. There was one historical voice and it was the privileged white male. The new social history brought many different voices into the mix and has dramatically altered the historiographical landscape. Yet, there is the yearning for the consensus narrative, the one ring that binds them all to borrow from J.R.R. Tolkien's *Lord of the Rings*. I believe that the one ring is the individual—the individual approach to history.

I know that my young students want excitement and what is more exciting than history? History is life. I will infuse my own personal history and stories into this book as we go through history in America since 1877. It is a personal approach because history is personal.

I want my students to feel empowered to make history, to take part, to truly know what it is to be free. I challenge my students on the first day of class to embark on a voyage of discovery by asking them: Who are you and why are you here? My 25-year journey as a history teacher has brought me here and I am dedicated, dear reader, to bring you something completely different that will stand other textbooks on their heads. *Making History* is essentially an anti-textbook. Are you ready to make history?

I want to thank those who taught, inspired, and empowered me: Dr. Sidney T. Mathews, Dr. Bruce Haulman, David Willson, my colleague Dr. David Lewis, my father Asbjørn Solheim, my mother Olaug Strand, my girl Ginger, Dr. Bernard Sternsher, Dr. Gary Hess, Colonel William V. Wenger, US Army (retired), my children, the rest of my family, my friends, and all of my students. This is a book I did not intend to write. At this point in my teaching career I had resigned myself to assigning standard, uninspiring American history textbooks and simply adding my own unique interpretations and personal approach to teaching history in the classroom. Students over the years have complained of boring, tedious, tiresome textbooks, high prices, and irrelevant narratives that seem so distant from real life. These books are bland, politically correct, spiritless, and clones of one another. Learned historians wrote them, or were purported to have written them, but there is nothing of them in those textbooks. It was time for a change. *Making History* is a departure from the traditional textbook. Consider a book where *The Education of Henry Adams* meets *On the Road*.

The journey begins.

STATES RIGHTS'

BY DR. BRUCE OLAV SOLHEIM WITH ART BY GARY DUMM

MY MENTOR, DR. SIDNEY T. MATHEWS...

...TAUGHT HISTORY AT CAMPBELL UNIVERSITY, FT. BRAGG, N.C. A GREAT STORY-TELLER, HE LOOKED LIKE COL. SANDERS. AS A COMBAT HISTORIAN, HE CO-WROTE THE U.S. ARMY'S HISTORY OF THE ITALIAN CAMPAIGN IN WORLD WAR II. HE MET AND INTERVIEWED FAMOUS GENERALS LIKE PATTON, CLARK, ALEXANDER, AND MONTGOMERY.

HIS MOST PRIZED POSSESSION WAS A PHOTO OF GENERAL PATTON...

...PEEING IN THE RHINE RIVER IN GERMANY.

IN CLASS IN 1984, DR. MATHEWS, IN HIS THICK SOUTHERN DRAWL, ASKED US IF WE KNEW WHY WE FOUGHT THE CIVIL WAR.

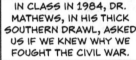

...TO END SLAVERY, SIR.

I SPOKE UP QUICKLY...

I THEN SAT DOWN SATISFIED THAT MY ANSWER WAS CORRECT. HE LOOKED AT ME AND SHOOK HIS HEAD.

WRONG. STATES' RIGHTS.

HUH? WHAT WAS STATES' RIGHTS? WHAT ABOUT HONEST ABE AND THE EMANCIPATION PROCLAMATION?

YES, I SAID FREE.

LINCOLN

STATES' RIGHTS WAS A STICKING POINT BACK IN THE 1780S. SOUTHERN STATES WANTED TO PRESERVE INDIVIDUAL RIGHTS (EXCEPT FOR SLAVES), SO THEY WERE AGAINST A STRONG FEDERAL GOVERNMENT. AS AMERICA EXPANDED WEST, CONFLICT ERUPTED BETWEEN PRO- AND ANTI-SLAVERY FORCES.

THE SOUTH ARGUED FOR STATES' RIGHTS IN ORDER TO RETAIN SLAVERY.

NEW STATES OUT WEST COULD TIP THE BALANCE EITHER WAY. HISTORY IS ALL ABOUT PERSPECTIVE—MINE WAS NORTHERN, AND DR. MATHEWS' WAS SOUTHERN. SO, DID NEARLY 700,000 AMERICANS DIE IN THE CIVIL WAR, BLACK AND WHITE, STRICTLY OVER THE ISSUE OF STATES' RIGHTS? NO. SLAVERY WAS AT THE HEART OF THE WAR AND IS THE GREAT EVIL IN AMERICAN HISTORY.

THE SCARS LEFT ON AMERICA'S PSYCHE FROM IT ARE PAINFUL AND ENDURING.

CHAPTER ONE

RECONSTRUCTION

OBJECTIVES

1. What was Reconstruction?
2. What was the impact of slavery?
3. What was the legal basis of Reconstruction?
4. Did Reconstruction fail?

PERSONAL HISTORY

After basic training at Lackland Air Force Base in Texas, my brother Alf was sent to radio school at Keesler Air Force Base in Biloxi, Mississippi. It was at Keesler where my brother became friends with a black airman from Detroit. One day they were downtown and decided to get haircuts. They walked into a barber shop, and all of the white patrons and the barbers froze in silence. Finally, one of the barbers said to my brother: "We can cut your hair, son, but the nigger has to go." That was my brother's first personal encounter with overt racism. That was in 1967. I remember getting angry when my brother told me the story. How could people act like that? My parents were big supporters of Dr. Martin Luther King, Jr., and the Civil Rights movement. A few years later, I decided that I was going to invite one of my friends from my biology class to come over after school. He was one of the few black kids at my school. We planned to shoot baskets, watch TV, and look at my baseball card and comic book collection. I told my mom, and she was happy that I was making new friends. He told me that his mom would bring him over. I came home from school and waited and waited, but he never showed up. I was disappointed. Had I insulted him? Had his parents said no? Was it too uncomfortable for him? Did he forget? I saw him at school, but since he did not bring it up, I did not ask him. I still wonder what happened.

INTRODUCTION

History is all about individual perspective, bias, and interpretation. First, we see the world around us. Because our view is limited by our experiences, education, travel, and many other factors, our view is like looking through a knothole in a fence. The more we broaden our perspective through education and experience, the bigger the knothole gets. Next, we judge and classify what we see. We do this by defining by opposites, hot and cold, dark and light, good and evil. These judgments become our biases. These biases narrowly frame our view. We try hard not to be biased, but biases are ingrained in us as we grow up and are socialized. Then, we spend our whole lives trying to learn the gray area between black and white. Finally, we construct our own realities and interpret the world around us. Each one of us sees a different reality. No two people are exactly the same. The study of history becomes even more challenging, because we all see the world differently. Arguments and disagreements can arise, and interpretations can change over time. As our perspective changes, our history changes. It is all a very individual process that has collective consequences.

This first chapter is dedicated to the Reconstruction era in America and the Civil War preceding it. It is always necessary to take one step back and then two steps forward when studying the past. From 1865 to 1877, Americans tried to change their perspective on the issue of slavery and attempted to heal from slavery's impact. In spite of that undertaking long ago, the legacy of the institution of slavery continues to haunt Americans like remnants of a terrible nightmare. We cannot progress as a people if we let the nightmare consume us or if we ignore its presence. Reconstruction was a noble effort to live up to the words of the Declaration of Independence: "We hold these truths to be self-evident, that all men are created equal, that they are endowed by their Creator with certain unalienable Rights, that among these are Life, Liberty and the pursuit of Happiness." What happened to that noble effort? We must be honest with ourselves, because racial divisions are still strong in America today. For instance, look at the debate over immigration or the Black Lives Matter movement. A Pew Research Center poll in 2015 showed that 59 percent of Americans believe that changes are needed to give African Americans equal rights. That is up from 46 percent in 2014. To tell the story of America, and more importantly, the story of us, as individual Americans, we have to look at how black Americans have been oppressed by white Americans and how that has impacted other ethnic minority groups. To do this, we have to look at the impact of the Civil War, the most terrible of all American wars.

THE CIVIL WAR

As the prologue to this book indicated, history begins and ends with the individual. For the Civil War, we can identify the first person killed and the last person killed. Private Daniel Hough was a Union soldier stationed at Ft. Sumter, South Carolina. He was the first person killed. Private John J. Williams, also a Union soldier, was killed in Brownsville, Texas. Private Williams was the last person killed in the Civil War. When Abraham Lincoln arrived in Washington, D.C., in March 1861 for his inauguration, the atmosphere was gloomy, and war was on the horizon. Lincoln's inaugural speech was a warning:

> *In your hands, my dissatisfied fellow-countrymen, and not in mine, is the momentous issue of civil war. The Government will not assail you. You can have no conflict without being yourselves the aggressors. You have no oath registered in heaven to destroy the Government, while I shall have the most solemn one to preserve, protect, and defend it. I am loath to close. We are not enemies, but friends. We must not be enemies. Though passion may have strained it must not break our bonds of affection. The mystic chords of memory, stretching from every battlefield and patriot grave to every living heart and hearthstone all over this broad land, will yet swell the chorus of the Union, when again touched, as surely they will be, by the better angels of our nature. (Lincoln, 1861)*

President Lincoln, although speaking to the entire nation, was directing his words specifically to the South. Unfortunately, his appeal to the better angels of our nature fell on deaf ears. The common belief is that the Civil War began with the attack on Ft. Sumter in Charleston Bay, South Carolina, but in reality, although unofficially, the war had already begun out West, in Kansas. Westward expansion led to a violent clash between pro-slavery and anti-slavery forces. Also, the Fugitive Slave Law of 1850 had made the Northern states complicit with the preservation of slavery in the South. Abolitionists were gaining momentum and strength and Lincoln represented, for the South, the end of their institution of slavery. The American Revolution had left two extremely important questions unanswered: Was the United States a confederation of sovereign states, and would slavery continue to exist? Slavery had divided America from the beginning. By the time it was over, the US Civil War had claimed nearly 700,000 lives, more than all other American wars combined.

The free states and the slave states could not agree on the power of the federal government to prohibit the growth of slavery in US territories that were yet to become states. Lincoln's campaign promise was to stop the growth of slavery in the western territories. As a result, the slave states seceded and formed the Confederate States of America. Lincoln and the majority of people in the North did not recognize the Confederacy and sought to preserve the Union. On April 12, 1861, the Confederate army attacked a federal garrison at Ft. Sumter. As 1861 came to an end, almost one million soldiers were deployed against each other. Epic battles took place in 1862, like those in Shiloh, Fredericksburg, Antietam, leading to bigger battles as the war dragged on in Gettysburg and Vicksburg. Lincoln's original call to restore the Union was coupled with his call to end slavery after the issuing of the Emancipation Proclamation in 1863.

Why did poor Southern whites fight to preserve slavery when they did not own any slaves? One reason is that the South gained great wealth from slave labor, which indirectly benefited poor whites as this wealth trickled down through the racial hierarchy in the South. Even though most Confederate soldiers realized that they would never get a fair share of the wealth of the upper classes in the South, at least they were not at the bottom of society like the slaves. They could feel superior to someone, in other words. The wealthy in the South remained wealthy after the Civil War when slavery had been abolished. Nothing changed for them, and poor whites supported the economic class division that kept them down. Another possible reason that poor Southerners fought in the Civil War is hyper-masculinity provoked by paranoia and fear-mongering. Evidence of this fear-mongering is most directly evident in the Georgia secession proclamation from January 29, 1861. Georgia addressed the perceived threat posed by President Lincoln and the Republican Party.

> *Because by their declared principles and policy they have outlawed $3,000,000,000 of our property in the common territories of the Union; put it under the ban of the Republic in the States where it exists and out of the protection of Federal law everywhere; because they give sanctuary to thieves and incendiaries who assail it to the whole extent of their power, in spite of their most solemn obligations and covenants; because their avowed purpose is to subvert our society and subject us not only to the loss of our property but the destruction of ourselves, our wives, and our children, and the desolation of our homes, our altars, and our firesides. (State of Georgia, 1861)*

When Confederate soldiers were asked why they were fighting, they would say simply: "Because y'all are down here."

By 1865, most of the Confederate armies had surrendered, and the Union army captured Confederate president Jefferson Davis. The war was over; however, President Lincoln did not survive to see the outcome. He was assassinated by an actor (and Confederate sympathizer) named John Wilkes Booth on April 14, 1865. Reconstruction would be left up to Andrew Johnson.

According to Civil War author Shelby Foote, one must understand the Civil War to understand America. In many ways, the Civil War was the completion of the American Revolution. As President Lincoln said in the Gettysburg Address, it was "a new birth of freedom." Shelby Foote noted that, "The Civil War made us an is." This is both a simple and a powerful statement. Prior to the Civil War, it was common to refer to the United States in the plural: "The United States are a nice place to live." After the Civil War, it was customary to refer to the United States in the singular: "The United States is a nice place to live." That simple change carries a whole lot of meaning: that we were now one nation. It is important to note some important and often misunderstood details about the Civil War:

1. The North went to war initially to preserve the Union, not explicitly to end slavery.
2. The South fought for states' rights to preserve slavery.
3. Western expansion was a primary catalyst in the start of the Civil War.
4. Most of the war was fought in the South.
5. More than 3 million men fought in the war.
6. Nearly two percent of the US population died in the war. The equivalent casualty rate today would add up to 7.5 million killed.
7. African Americans constituted less than one percent of the northern population, yet by the end of the war made up 10 percent of the Union Army.
8. The words "In God We Trust" first appeared on a US coin in 1864.
9. Officially, the Civil War started April 12, 1861, at Fort Sumter, South Carolina, and ended April 9, 1865, at Appomattox Courthouse, Virginia.
10. Most battlefield wounds were treated by traumatic amputations with no anesthesia.
11. Most of the generals knew each other and went to military academies together.
12. The Emancipation Proclamation (1863) made the war a war to end slavery and restore the Union.
13. The Confederate government under President Jefferson Davis abandoned the concept of states' rights and became even more centralized than the US government.

Many textbooks published from 1890 to 1970 downplayed the horrors of slavery and the intent of the South in the Civil War. Some would go as far as to call the Civil War "the War between the States" or even worse, "the War of Northern Aggression." The issue, according to these outdated and incorrect textbooks, was states' rights, not slavery.

STATES' RIGHTS

During the constitutional phase of American history after the Revolutionary War, the white people of the Southern states demanded the Bill of Rights (first ten amendments to the Constitution) because of their fears of the federal government being too powerful. In theory, protecting states' rights thereby protects individual rights. An exception was made to exclude slavery in the discussion of individual rights. This general concept of states' rights emerges from that argument. The Founding Fathers divided on the issue of states' rights fell into two argumentative camps: Federalists and Anti-Federalists. John Adams, Alexander Hamilton, Benjamin Franklin, George Washington, and James Madison were all Federalists. Thomas Jefferson, Thomas Paine, Richard Henry Lee, Patrick Henry, and Samuel Adams were all Anti-Federalists.

The power of the federal government was also tested during the time of President Andrew Jackson. The Nullification Crisis of 1832–1833 involved South Carolina challenging the federal government in a dispute over federal tariffs. South Carolina asserted that it could overturn any federal law dealing with tariffs if such tariffs were found to be harmful to the state. The crisis was averted, but the legacy of anti-federalism and states' rights still haunted America.

RECONSTRUCTION AND SLAVERY

Defined, Reconstruction was the process of bringing the North and South back together after the Civil War and integrating former slaves into the mainstream of American society. That was an ambitious undertaking. Even if one looks at the first part of this definition, bringing the North and South back together, that alone was difficult enough. The Civil War cost the lives of nearly 700,000 Americans. And these were not Americans being killed by some foreign army on foreign soil; these were Americans killing Americans in America. To this day, the Civil War is an emotional issue in the South. The second part, integrating former slaves, was equally difficult. It would be difficult for the slave who has not been allowed to learn to read nor write and who decends from nearly 250 years' worth of socialization as a slave. It would not be easy for whites who were accustomed to a system that put blacks at the bottom. It should be noted that not everyone in the North was an abolitionist and even those who favored abolition did not necessarily advocate equal rights for former slaves. The transition would be tough for everyone. Because slavery had existed in America for nearly five generations, it is important to look at its impact on American society.

DEHUMANIZATION AND SLAVERY

In 1526, in what is now South Carolina, 500 Spaniards arrived with 150 black slaves. The Native Americans in that area did not accept the Spanish settlement, and conflict began. Eventually, the black slaves revolted and escaped. The remaining Spanish colonists fled to Haiti. The escaped slaves blended into Native American tribes. Those escaped slaves, then, became the first non-native residents of what would become America.

In order to enslave another human being, you would have to desensitize yourself to human suffering. In other words, you would have to think of the slave as less than human in order to justify their mistreatment. This process is known as dehumanization. The first step in dehumanization is to use cruel and hurtful names to describe the people you are dehumanizing. Once that is an accepted practice, the next step is to treat them differently than you would wish to be treated. Third, the different treatment and status is codified and put into law or custom. Fourth, the dehumanized people are segregated and separated from others. Finally, the dehumanized people are exterminated. The Nazi treatment of the Jews is an example. It is surprising to many people that dehumanization begins simply with a derogatory name given to a certain group. The first step in dealing with this innate human ability to dehumanize is not to accept using such derogatory language and names. The golden rule, the ancient axiom that is found in many cultures and that most people are taught in kindergarten, applies: do unto others as you would have them do unto you.

When African slaves were brought to America, they came through the Caribbean first where they went through a period of "seasoning." The first rationale used to justify their enslavement was not race or color, it was religion. It was okay to enslave non-Christians. However, once slaves began to adopt Christianity, the rationale had to change. It then became racial. During the time of slavery, it was illegal to teach a slave to read or write. It was also illegal for slaves to look at white people directly, eye to eye. The reason for this was to keep the slave dependent on the slave master and to protect the slave master from seeing the suffering. It is often said that eyes are the windows to the soul. It is easy to see if someone is suffering when you look them in the eyes. Also, as it is in the animal kingdom, eye to eye contact assumes equality. When two dogs approach each other and stare each other down, one inevitably backs down, lowers its body and looks down to show submission to the dominant animal.

It is important to note that most African slaves ended up in Latin America, Brazil being the country receiving the most slaves. Slavery was also tied into sugar production and eventually the manufacture of chocolate. High demand for these commodities led to a high demand for people to work the sugar cane fields. The first African slaves to reach America landed in 1619 in the Jamestown Colony. That was the beginning of American slavery.

EVOLUTION OF ABOLITIONISM

An Abolitionist was a person who believed that slavery in the United States should end immediately. With the writing of the Constitution some of the founding fathers, like Thomas Jefferson, attempted to put anti-slavery language in an early draft (even though he held slaves himself). This attempt was not successful due to protests from the Southern colonies. Benjamin Franklin, who was also a slaveholder, was a member of one of the first anti-slavery organizations in the United States—the Pennsylvania Society for the Abolition of Slavery.

Following the Revolutionary War, the Northern states began to abolish slavery. By 1804, all the Northern states had abolished slavery. Many individual slaveholders in the Upper South made provisions in their wills to free their slaves, supposedly moved by the revolutionary ideals of equality expressed in the Declaration of Independence and the US Constitution. The percentage of free black people in the Upper South increased from less than one percent to nearly 10 percent from 1790 to 1810. President Thomas Jefferson signed the Act Prohibiting the Importation of Slaves in 1807, and he privately supported the Missouri Compromise in 1820 that prohibited slavery north of 36 degrees, 30 minutes North, excluding Missouri.

William Lloyd Garrison was the founder of the American Anti-Slavery Society in 1833. The Virginia legislature debated abolition from 1829 to 1831, and in the North, there were serious discussions about freeing the slaves and sending them to Africa for settlement. This led to the founding of the African country of Liberia. Between 1822 and the end of the Civil War, more than 15,000 freed and free-born American blacks settled in Liberia (which declared its independence in 1847).

Nat Turner, born a slave, led a rebellion of slaves in Virginia in August 1831. More than 80 slaves joined in, and they murdered 60 white people. There were several slave rebellions between 1776 and 1865, but Nat Turner's was the most violent and had the greatest impact. As a result of the rebellion, pro-slavery forces tightened their grip on the slaves, and anti-slavery forces noted that only more blood would spill until slavery was abolished. Congress passed the Fugitive Slave Law in 1850 that made it illegal to provide assistance to runaway slaves, even in the North. This law made the Northern states complicit with slavery in the South and further divided the nation. In the 1850s the 15 states that constituted the American South still supported slavery, especially in the agricultural areas and less so in the border states and urban areas. In 1860, there were 4 million slaves in the United States.

On March 6, 1857, the US Supreme Court decided that slave owners had the right to take their slaves into Western territories. The most important issue of the 1850s was whether slavery should be allowed in the West. The Compromise of 1850 allowed new territories to decide for themselves on the issue of slavery by popular vote. When this process was tested in Kansas, violence broke out. Dred Scott was a slave whose owner had lived in Illinois (which was a free state) and Wisconsin, which was a free territory when Scott lived there. The court ruled that Scott was not free based on his residence, because he was not considered a person under the law. Dred Scott was considered to be the property of his owner, which could not be taken away without due process of law. The justices were trying to end the debate about slavery in the West and overlooked that fact that there were many free black people living in the North.

Former slave Frederick Douglass, free blacks Charles Henry Langston and John Mercer Langston (brothers), William Lloyd Garrison, and Harriet Beecher Stowe were all leading abolitionists in the North. When President Lincoln was introduced to author Harriet Beecher Stowe, he allegedly said: "So you're the little woman who wrote the book that made this great war!" Her novel, *Uncle Tom's Cabin*, was published in 1852 and served to galvanize the abolitionist movement.

The purpose of *Uncle Tom's Cabin* was to educate people about the horrors of slavery. Stowe showed that slavery impacted everyone in America, including people in the North, and hoped to change hearts and minds in the South, as well. Although *Uncle Tom's Cabin* did, unfortunately, popularize some stereotypes of black people, it also proved that literature can be an agent of social change.

Frederick Douglass was a famous American abolitionist, statesman, speaker, and author. Douglass escaped from slavery at age 20, and his three autobiographical books are essential reading in American history. Douglass was born into slavery around 1818 in Maryland. He

FIGURE 1.1. Harriet Beecher Stowe

FIGURE 1.2. Frederick Douglass

became one of the most famous intellectuals of the latter 19th century in America. He was an advisor to presidents and lectured on a wide variety of topics, including women's rights. He died on February 20, 1895. Douglass said, "No man can put a chain about the ankle of his fellow man without at last finding the other end fastened about his own neck." This quote truly captures the spirit of the anti-slavery movement. Not only was slavery harmful to the slave, it was also harmful to the slave owner and the country. Douglass was probably the most distinguished and eloquent speaker regarding the evils of slavery. His words ring as true today as they did over 150 years ago. "Where justice is denied, where poverty is enforced, where ignorance prevails, and where any one class is made to feel that society is an organized conspiracy to oppress, rob and degrade them, neither persons nor property will be safe."

John Brown did not believe in a slow evolutionary approach to ending slavery; he believed in the violent overthrow of the slavery system. Brown took part in the anti-slavery conflicts in Kansas and believed that he and his sons were doing the will of God. By 1858, he had recruited some more radical abolitionists who were bent on creating a slave rebellion. In 1859, John Brown and nearly two dozen of his followers attacked and took over a federal arsenal at Harpers Ferry in Virginia. He intended to seize weapons and supplies to support his planned slave rebellion. He was not successful, and several were killed, including most of his men and his two sons. The US Marines, under the command of Robert E. Lee, put down the uprising. John Brown was captured and sentenced to death for murder, inciting slave insurrection, and treason. After

FIGURE 1.3. John Brown

sentencing Brown pronounced, "If it is deemed necessary that I should forfeit my life for the furtherance of the ends of justice, and mingle my blood further with the blood of my children and with the blood of millions in this slave country whose rights are disregarded by wicked, cruel, and unjust enactments—I submit; so let it be done!" John Brown was hanged on December 2, 1859, after allegedly passing on these final words in a note, "I, John Brown, am now quite certain that the crimes of this guilty land will never be purged away but with blood." Many textbooks portray Brown as a villain and a madman who went crazy and turned into a murdering extremist. Since the 1970s, most history books began to take a different look at this extremely committed and complicated man. Frederick Douglass offered this: "His zeal in the cause of my race was far greater than mine—it was as the burning sun to my taper light—mine was bounded by time, his stretched away to the boundless shores of eternity. I could live for the slave, but he could die for him." American novelist Herman Melville called him "the meteor of the war."

EASING INTO ABOLITION

Many in the Republican Party believed that market forces would destroy slavery. Southern leaders believed that blocking the expansion of slavery in the West challenged their livelihoods. With the election of Abraham Lincoln, seven of the Southern states decided to secede from the Union and form a new nation. After President Lincoln had started the call for troops to stop the rebellion, four more Southern states seceded.

President Lincoln invoked the concept of pre-determination in this second inaugural speech (1865), which was a clear indictment of America's sins against black people. Lincoln believed, as did many others, that the United States was being punished for the sin of slavery. Black people fighting for the Union army changed a lot of people's minds, especially Union soldiers. They became more supportive of equality. A change of hearts and minds. As the war dragged on, even southerners joined the Union, realizing that they were on the losing side and inspired by the cause to free the slaves.

> *If we shall suppose that American slavery is one of those offenses which, in the providence of God, must needs come, but which, having continued through His appointed time, He now wills to remove, and that He gives to both North and South this terrible war as the woe due to those by whom the offense came, shall we discern therein any departure from those divine attributes which the believers in a living God always ascribe to Him? Fondly do we hope, fervently do we pray, that this mighty scourge of war may speedily pass away. Yet, if God wills that it continue until all the wealth piled by the bondsman's two hundred and fifty years of unrequited toil shall be sunk, and until every drop of blood drawn with the lash shall be paid by another drawn with the sword, as was said three thousand years ago, so still it must be said 'the judgments of the Lord are true and righteous altogether. (Lincoln, 1865)*

President Lincoln issued the Emancipation Proclamation on January 1, 1863, and changed the legal status of slaves in the Confederacy to free people. Freed blacks escaped to join the Union troops, and many joined the Union army. Plantation owners tried to hide their slaves by moving farther South, but by June 19, 1865, the Union army controlled all Confederate territory and had liberated all slaves.

In February 1863, Governor John A. Andrew of Massachusetts called for the formation of the 54th Massachusetts Infantry Regiment. The regiment was made up of 1,000 volunteer black soldiers from Massachusetts and other states (including slave states) and even Canada. Frederick Douglass's two sons enlisted. Blacks were not allowed to be officers, so Robert Gould Shaw was named the commander. Shaw had fought at the Battle of Antietam. The regiment had great esprit de corps. All of the white officers and men refused to take any pay until the pay was made equal among white and black soldiers. The 54th fought bravely at Fort Wagner near the Port of Charleston on July 18, 1863. The regiment was decimated with nearly one-half of its soldiers being killed in the attack. Shaw was also killed leading his men. The Confederates dumped all of the bodies into a mass grave and sent a message to the Union: "We buried Shaw with his niggers." Shaw's parents replied that there could be "no holier place" to be buried than "surrounded by ... brave and devoted soldiers."

RECONSTRUCTION AFTER THE CIVIL WAR

Many abolitionists were upset with President Lincoln when he did not make ending slavery the primary goal of the Union war effort. Lincoln was afraid that border slave states that were still loyal to the Union would move to the Confederacy, and he was also worried that conservative northerners would not be supportive of the cause. The bottom line was that most everyone in the North believed in restoring the Union, but freeing the slaves was another matter. Thousands of slaves joined the Union as Lincoln's army marched through the South, thereby pushing the agenda of abolition and showing that the Southern concept of the contented slave was a cruel and inaccurate myth.

President Lincoln knew that the time was right and emancipation had become a political, moral, and military imperative. The Emancipation Proclamation freed 3 million slaves, and nearly 200,000 blacks joined the Union Army, which led to a social revolution in the South. Although the Emancipation Proclamation did not end slavery in the nation, it captured the hearts and imaginations of millions of Americans and fundamentally transformed the character of the war.

Hoping to shorten the war, in December 1863, Lincoln offered what he called the Ten Percent Plan. The plan held that a state could be reintegrated in the Union if 10 percent of the population of that state had taken an oath of allegiance and swore to uphold Emancipation. In that case, everyone would be granted amnesty. Moderate Republicans supported the plan, and Radical Republicans did not. They felt that the plan was too lenient. Radical Republicans passed a counter plan known as the Wade-Davis Bill in the summer of 1864. The bill demanded that a majority of the state would have to take a loyalty oath, not just 10 percent. Lincoln pocket-vetoed the Wade-Davis Bill.

In the Gettysburg Address on November 19, 1863, Lincoln declared " ... that this nation, under God, shall have a new birth of freedom—and that government of the people, by the people, for the people, shall not perish from the earth." Lincoln looked at the Civil War as the completion of the American Revolution. Both the Emancipation Proclamation and the Gettysburg Address set the stage for what was to come. Lincoln contemplated many ideas of how to implement Reconstruction but still had no clear plan as the war wound down in 1865. In a speech he gave on April 11, 1865, Lincoln said that free blacks and those who fought deserved the right to vote. He was killed by John Wilkes Booth, a Confederate supporter and actor, three days later. When Booth shot Lincoln, the assassin lept from the theater balcony and purportedly yelled to the crowd: "Sic semper tyrannis!" Translated from Latin, it means, "thus be it to tyrants." This phrase is also the state motto of Virginia.

The Thirteenth Amendment was ratified December 6, 1865. "Neither slavery nor involuntary servitude, except as a punishment for crime whereof the party shall have been duly convicted, shall exist within the United States, or any place subject to their jurisdiction." The Thirteenth Amendment completed the abolition of slavery in the United States, which had begun with President Abraham Lincoln issuing the Emancipation Proclamation in 1863.

PRESIDENTIAL RECONSTRUCTION

In May 1865, President Andrew Johnson, who had succeeded Lincoln after the assassination, made his plans for Reconstruction known. Johnson believed in the Union, but also in states' rights. According to President Johnson, the Southern states, even though they had seceded, had not given up their right to govern themselves. He did not believe the federal government had any right to determine voting rights at the state level. President Johnson's Presidential Reconstruction required that all land confiscated by the Union army and given to freed slaves had to go back to the original owners. Although state governments in the South were required to honor the abolition of slavery, swear loyalty oaths, and pay war debt, they were largely given the right to reconstruct themselves. Without proper oversight and true reconstruction, Southern states enacted "black codes" designed to restrict and control freed slaves and trap them as an agricultural labor force. Black codes angered many in the North and led to the Freedmen's Bureau and Civil Rights Bills of 1866. The Civil Rights Act of 1866 declared black people citizens and guaranteed them equal protection under the laws. It was passed by Congress on April 9, 1866, over the veto of President Andrew Johnson. The act declared that all persons born in the United States were citizens without regard to race, color, or previous condition. The activities of terrorist organizations, such as the Ku Klux Klan (KKK), undermined the purpose of this act. Johnson vetoed the bill, leading to his impeachment in 1868. The Civil Rights Act of 1866 became the first major bill to become law after a presidential veto.

RADICAL RECONSTRUCTION

In the 1866 congressional elections, voters in the North rejected President Johnson's policies and Republicans in Congress took control of Reconstruction in the South. In March 1867, Congress passed the Reconstruction Act that divided the South into five military districts and prescribed how voting (for men only) would be conducted. The Reconstruction Act also required Southern states to ratify the Fourteenth Amendment before they could rejoin the Union. The Fourteenth Amendment to the Constitution was ratified on July 9, 1868, and granted citizenship to "all persons born or naturalized in the United States," which included former slaves recently freed. In addition, it forbade states from denying any person "life, liberty or property, without due process of law" or to "deny to any person within its jurisdiction the equal protection of the laws." By directly outlining the role of the states, this amendment greatly ensured civil rights for all Americans and is cited in more court cases than any other amendment. The only problem was that it only applied to men, not to women.

In February 1869, Congress approved the Fifteenth Amendment (ratified in 1870). The Fifteenth Amendment to the Constitution granted black men the right to vote by declaring that the "right of citizens of the United States to vote shall not be denied or abridged by the United States or by any state on account of race, color, or previous condition of servitude." Although it became the law of the land, the promise of the amendment would not be fully implemented until the 1960s. White people in the Southern states used poll taxes, literacy tests, and other devious means to effectively deny black people the vote.

After 1870, all former Confederate states had been readmitted to the Union, and blacks were able to participate in politics for the first time. Black people won elections in state governments and even the US Congress during this time. In 1870, Joseph Rainey of South Carolina was the first black person elected to the House of Representatives. In the same year, Hiram Revels of Mississippi was elected as the first black US senator. Reconstruction also provided for the first state-funded public school systems in the South, more equitable tax laws, and ultimately, the passage of the Civil Rights Act of 1875, which outlawed racial segregation in transportation and public accommodations and prevented exclusion of blacks from jury service. Unfortunately, in 1883, the Supreme Court declared that the act was unconstitutional and held that Congress did not have the power to regulate the conduct and transactions of individual people.

After 1867, many southern whites used violence to counter the revolutionary and necessary changes to society brought about by Reconstruction. The KKK and other white supremacist organizations targeted white and black Republican leaders and any black people who simply were exercising their rights. President Ulysses S. Grant attempted to curb the KKK and other white supremacy groups, but by the early 1870s, those hate groups continued to interfere with black voting and equal rights, and support for Reconstruction began to dissipate. A severe economic depression in 1874 helped bring the Democratic Party back and put it in control of the House of Representatives for the first time since the Civil War. Democrats in Mississippi used violence to control black people and effectively end Reconstruction. President Grant did not send federal support. The contested election of 1876 and the removal of Union troops spelled doom for Reconstruction.

THE GREAT BETRAYAL

The presidential election of 1876 was decided by an appointed commission after disputed returns from Florida, Louisiana, and South Carolina—the only three states in the South with Reconstruction-era Republican governments still in power—could not be counted in the electoral column for either candidate. A bipartisan congressional commission debated over the outcome as the representatives from Republican Party candidate Rutherford B. Hayes met secretly with moderate Southern Democrats. The Democrats agreed to support Hayes on the condition that he withdraw all federal troops from the South, leaving the Southern Democrats in control of the region. This would mark the end of the Reconstruction era.

Southern states had been under occupation by the Union army since the end of the Civil War. The Union army enforced African American suffrage and political equality. As white Southerners reacted to these radical changes, segregation policies emerged (i.e., Black Codes and Jim Crow laws). The Civil Rights Act of 1866 gave African Americans the same rights as white Americans, but it was never enforced by President Ulysses S. Grant. Jim Crow laws, backed up by Ku Klux Klan terrorist activities, crippled efforts to enforce federal laws. In 1874, the Democratic Party took control of the House of Representatives due to an economic depression, Grant administration scandals, and growing frustration over the process of Reconstruction.

In 1876, Samuel J. Tilden was the Democratic Party candidate for president. He wanted to remove the Union Army from the South. The Republicans nominated Rutherford B. Hayes. Althought Tilden won the popular vote, neither candidate had enough electoral votes. A candidate needed 185 electoral votes to win. There were disputed electoral votes in South Carolina, Florida, and Louisiana. Congress appointed a federal commission to decide who would be the new president. The electoral commission that came together in January 1877 was made up of five US representatives, five Supreme Court justices, and five US senators. A deal was made during the commission's deliberations. Republicans and Southern Democrats met in secret, and Hayes agreed to remove the Union troops from the South in exchange for a promise from the Democrats to respect African American political rights. This solidified Democratic control of the South. Hayes also agreed to add a Southerner to his presidential cabinet and support a southern transcontinental line. The commission then awarded Hayes all of the disputed votes, which gave him enough electoral votes to win.

The question remains, why did the Democrats give up the presidency that they had probably legitimately won? No one knows for sure, since the deal was made in secret and was not fully documented for history. The answer may be that people in both the South and the

North were more interested in restoring their way of life and wealth and were less concerned with civil rights for African Americans. Politics won out over doing what was right. The abandoned goals of Reconstruction were resurrected in the 1950s, with the 1954 *Brown v. Board of Education* Supreme Court decision and the passage of the Civil Rights Act of 1957. Alexander Hamilton dreamed of a powerful industrial America with a strong centralized government. This vision was championed by Northern politicians in the Republican Party, who had their roots in the Federalist and Whig parties. The Democrats of the South prevented this vision from becoming reality, using their agrarian financial power subsidized by slave labor. Their vision came from Thomas Jefferson—small government, free trade, a nation of yeoman farmers. Lincoln's election signaled the beginning of the end of Jefferson's vision, as power shifted from the South to the North. Once the Union troops were removed from the South, rigid segregation took hold in America.

PLESSY V. FERGUSON

The Supreme Court decided on *Plessy v. Ferguson* in 1896. Homer Plessy was 7/8 white, called an "octoroon" in the language of the time. Plessy's case was chosen, because his light complexion was thought to make him a more sympathetic plaintiff. He was recruited by the Citizens' Committee of New Orleans to challenge the Louisiana separate car law. The Supreme Court was not moved by the legal appeal and rendered its "Separate but Equal" ruling. Justice Henry B. Brown declared, "We consider the underlying fallacy of the plaintiff's argument to consist in the assumption that the enforced separation of the two races stamps the colored race with a badge of inferiority. If this be so, it is not by reason of anything found in the act, but solely because the colored race chooses to put that construction upon it."

The *Plessy* ruling cemented segregation into American law, custom, and social life. In some ways it can be looked at as a victory for the South. But one cannot only blame the white folks in the South, because people in the North also failed to stop the rise of segregation. Of course, facilities were not equal and became even less so as time went on. The ruling seems to blame the victim in its argument as if any harm coming from segregation is only in the mind of black people in America. It would take until 1954 to overturn *Plessy v. Ferguson*.

CONCLUSION

As an Army private in March 1979, I was sent to Charleston Air Force Base, South Carolina, to await overseas movement to Germany. I thought about my brother Alf's assignment at Charleston Air Force Base during the Vietnam War—he had hated South Carolina. I had this idea that the Air Force was different from the Army, and when I met an Air Force firefighter at the airport, I asked him what his Military Occupational Specialty (MOS) was. He told me that in the Air Force people have jobs, not an MOS. I had a 24-hour layover, and it was during this time that I met two other young soldiers awaiting travel to Germany. They looked like trouble, but I was young, naïve, and bored. Sam was short and white, and James was tall, black, and had startlingly blue eyes. We hired a cab and headed toward the old waterfront district in Charleston. James told me that he had met the son of a wealthy man and that he had been invited over. We thought he was probably lying, but then the cab stopped in front of a huge mansion on the water overlooking Ft. Sumter. I thought about the historical significance of this location. A time-worn cannon stood nearby, probably commemorating the Confederate firing on Ft. Sumter that started the Civil War.

"This is it!" James said, "Let's go in." I was beginning to get suspicious.

We walked into the grand old house, and on an antique chair sat a white man in his 60s. He was unconscious and had a pistol in his hand and a bottle of whiskey near his feet.

"I grew up in the projects, I've never seen anything like this," said James.

I had not seen anything like that either. I guess it was what you call old money. James hurried upstairs and came down with a young man who told us he was the son of the old guy. James introduced him as Rick.

"He's always drunk," Rick said as he pointed at his father.

"We can't let my dad see your black friend," said Rick to me almost under his breath, "he'll most likely shoot him."

There was talk of getting some marijuana and getting the young man's sister to come with us on some adventure. I grew anxious. When Rick and Sam left to get some pot, James went upstairs again, and it sounded like he was rifling through their drawers. I decided to leave. After all, this was the deep south, we were in a rich white man's mansion who apparently hated blacks, he was armed with a pistol and was drunk, my companions were dealing with drugs, and my black companion was planning a liaison with the rich white guy's daughter. All of this seemed to indicate that there might be trouble. I began to walk down the broad street overlooking the bay. I imagined the old cannon firing and the naïve excitement of the Confederate soldiers, not knowing that the Civil War they were starting would eventually take the lives of nearly 700,000 soldiers. A taxi drove by, and I hailed it. I returned to the base and slept a little. The next morning, I took my flight to Germany. I did not see my two companions on the flight.

I really did not think much about that day until one year later when I was already working at the US Military Confinement Facility in Mannheim, West Germany. I was walking in the hallway of the prison when someone said: "Hey, don't I know you?" I turned around, and there was James. He was a prisoner. James explained how he had eventually made it out of the sticky situation in Charleston. He took some money and ran before the rich old white guy noticed. James told me how he became a drug dealer in his infantry unit in Germany and was finally caught.

"I had a BMW though," he told me.

"Yes indeed, I was livin' mighty high."

"What happened to Sam? Weren't you guys going to the same unit in Germany," I asked.

"He ratted me out and got away with it, man . . . life ain't fair and it's a mean old world," said James.

He was heading for the military prison at Ft. Leavenworth, Kansas, to make big rocks into little rocks for a few years. I could not help but think that being black in America was something that I knew nothing about, but I would have to do my best to learn. Serving in the US Army with nearly 40 percent of the soldiers being minorities would give me that opportunity to learn.

According to Ohio State University law professor and civil rights activist Michelle Alexander, in 2011, there were more African Americans in prison or "under the watch" of the justice system than were enslaved in the United States in 1850. Currently in America, 40 percent of the prison population are black, 19 percent are Hispanic, and 39 percent are white. Whites constitute 64 percent of the entire population, and Hispanics 16 percent. Blacks constitute only 13 percent of the entire population, so the incarceration rates are way out of proportion. As James said: "Life ain't fair and it's a mean old world."

References

Georgia, State of. 1861. Ordinance of Secession. *Journal of the Georgia Convention*. Hargrett Rare Book and Manuscript Library. University of Georgia. http://www.libs.uga.edu/hargrett/selections/confed/ord.html

Lincoln, Abraham. 1861. First Inaugural Address. The American Presidency Project. http://www.presidency.ucsb.edu/ws/?pid=25818

Lincoln, Abraham. 1865. Second Inaugural Address. The Avalon Project. http://avalon.law.yale.edu/19th_century/lincoln2.asp

Timeline

1860

December 20: South Carolina is the first to secede from the Union.

1861

March 4: Abraham Lincoln is inaugurated president.

March 11: The Confederate States of America adopts a Constitution. The Confederacy includes Alabama, Florida, Georgia, Louisiana, Mississippi, South Carolina, and Texas.

April 12: South Carolina troops fire on Fort Sumter, and the Civil War begins.

July 2: President Lincoln issues his suspension of habeas corpus in certain cases.

July 22: US Congress passes a resolution declaring that the war is being fought to "preserve the Union," not to destroy slavery.

November 1: President Lincoln declares George McClellan General-in-Chief of the Union army.

1862

April 25: Union soldiers capture New Orleans.

May 20: President Lincoln signs the Homestead Act.

July: Congress passes the Militia act, authorizing Lincoln to use black soldiers.

September 17: The Battle of Antietam, Maryland, is the bloodiest battle of the Civil War.

September 23: Lincoln's Emancipation Proclamation is published.

1863

January 1: The Emancipation Proclamation takes effect.

March 3: The Conscription Act (Enrollment Act) is passed, drafting men (20–45) in the Union army. Draft exemptions can be bought for $300.

June 20: West Virginia is admitted as the 35th state, becoming part of the Union.

July 3: The Battle of Gettysburg is a Union victory, but more than 50,000 are dead. General Lee is in retreat.

July 4: The Battle of Vicksburg ends, 29,000 rebel troops surrender, and the Confederacy is split in two.

July 13: The New York Draft Riots begin.

November 19: Lincoln delivers the Gettysburg Address.

December 8: Lincoln issues the Proclamation of Amnesty and Reconstruction (Ten Percent Plan) that offers pardons to Confederates who take a loyalty oath.

1864

July 4: Lincoln pocket vetoes the Wade-Davis Bill.

September 2: Union general Sherman burns Atlanta and continues his march to the sea.

November 8: Lincoln defeats Democrat George McClellan in the presidential election of 1864.

December 22: Union general Sherman enters Savannah, completing his march to the sea.

1865

February 1: Congress proposes the Thirteenth Amendment, outlawing slavery and involuntary servitude everywhere in the United States.

March 3: Freedmen's Bureau is founded to aid former slaves.

March 4: Lincoln is inaugurated for his second term with Andrew Johnson as vice president.

April 8: General Lee surrenders to General Grant at Appomattox, Virginia.

April 14: President Lincoln is assassinated at Ford's Theater by John Wilkes Booth.

April 18: General Johnston surrenders to General Sherman in North Carolina, effectively ending the Civil War.

May 29: President Johnson moves to reconstruct the South on his own initiative calling it Restoration.

June: Southern states begin to pass Black Codes.

December 24: The Ku Klux Klan is formed in Tennessee.

December 18: The Thirteenth Amendment is ratified.

1866

April 9: The Civil Rights Act passed despite Johnson's earlier veto.

May 1: The Memphis Race Riot/Massacre occurs.

June 13: The Fourteenth Amendment to the Constitution approved by Congress.

July 24: Tennessee is the first Southern state admitted to the Union.

July 30: The New Orleans Race Riot/Massacre occurs.

November: Radical Republicans take over Congress. All Southern states except Tennessee refuse to ratify the Fourteenth Amendment.

1867

March 2: The First Reconstruction Act and Tenure of Office Act is passed over President Johnson's veto.

March 23: The Second Reconstruction Act is passed over President Johnson's veto.

July 11: The Republican convention in New Orleans occurs. The party platform includes equality for African Americans.

July 19: The Third Reconstruction Act is passed over President Johnson's veto.

December: President Johnson continues to oppose congressional policy and tries to remove radical Secretary of War Edwin M. Stanton.

1868

March 11: The Fourth Reconstruction Act is passed.

March 30: The impeachment trial of Andrew Johnson begins.

July 28: The Fourteenth Amendment is ratified.

August: Arkansas, North Carolina, South Carolina, Louisiana, Alabama, and Florida are readmitted to the Union.

September 28: Nearly 300 African Americans are killed in the Opelousas Massacre in Louisiana.

November 3: John W. Menard of Louisiana is the first African American elected to the US Congress but is never seated and is barred by white members of Congress.

November 3: Former slave Oscar J. Dunn is elected lieutenant governor of Louisiana.

November 3: Ulysses S. Grant is elected president.

1869

February 26: The Fifteenth Amendment is approved by Congress. This amendment prohibits any state from denying a citizen the right to vote because of race, color, or previous condition of servitude.

March 4: Grant is inaugurated as president.

May 10: The transcontinental railroad is completed.

July 1: The Freedmen's Bureau ends.

1870

February 3: The Fifteenth Amendment is ratified.

February 23: Hiram Revels elected to US Senate as the first black senator.

May 31: The Enforcement Act (targeting the Ku Klux Klan) is passed by Congress.

December 12: Joseph H. Rainey is sworn in as the first black member of the US House of Representatives.

1871

April 20: The Third Enforcement Act (Ku Klux Klan Act) is passed.

1872

May 22: President Grant signs the Amnesty Act for former Confederates.

November 5: Grant wins a second term as president, defeating Horace Greeley.

December 9: P.B.S. Pinchback, acting governor of Louisiana, is the first African American to serve as a state governor.

1873

The financial Panic of 1873 drives the nation into a depression.

1875

March 1: The Civil Rights Act of 1875 provides blacks with the right to equal treatment in public places and transportation.

November: The disputed election between Rutherford B. Hayes and Samuel J. Tilden is resolved in favor of Republican Hayes through a secret backroom deal.

1877

March: President Hayes removes Union troops from the South, signaling the end of Reconstruction.

1896

May 18: The *Plessy v. Ferguson* Supreme Court decision upholds Louisiana statute requiring "separate but equal" accommodations on railroads. The Supreme Court holds that segregation is not necessarily discrimination.

CREDITS

1. Fig. 1.1. "Harriet Beecher Stowe," https://commons.wikimedia.org/wiki/File:Beecher-Stowe_3.jpg. Copyright in the Public Domain.
2. Fig. 1.2. "Frederick Douglass," https://commons.wikimedia.org/wiki/File:Motto_frederick_douglass_2.jpg. Copyright in the Public Domain.
3. Fig. 1.3. "John Brown," https://commons.wikimedia.org/wiki/File:John_Brown.jpg. Copyright in the Public Domain.

WORKING CLASS

BY DR. BRUCE OLAV SOLHEIM WITH ART BY GARY DUMM

MY PARENTS CAME TO THE UNITED STATES FROM NORWAY IN 1948 WITH LITTLE MONEY IN THEIR POCKETS AND BIG DREAMS.

THEY SETTLED IN SEATTLE. THEY DID NOT SPEAK ENGLISH AND HAD TO LIVE WITH RELATIVES AND WORKED HARD TO GET BY.

MY MOTHER WORKED AS A MAID IN THIS HOUSE ...

... WHILE MY DAD WAS A COMMERCIAL FISHERMAN IN ALASKA.

WHEN I WAS BORN IN 1958, WE HAD A MODEST HOUSE IN KENMORE, WA. MY MOTHER DID NOT HAVE TO WORK AS A MAID ANYMORE BECAUSE MY FATHER HAD A UNION CARPENTER JOB WITH BENEFITS.

OUR FAMILY OF FOUR LIVED ON ONE WORKING CLASS UNION MEMBER'S WAGE. THAT IS NO LONGER POSSIBLE IN AMERICA. I BELIEVE YOUNG PEOPLE TODAY DESERVE TO KNOW WHY.

CHAPTER TWO

RAPID INDUSTRIALIZATION

OBJECTIVES

1. Understand the forces that led to rapid industrialization.
2. Understand the political culture that existed during rapid industrialization.
3. Understand the closing of the western frontier and the concept of Manifest Destiny.
4. Understand the changes in gender and family relations that occurred during rapid industrialization.

PERSONAL HISTORY

I have experience in the corporate world. I spent five years working at the Boeing Company, both the military and the commercial sides of that giant aerospace corporation. I found the military side to be a more pleasant working environment. Maybe I felt that way, because I had spent six years in the US Army, and working with government contracts at Boeing was an easy transition. The pace was steadier, the atmosphere more relaxed. When I transferred to the commercial side of the company, the differences were immediately apparent. For one thing, the pace was either boom or bust. Boeing commercial was either ramping up at breakneck speed with massive overtime, or they were laying off workers. There was not much in between. You did not have time to nurture long-term relationships, because people came and went quickly, and there was a lot of backstabbing to get ahead and avoid layoffs. The management style reflected this cutthroat environment.

While on the military side of Boeing, I worked as a buyer on the B-1B bomber project. We took our time to do the documentation and conduct our negotiations properly and correctly according to Federal Acquisition Regulations and Defense Acquisition Regulations. The government was not in a big hurry, so neither were we. On the commercial side, I worked on the engineering change board as a materiel representative. We sat in endless meetings discussing schedules and parts delivery lead times. I then switched to buying small machine parts, and the pace was even more hectic. I remember going to schedule meetings where management did not provide enough chairs for the buyers, and they deliberately turned off the air conditioning in the windowless room. The environment was hot, crowded, and uncomfortable. Then, the second-level manager would start yelling at us if our parts were behind schedule. The yelling could get very loud, mean, and nasty. We called this "the wire brush treatment."

"Where are those parts, goddammit!" was what the big boss usually said.

"I could do your job with my eyes closed, now get it done! Today!" was also a familiar refrain. When we were ramping up because of large orders, the management would order mandatory overtime. Now, just to make it clear, it is not legal to make workers work overtime, so they would say that it was not mandatory. However, if you did not work the "non-mandatory" overtime, you would suffer when it came to promotions and layoffs. One day, after working mandatory overtime, I was both exhausted and stressed out. The big boss was again in charge of the delivery meeting and was in rare form. He was surrounded by his sycophant crony first-line managers, of course.

"Where are my god damn parts!" he said staring directly at me with glaring eyes.

"They are still in production," I said calmly.

"At what stage are they at this minute?" he screamed.

"The production line is shut down," I said.

"What?! What the hell is wrong with you! You need to get those parts here today!" he screamed at the top of his lungs as he pounded the table.

"Why is the line shut down?!" he added in exasperation.

"They're having a company party today," I said.

"What?!" he screamed.

"A Mexican fiesta with piñatas and everything," I said with a smirk knowing that this would take him over the top. Sure enough, the big boss threw his clipboard down on the table, which knocked over a coffee cup that spilled coffee all over the papers on the table and then crashed to the floor breaking into little pieces. There was quiet in the room as his fury grew and his face turned dark red and veins popped up in his forehead. He then started to tremble violently and shook his finger at me.

"I'll have your ass, you prick! You get over there and get that line moving again, you asshole!" he yelled so that even the floors above and below us could hear him. I thought for a moment, picked up my papers, and started to leave.

"Where the hell do you think you're going? I'm not done with you!" he screamed.

"I think you need to work on your people skills, and I'm going back to work," I said as I left the hot, stuffy room. The other buyers stood in stunned silence. Later, my immediate supervisor came up to me and said no one has ever talked to the big boss like that. I could not tell if he was impressed or mad at me—maybe a little of both. I think Boeing is probably typical of most of corporate America. Type A personality managers (like our big boss) dominate and move up the corporate ladder. Corporations, led by such type A personality managers operating in a cut-throat environment, seem to be able to get away with almost anything and have a stranglehold on our political system guided by the motto: might makes right. Corporations are vital to the growth of the United States, but unchecked power leads to corruption, scandal, and becomes a detriment to our society. Sometimes, for the sake of all of us, the little guy has to stand up for himself or herself and be recognized.

The story of how America came out of its bloody Civil War still a backward agrarian country and emerged in 1900 as an up-and-coming world power is critical to understanding America today. The period from 1865 to 1901 is commonly called the "Gilded Age." The name was taken from a Mark Twain novel that satirized greed and political corruption in post–Civil War America. America's gross national product quadrupled between 1865 and 1900. This is not surprising, since almost everything Americans do, they do quickly. Nothing, however, comes without a price. The balance of power among government, big business, and labor that America enjoyed from the Great Depression until the mid-1970s is gone. The America that I was born in, no longer exists. In terms of the power of big business, America today is more like America during the Gilded Age. How did this happen to my country?

FORCES OF EXPANSION

In order for the United States to become a world power, sacrifices had to be made. Nothing comes without a price. The establishment of a mass transportation system, the rise of the cities, the rise of mass production and corporate America, and massive waves of immigrant workers were the raw materials needed to transform America into a modern industrial world power.

MASS TRANSPORTATION

The First Transcontinental Railroad (originally the Pacific Railroad and later the Overland Route) was a 1,907-mile railroad line constructed between 1863 and 1869 that connected San Francisco Bay to Council Bluffs, Iowa, on the Missouri River. The rail line was built by three private companies: the original Western Pacific Railroad Company built between Oakland and Sacramento, California (132 miles), the Central Pacific built eastward from Sacramento to Promontory Summit, Utah (690 miles), and the Union Pacific Railroad Company built westward to Promontory Summit from Council Bluffs (1,085 miles). Opened for through traffic on May 10, 1869, with the driving of the Golden Spike at Promontory Summit, the transcontinental railroad promoted the settlement and economy of the American West by making transportation much quicker, and cheaper from coast to coast.

Prior to the completion of the transcontinental railway in 1869, the only way to reach the West Coast of the United States from the East was to travel overland or by ship. In order to travel by ship, you would have to plan on eight months at sea. This was prior to the opening of the Panama Canal, so you had to sail around the southern tip of South America. This sea voyage was also quite expensive. You could opt instead for the overland route, which was fraught with numerous perils and would take six months. Once the transcontinental was completed, travel time from East to West was cut to eight days. California's population exploded.

If you look at this from a business perspective, after the completion of the transcontinental railway, an East Coast manufacturer could ship goods fairly inexpensively and quickly across the nation. Prior to 1871, approximately 45,000 miles of track had been laid. Between 1871 and 1900, another 170,000 miles were added to the nation's railroad system. All the points between were also tied together in a network of railways.

It is said that lines of communication follow lines of transportation. For instance, to get word to your West Coast sweetheart prior to the transcontinental, it would take six to eight months from the East Coast. A lot can happen in six to eight months. The railways sped up communication—letters could travel cross country in eight days. Even quicker was the telegraph. Telegraph lines followed the railways and provided instant electronic communication capability. If you consider how business could now communicate with such speed, you'll realize that the boon to business was exponential. The basic transportation and communication infrastructure for modern America was ready.

MASS CONSUMPTION

The construction of a railway transportation network throughout the nation allowed cities to rise up along the way. People moved from small towns and farms to the city, something we call urbanization. Urban dwellers are considered consumers because they lack the capability of producing their own food and other items. Farmers were largely self-sufficient. Urban and suburban people are not, they are dependent on manufactured goods. The more people moved to cities, the more consumers, the more the need for manufactured goods transported on cheap railway networks subsidized by the government. More consumers meant more factories, and more factories meant more urban jobs. None of this would have been possible without mass production techniques and the factory. By 1880 America's population was 30 percent urban.

MASS PRODUCTION

Mass production was made possible by the development of the assembly line and interchangeable parts. Prior to mass production, everything was made one-off and unique. This was a slow, laborious, and expensive process. Urban consumers needed factory goods and also worked in the factories that were being built in the cities. Many of the factory workers came from overseas. American corporations enjoyed free reign as they had government in their pocket, held labor movements at bay, and had caretaker presidents at the helm.

MASS IMMIGRATION

Immigration increased dramatically—the number of foreign born people in America doubled between 1870 and 1900. By 1900, 20 percent of Americans were foreign born. Immigrants settled on farms and in cities, and the transcontinental railway was built primarily with immigrant labor: Irish work gangs, along with former slaves, from the East and Chinese work gangs from the West, over the mountains. These four ingredients multiplied and fed off of each other, accelerating the process of industrialization, urbanization, and the rise of big business.

THE PRICE PAID

British philosopher and sociologist Herbert Spencer believed the poor were genetically inferior to the rich and should not be helped in any way. He postulated that this was a variation on Charles Darwin's theories of natural selection and the concept of survival of the fittest. Spencer called his concept Social Darwinism. John Rockefeller once said, "God gave me my money." During the Gilded Age, the previous practice of local government providing welfare services to the poor and unemployed was abolished. The unemployed were called "tramps." Railway workers had their wages cut to the point that they could not feed their families. This led to one of the most violent strikes in American history, the Great Railroad Strike of 1877. The strike started in Martinsburg, West Virginia, and then spread. President Rutherford B. Hayes sent in the army to preserve order but not break the strike. After the strike, trade unions began to spring up and business became more and more anti-union. Terrence Powderly organized the Knights of Labor, who advocated Christian socialism. Their members included skilled and unskilled laborers, male and female, and all races. In the Midwest, farmers organized granges (an association of farmers) and supported the Greenback Party. They wanted economic stimulus and federal regulation of the railroads. What was very clear was that the United States gained strength and power on the backs of the working class, including immigrants, women, and children.

DISTRIBUTION OF WEALTH

In the 1870s in America, private charities cared for the poor and unemployed. However, many charities were run by wealthy businessmen with little sympathy for the poor. Many Americans agreed with them during the Gilded Age. Even the middle class looked down on the poor and idealized the rich. Those who questioned laissez-faire capitalism (where businesses basically do whatever they want without government interference) were considered dangerous

Table 2.1. Distribution of Wealth in America in 1900, 1960, and 2010

	1900 (% OF THE WEALTH)	1960 (% OF THE WEALTH)	2010 (% OF THE WEALTH)
Top 1 % of the people	50	25	35
Next 9 % of the people	40	35	35
Middle 40 % of the people	5	35	25
Bottom 50 % of the people	5	5	5

radicals. Civil War veterans received pensions, but only those who fought for the Union. Southern veterans got pensions from Southern states. The poor put their trust in the political bosses who ran all large cities. These bosses rigged elections, made questionable deals, lined their own pockets, and undermined the democratic process.

The following table shows what the distribution of wealth was in America in 1900, 1960, and 2010.

Based on Table 2.1, one can see that wealth inequality in the United States today is approaching 1900 levels. By contrast, one can see that in 1960 things were quite different, there was a strong middle class, labor unions were strong, and the wealthiest Americans paid much higher taxes than they do today. This all changed with the start of the Conservative Revolution in 1981 which will be discussed in a later chapter.

POLITICAL CULTURE

Who we elect as president says a lot about America at any given time. We will look at the US presidents between Abraham Lincoln and Theodore Roosevelt. During the time of Rapid Industrialization, Americans elected weak and ineffective chief executives who let big business do whatever it wanted to do. By 1900, it was time for a change.

ABRAHAM LINCOLN

Lincoln is ranked as the third best president by the American Historical Association. Lincoln understood what needed to be done to bring the North and South back together. He wanted to treat the South humanely after the war. He expressed this in his second inaugural address on March 4, 1865: "With malice toward none; with charity for all … to bind up the nation's wounds … to do all which may achieve and cherish a just and lasting peace, among ourselves, and with all nations." We will never know if Lincoln's version of Reconstruction would have worked, since he was assassinated by John Wilkes Booth on April 14, 1865.

FIGURE 2.1. Abraham Lincoln

ANDREW JOHNSON

Ranked near the bottom at number 43 by the American Historical Association, Andrew Johnson was no Lincoln. He was a pro-slavery Tennessee Democrat who differed from Confederate President Jefferson Davis only in that he supported the Union. Lincoln used him on the ticket to secure some Democratic votes. Johnson liked Lincoln's concept of leniency, but did not care for his ideas of equality for the former slaves. Many Union veterans were upset with Johnson as former Southern leaders returned to power. Congress tried unsuccessfully to remove Johnson from office through impeachment, but Johnson was able to finish his term, although he was weakened politically and lost the confidence of the people. Andrew Johnson set the stage for a succession of weak, ineffective, and pro-business presidents.

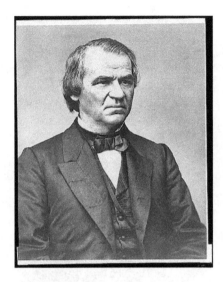

FIGURE 2.2. Andrew Johnson

ULYSSES S. GRANT

Grant is ranked number 26 by the American Historical Association, largely because he was a great general. His presidency was not so great. Grant won the presidency with Republicans in control of Congress, but his victory over Democrat Horatio Seymour would have been in question if Texas, Mississippi, and Virginia had been allowed to vote. Carpetbagger governments in the South allowed Grant to win. Clearly, Grant was a soldier, not a politician. He trusted those under him too much. To his credit, Grant tried very hard to battle the terror caused by the Ku Klux Klan in the South. By 1870, all Southern states were readmitted to the union. Railroads were booming and helping forge an industrial economy and President Grant did not stand in their way. Grant won reelection but realized that the North could not impose its will on the South. Many Republicans who demanded civil service reform began to lose interest in keeping Union troops in the South. A devastating economic depression began in 1873 that spread panic from Europe to the United States. The railroad boom stalled and iron and steel production decreased dramatically. This depression changed American politics and split the Republican Party. Republicans in the North favored a strict return to the gold standard (a monetary system based on a fixed quantity of gold) and economic austerity. In the Midwest, Republicans wanted economic stimulus in the form of paper greenbacks (government-issued paper currency not based on the gold standard). In the 1874 election the Democrats took advantage of the split, and the House shifted from 70 percent Republican to only 37 percent. Scandals in the Grant administration further hurt the Republicans. America became more conservative and big business, especially the railroads, held more power than ever.

FIGURE 2.3. Ulysses S. Grant

RUTHERFORD B. HAYES

Hayes is ranked number 31 by the American Historical Association. The year 1876 was to be a celebratory year, since it was the US centennial, but it turned out that the contentious presidential election dampened much of the patriotic zeal. Because of the disputed election

FIGURE 2.4. Rutherford B. Hayes

of 1876, where Tilden won the popular vote, but lost the election, Hayes was distrusted. Hayes ended Reconstruction by removing the last Union troops that had enforced it. Hayes naively hoped that the South would respect civil rights for black people, but he also knew that his power to make a difference was extremely limited. He expressed interest in limiting the power of corporations and Wall Street, but ultimately did nothing as he found his power to be limited. Hayes inherited a nation divided by North and South, and rich and poor. The economic depression lingered on and the nation moved farther to the right politically.

JAMES GARFIELD

James Garfield, a former Union general, was elected president in 1880 and was assassinated while in office. Garfield was the second of four US presidents who were assassinated. He was shot by Charles J. Guiteau, a disgruntled federal office seeker. Garfield is ranked number 27 among American presidents by the American Historical Association. Garfield reluctantly accepted the Republican nomination. Republicans at that time tended to be Union veterans, businessmen, Northern evangelicals, descendants of New England puritans, and African Americans. The Democrats tended to be Confederate veterans, workers, Southern evangelicals, Catholics, and Lutheran immigrants. Garfield was the only ordained minister ever to be elected. He was also a war hero who promised to defend freed blacks and civil rights. He even

FIGURE 2.5. James Garfield

appointed four blacks to his administration, including Frederick Douglass. Garfield may have stood out among the do-nothing presidents between Lincoln and Theodore Roosevelt, but his assassination ended his chance of rising above the others. Garfield was shot on July 2, 1881, and lived for another two months.

CHESTER ARTHUR

Arthur is not a very well-known president. He is ranked number 25 by the American Historical Association. Arthur assumed the presidency upon Garfield's death. This terrified many Americans, including Arthur himself. He was put on the ticket to satisfy the conservative Stalwart Republicans, and was known for his corruption and cronyism. He changed his tune once he became president and started civil service reforms. Arthur reflected the business-first mentality of the Gilded Age. America was changing rapidly, with big cities, electric lights, streetcars, skyscrapers, suburbs, oil, steel, tenements, immigrants, telephones, corporations, and millionaires. Only 1 percent ever became rich during the Gilded Age. Many Americans believed in the Horatio Alger ideal. Alger's stories popularized the rags to riches myth. The ideal was that only through free enterprise could someone reach wealth from poverty, through self-reliance.

FIGURE 2.6. Chester Arthur

GROVER CLEVELAND

Grover Cleveland is the only president to serve two non-consecutive terms. He is ranked number 20 by the American Historical Association. Cleveland was the Democratic governor of New York and a reformer. Democrats still held the House in 1884, but Republicans were making gains. Former Confederates became the ruling class in the South, replacing Reconstruction-era politicians. These Democrats were known as Redeemers and Bourbon Democrats. Mississippi, Alabama, and Georgia all put Confederate logos on their state flags. The Supreme Court struck down Grant's Civil Rights Act, which meant Reconstruction was officially dead. The healing from the Civil War came at the price of civil rights. Former confederate rebels were restored to hero status. In the North blacks voted, in the South Redeemer Democrats disenfranchised them through various methods. *Plessy v. Ferguson* gave the Supreme Court's blessing to segregation. Cleveland wanted to return to the democratic ideals of Jefferson and Jackson—balancing the budget, sound fiscal policies, downsizing of government. Cleveland was very conservative and pro-business. John D. Rockefeller used the 1870s depression to gobble up 90 percent of America's oil refineries. He circumvented strict monopoly laws by forming a trust. J.P. Morgan controlled the nation's banking, and even bailed out the US government at one point.

FIGURE 2.7. Grover Cleveland

BENJAMIN HARRISON

Harrison was the grandson of William Henry Harrison, who died after only 30 days in office. Harrison was a former Union general and a well-known American Indian fighter. Ranked number 34 among presidents by the American Historical Association, Harrison was a conservative Republican and very unsociable. When asked if he could be more human, he said, "I tried, but I failed." He increased tariffs, and supported pensions for war veterans, including their children. The West was the major focus during his presidency, and Harrison went after American Indians, moving them to reservations. During his time in office, the Populist Party arose from the Midwest, West, and South.

FIGURE 2.8. Benjamin Harrison

WILLIAM MCKINLEY

McKinley was the last president to have fought in the Civil War. He was assassinated by an anarchist named Leon Czolgosz. McKinley is ranked number 21 among presidents by the American Historical Association, mainly because he was assassinated—assassinations tend to give presidents a bump in the polls. Favoring big business, McKinley had presided over a tremendous recovery and was expanding American power into the Pacific and the Caribbean. In the fall of 1901, McKinley spoke at an exhibition in Buffalo, New York, in which he praised the success of American industry. Leon Czolgosz, son of Polish immigrants, worked hard to

FIGURE 2.9. William McKinley

achieve the American Dream, but the 1893 depression ended his hopes. Czolgosz then turned to anarchism. Hoping to inspire the overthrow of capitalism, he shot McKinley at point-blank range. McKinley died soon after.

THEODORE ROOSEVELT

One of the greatest presidents in American history, Theodore Roosevelt is ranked number two by the American Historical Association. Although he is known as the champion of the working class, Roosevelt was born into wealth. He was a weak and sickly child, yet he went on to become police commissioner of New York City, governor of New York, assistant secretary of the Navy, and vice president of the United States. He served in the Spanish-American War as a cavalry colonel of the Rough Riders. "Teddy" Roosevelt (also known as TR) was one of the smartest men to occupy the White House. He was an author, naturalist, explorer, historian, and politician. Roosevelt was a progressive republican who had a wide range of interests and a dynamic personality.

Roosevelt seized an opportunity for glory in the run up to the Spanish-American War. By 1897 Roosevelt was in effect running the Navy Department as the assistant secretary of the Navy. When war broke out in 1898, he formed the Rough Riders, an odd collection of his wealthy friends, cowboys, and other admirers. He showed courage and gained fame in battle in Cuba, and then returned to be elected governor of New York. Roosevelt became president after McKinley was assassinated. He was inaugurated at age 42, the youngest person to become

FIGURE 2.10. Theodore Roosevelt

president. He attempted to move the Republican Party toward Progressivism, including trust busting and increased regulation of businesses. In November 1904 he was reelected and pushed for more reforms with his Square Deal program. Roosevelt looked to protect the average worker, break up monopolies, regulate railroad rates, and protect the nation's food and drug supply. He was the first conservationist president and expanded national parks and forests. He wanted more radical reforms, but the conservative Republicans would not allow it. He focused his foreign policy on the Caribbean and the building of the Panama Canal. There were no wars, but his slogan, "Speak softly and carry a big stick," was reinforced by sending the expanded US Navy—the Great White Fleet—on a world tour. He negotiated an end to the Russo-Japanese War, for which he won the Nobel Peace Prize. His presidency signaled the end of the Gilded Age.

What is apparent in looking at the American presidents during the time of rapid industrialization is that the presidents between Lincoln and TR were weak, ineffective, and merely served as business agents for American corporations. Theodore Roosevelt signaled the beginning of the Progressive Era and a re-balancing of American society.

LABOR MILITANCY

Industrial production in the United States grew rapidly after the Civil War and Chicago was a major industrial city and the hub of labor union activity. There were tens of thousands of immigrant workers who worked under horrible conditions and at low wages ($1.50 a day). The workers wanted better working conditions and higher wages. Employers responded with intimidation, other repressive tactics, and violence. Fights erupted and were covered by the mainstream press, which favored the employers.

HAYMARKET AFFAIR

The Haymarket Affair (or Haymarket Riot) took place after a bombing at a labor demonstration on Tuesday, May 4, 1886, at Haymarket Square in Chicago. The day began peacefully, with workers rallying in support of strikers demanding an eight-hour day. An unknown person threw a dynamite bomb at the police as they dispersed the crowd. The bomb blast and subsequent gunfire killed seven police officers and at least four civilians and many more people were wounded. The police responded by conducting raids without warrants and civil rights were suspended in an atmosphere of panic. Much of the police investigative focus was on recent immigrant workers. In the show trial that followed, eight anarchists were convicted of conspiracy. The evidence showed that one of the defendants may have built the bomb, but none of those on trial had thrown it. Seven of the defendants were sentenced to death, but Illinois governor Richard J. Oglesby commuted two of the sentences to life in prison. The death sentences of two of the defendants were commuted to life in prison by Illinois governor Richard J. Oglesby. Another defendant committed suicide in jail. Four defendants were hanged on November 11, 1887. The Haymarket Affair is considered the origin of international May Day observances for workers. The Haymarket Affair site was designated a Chicago Landmark in 1992. The Haymarket Affair has influenced labor–management relationships ever since. "The boisterous sea of liberty," Thomas Jefferson wrote in 1820, "is never without a wave."

MANIFEST DESTINY

In 1845 John L. O'Sullivan, a newspaper editor, wrote that, "Our claim is by the right of our manifest destiny to overspread and to possess the whole of the continent which Providence

has given us for the development of the great experiment of liberty and federative self government entrusted to us … In our hands it must fast fill in with a population destined to establish
a noble young empire." O'Sullivan coined the term Manifest Destiny, which still drives US
foreign policy today.

Expanding the nation westward seemed perfectly natural to most Americans in the mid-
nineteenth century. Guided by the spirit of the Puritans of New England, Americans believed
that they had a divine obligation to spread their good progress to the Pacific Ocean. Many
Americans believed that conquering the North American continent and forging the American
nation was by divine right bestowed by God. The Native Americans and others were simply in
the way. American missionaries, whose purpose was to save heathen souls, were soon followed
by soldiers and businessmen who had other interests. The economic incentive was paramount
as the Southern states wanted to expand cotton cultivation westward and make new states
into slave states. Westward expansion in that sense helped lead to the Civil War. Moreover,
Manifest Destiny fit nicely into our foreign policy as we gained power and projected that
power around the world. Accordingly, the United States was destined by God to spread its
form of government and way of life to the rest of the world. It was believed that by increasing
the American influence in foreign countries, the United States was bringing the blessings of
liberty to those countries.

FIGURE 2.11. American Progress (1872) by John Gast

GENDER AND FAMILY RELATIONS

Industrialization and urban expansion helped shape America into the technologically advanced society it is today, but it also led to:

1. insufficient housing in the cities,
2. environmental damage,
3. disease,
4. dangerous working environments, and
5. a rise in social problems such as alcoholism, crime, prostitution, gambling, and spousal abuse.

Families that had worked side by side on the farm were now crammed into tenement buildings. On the farm everyone contributed and their worlds were intertwined. In the city men and women were separated, children shoved off to factories, and old people left to rot. This put tremendous pressure on families, who lived on starvation wages in urban squalor. One of the most terrible legacies of urbanization is spousal abuse, or what is now called domestic violence.

Until the mid-1800s in America, most states accepted wife beating as a valid means for a husband to exercise authority over his wife. In 1850, Tennessee became the first state to outlaw wife beating. Other states followed. By the early twentieth century, it was common for the police to intervene in cases of domestic violence, but arrests were not common. Wife beating was made illegal in all states by 1920.

Domestic violence is a form of violence by one partner against another partner in an intimate relationship. Violence Against Women Acts have been passed by Congress in an attempt to reduce domestic violence. In 2000, statistics from a Department of Justice report showed that 22.1 percent of women and 7.4 percent of men have been the victim of domestic violence. The statistics cross all boundaries of race, income, and sexual orientation. However, a larger percentage of socially and economically disadvantaged groups in the United States regularly face higher rates of domestic violence than other groups. For example, about 60 percent of Native American women are physically assaulted in their lifetime by a partner or spouse.

CONCLUSION

By 1900, America was out of balance. There was too much power in the hands of too few people. Rapid industrialization had indeed created a powerful America, but this was done on the backs of children, women, immigrants, and the disenfranchised working class. The Gilded Age, unfortunately, has returned in our time. The distribution of income is not unlike it was in 1900. Americans work longer hours, take fewer vacations, and have less union representation than any other modern industrial nation. The real strength of America is in its people. I witnessed how hard my parents worked to reach the middle class. They came to America when it was still possible to get ahead. One can learn from the past and see what ordinary Americans did in 1900 when faced with such imbalance and unfairness—they took their country back from the privileged few.

TIMELINE

1868

June 25: Congress enacts an eight-hour workday for government workers.

July 28: The Fourteenth Amendment to the US Constitution grants citizenship to anyone born in the United States and guarantees due process and equal protection of the laws.

November 3: Republican Ulysses S. Grant is elected president of the United States.

1869

January: General Philip H. Sheridan says, "The only good Indian is a dead Indian."

May 10: The golden spike is driven into a railroad tie at Promontory Summit, Utah, completing the transcontinental railroad.

1870

US population reaches 39,818,449.

January 10: John D. Rockefeller's Standard Oil Company is incorporated in Ohio.

February 25: Hiram R. Revels of Mississippi becomes the first African American US senator. Joseph H. Rainey of South Carolina becomes the first African American elected to the House of Representatives.

March 30: The Fifteenth Amendment to the US Constitution guarantees the right to vote regardless of "race, color, or previous condition of servitude."

1871

January: Victoria Woodhull demands that women receive the vote under the Fourteenth Amendment.

March 3: Congress declares that American Indian tribes will no longer be treated as independent nations.

April 10: P.T. Barnum opens his three-ring circus, hailing it as the "Greatest Show on Earth."

October 8: The Great Chicago Fire kills 250 people and destroys 17,500 buildings.

1872

Andrew Carnegie visits Henry Bessemer's steel plant in England, and returns home to expand the steel industry.

August: Montgomery Ward begins to sell goods to rural customers by mail.

September 4: Crédit Mobilier Scandal.

November 5: Susan B. Anthony and others are arrested for trying to vote in Rochester, New York.

November 5: President Ulysses S. Grant is reelected to a second term as president of the United States.

1873

Mark Twain and Charles Dudley Warner publish *The Gilded Age: A Tale of Today*, a satire of contemporary greed and corruption.

March 3: The Comstock Act prohibits the mailing of obscene literature.

September 18: The Financial Panic of 1873 begins, in which 5,183 business fail.

1874

Barbed wire is used to fence in cattle on the Great Plains.

The discovery of gold leads thousands of prospectors to trespass on American Indian lands in the Black Hills in Dakota territory.

November: The Women's Christian Temperance Union is founded.

1875

March 1: Congress passes the Civil Rights Act of 1875, guaranteeing equal use of public accommodations and places of public amusement. It also forbids the exclusion of African Americans from jury duty.

May 10: A federal grand jury indicts 238 for conspiring to defraud the US government of tax revenues.

1876

February 14: Alexander Graham Bell patents the telephone.

May: The nation celebrates its centennial by opening an International Exhibition in Philadelphia.

June 25: General George A. Custer and 265 officers and enlisted men are killed by Sioux Indians, led by Sitting Bull and Crazy Horse, at the Little Bighorn River in Montana.

1877

Charles Elmer Hires introduces root beer.

February 27: An electoral commission declares Rutherford B. Hayes the winner of the disputed presidential election.

April 10: President Hayes begins to withdraw federal troops from the South, signaling the official end of Reconstruction.

June to October: Federal troops pursue and capture Chief Joseph and the Nez Perce Indians of Oregon and force them to live on an Oklahoma reservation.

July 16: The Great Railroad Strike begins in Martinsburg, West Virginia, after the Baltimore and Ohio Railroad imposes a 10 percent wage cut.

December 6: Thomas Edison invents the phonograph.

1878

German engineer Karl Benz produces the first automobile powered by an internal combustion engine.

January 10: The Senate defeats a women's suffrage amendment 34–16.

1879

February 15: Congress grants female attorneys the right to argue cases before the Supreme Court.

October 21: Thomas Edison invents the light bulb.

1880

US population reaches 50,155,783.

November 2: Republican James Garfield is elected president of the United States.

1 8 8 1

Helen Hunt Jackson's book *Century of Dishonor* reveals the government's unjust treatment of Native Americans.

Cyrus McCormick introduces a mechanical harvester and twine binder that increases agricultural productivity.

July 2: President James Garfield is shot by Charles J. Guiteau, a disgruntled office seeker. Garfield dies on September 19.

July 4: Booker T. Washington opens the Tuskegee Institute.

July 19: Sitting Bull and other Sioux Indians return to the United States from Canada.

1 8 8 2

Attorney Samuel Dodd invents the trust.

May 6: Congress passes the Chinese Exclusion Act, barring Chinese immigration for 10 years.

1 8 8 3

Joseph Pulitzer buys the *New York World* from Jay Gould.

January 16: Congress passes the Pendleton Act, creating a Civil Service Commission and filling government positions by a merit and examination system.

May 19: Buffalo Bill Cody opens his Wild West show in Omaha, Nebraska.

October 15: The Supreme Court rules that the Civil Rights Act of 1875 only forbids state-imposed discrimination, not that by individuals or corporations.

November 18: Railroads in the United States and Canada adopt a system of standard time.

1 8 8 4

The Knights of Labor strike against the Wabash Railroad.

May 1: First skyscraper in the United States is being built in Chicago.

November 4: Democrat Grover Cleveland defeats Republican James Blaine and is elected president of the United States.

1 8 8 6

Dr. Stanton Coit provides services to the poor when he opens the first settlement house.

May 1: Over 300,000 workers demonstrate for an eight-hour work day.

May 4: The Haymarket Square bombing in Chicago kills 7 police officers, several citizens, and wounds 60.

May 10: The Supreme Court holds that corporations are persons covered by the Fourteenth Amendment, and are entitled to due process.

May 31: Most Southern railroads adopt the standard rail gauge.

October 28: President Grover Cleveland unveils the Statue of Liberty.

December 8: The American Federation of Labor is founded, with Samuel Gompers as president.

1887

February 4: The Interstate Commerce Act requires railroads to charge reasonable rates and forbids them from offering rate reductions to preferred customers.

February 8: The Dawes Severalty Act subdivides American Indian reservations into individual plots and some lands are sold to white settlers.

1888

Edward Bellamy publishes his utopian novel, *Looking Backward.*

November 6: Republican Benjamin Harrison is elected president of the United States, despite receiving 100,000 fewer votes than Democratic incumbent Grover Cleveland.

1889

New Jersey permits holding companies to buy up the stock of other corporations.

April 22: President Benjamin Harrison opens a portion of Oklahoma to white settlement.

May 31: Johnstown Flood. An abandoned reservoir breaks, flooding the city of Johnstown, Pennsylvania, and killing 2,295 people.

June: Industrialist Andrew Carnegie publishes an essay entitled "The Gospel of Wealth."

1890

US population reaches 62,947,714.

The US Bureau of the Census announces that the Western frontier is now closed.

July 2: Congress passes the Sherman Antitrust Act.

November 1: Mississippi restricts black suffrage by requiring voters to demonstrate an ability to read and interpret the US Constitution.

December 15: American Indian police kill Sitting Bull in South Dakota.

December 29: More than 200 Lakota men, women, and children are killed on the Pine Ridge Indian Reservation by the US Cavalry. This is known as the Wounded Knee Massacre.

1891

James Naismith, a physical education instructor at the YMCA Training College in Springfield, Massachusetts, invents basketball.

March 14: A New Orleans mob breaks into a prison and kills 11 Sicilian immigrants accused of murdering the city's police chief.

May 19: The Populist Party is founded in Cincinnati, Ohio.

September 22: A total of 900,000 acres of land that had been given to the Sauk, Fox, and Pottawatomi Indians is opened to white settlement.

1892

The boll weevil (a type of beetle that feeds on cotton plant buds) arrives in Texas.

January 1: Ellis Island opens to screen immigrants.

July 2: A cut in wages at Andrew Carnegie's steelworks at Homestead, Pennsylvania, causes a labor strike.

October 12: The World's Columbian Exhibition opens in Chicago to commemorate the 300th anniversary of Columbus's discovery of the New World and features the first Ferris Wheel.

Fall: College football emerges as a national sport.

November 8: Democrat Grover Cleveland is elected president of the United States, becoming the only president to serve two non-consecutive terms.

1893

Frederick Jackson Turner proposes his thesis on the frontier experience's role in shaping the American character.

January 17: Pro-American interests depose Queen Liliuokalani of Hawaii.

1894

May 1: Jacob Coxey leads a march on Washington by the unemployed (known as Coxey's Army).

May 10: Workers at the Pullman sleeping car plant in Chicago go on strike.

June 26: The American Railway Union, led by Eugene Debs, begins to boycott trains carrying Pullman cars.

July 3: Federal troops enforce a court injunction forbidding the American Railway Union from interfering with interstate commerce and delivery of the mail. The Pullman Strike ends as Eugene Debs is arrested.

1895

May 20: The Supreme Court strikes down an income tax.

1896

May 18: In a case known as *Plessy v. Ferguson,* the US Supreme Court rules that segregation of blacks and whites is permitted under the Constitution so long as both races receive equal facilities. This becomes known as "separate but equal."

July 7: William Jennings Bryan electrified the Democratic convention with his "Cross of Gold" speech and received the party's nomination.

November 3: Republican William McKinley is elected president of the United States.

CREDITS

1. Fig. 2.1. Anthony Berger, "Abraham Lincoln," http://www.loc.gov/pictures/resource/ppmsca.19305/. Copyright in the Public Domain.
2. Fig. 2.2. "Andrew Johnson," http://www.loc.gov/pictures/item/96522530/. Copyright in the Public Domain.
3. Fig. 2.3. "Ulysses S. Grant," http://www.loc.gov/pictures/resource/cph.3c10720/. Copyright in the Public Domain.
4. Fig. 2.4. "Rutherford B. Hayes," http://www.loc.gov/pictures/resource/cph.3a53292/. Copyright in the Public Domain.
5. Fig. 2.5. "James Garfield," http://www.loc.gov/pictures/item/brh2003000342/PP/. Copyright in the Public Domain.
6. Fig. 2.6. "Chester Arthur," http://www.loc.gov/pictures/item/96524270/. Copyright in the Public Domain.

7. Fig. 2.7. "Grover Cleveland," http://www.loc.gov/pictures/item/00651299/. Copyright in the Public Domain.

8. Fig. 2.8. "Benjamin Harrison," http://www.loc.gov/pictures/item/96521670/. Copyright in the Public Domain.

9. Fig. 2.9. "William McKinley," http://www.loc.gov/pictures/item/91738541/. Copyright in the Public Domain.

10. Fig. 2.10. "Theodore Roosevelt," http://commons.wikimedia.org/wiki/File:Teddy_Roosevelt_portrait. jpg. Copyright in the Public Domain.

11. Fig. 2.11. "American Progress (1872) by John Gast," http://commons.wikimedia.org/wiki/File:American_progress.JPG. Copyright in the Public Domain.

AMERICAN ASSHOLE?

BY DR. BRUCE OLAV SOLHEIM WITH ART BY GARY DUMM

IN 2003, I TAUGHT AMERICAN HISTORY AS A FULBRIGHT PROFESSOR AT THE UNIVERSITY OF TROMSØ IN NORTHERN NORWAY— THE NORTHERNMOST UNIVERSITY IN THE WORLD.

TROMSO

ARCTIC CIRCLE

MAP OF NORWAY

WE HAD JUST INVADED IRAQ, AND MANY NORWEGIANS WERE CRITICAL OF U.S. FOREIGN POLICY, INCLUDING MY COLLEAGUES.

MY DAUGHTER WAS CALLED "AN AMERICAN ASSHOLE" BY ONE OF HER CLASSMATES. THAT MADE ME MAD.

THEN, A NORWEGIAN IN A YANKEES HAT YELLED AT ME IN THE GROCERY STORE.

GO HOME AMERICAN IMPERIALIST WAR PIG!!

I WAS STARTING TO TAKE IT PERSONALLY.

BUT THEN I BEGAN TO NOTICE HOW QUIET AND PEACEFUL LIVING IN NORWAY WAS COMPARED TO POST-9/11 AMERICA. I STARTED TO WONDER...

SPEAK SOFTLY AND CARRY A BIG STICK.

WELL, WE DO HAVE BIGGER STICKS NOW!

PRESIDENT THEODORE ROOSEVELT WAS A COWBOY, AN AUTHOR, A BIRD-WATCHER, A NATURALIST, A BIG GAME HUNTER, AND A WARRIOR. IS THE UNITED STATES AN IMPERIALIST NATION?

CHAPTER THREE

US IMPERIALISM AND THE SPANISH-AMERICAN WAR

OBJECTIVES

1. Define imperialism and foreign policy.
2. Identify the traditional forces in US foreign policy.
3. Understand why the United States fought the Spanish-American War.
4. Determine how US foreign policy has changed since 1898.

PERSONAL HISTORY

I served for six years in the United States Army as both an enlisted man and as an officer. It was not until my final year or two that I began to think that maybe we were being used for some other reason than to preserve and protect freedom and liberty around the world. When I was stationed in West Germany in 1980, I drove by US Army Europe (USAREUR) headquarters. German workmen had taken down huge shields with a flaming sword crest symbolizing the Army command in Europe on the two gigantic pillars at the wrought iron entrance gate. They were apparently going to repaint the shields. I looked more carefully and could not believe my eyes. There, where the shields had been, I could clearly see the shadows of Nazi eagles and swastikas. USAREUR headquarters was previously the Nazi headquarters for the 110th Infantry Regiment. I wish I had taken a picture: the USAREUR sign flanked by two Nazi swastika–emblazoned pillars. I am not sure if it was just irony or something else.

INTRODUCTION

Foreign policy is simply the actions a government takes concerning everything outside of its borders. US foreign policy is a complex mixture of various powerful interests and concepts. Other countries have accused the United States of imperialism over the years. These criticisms are not without some validity. The United States does not set out to be imperialistic, but, in the process of carrying out its foreign policy, it often acts imperialistically. Classic military imperialism (i.e., that of the Roman Empire) was driven by the concept that "might makes right." The Romans offered no apologies for taking over other lands. The United States, on the other hand, does not set out to conquer other lands merely to demonstrate its power or to gain riches by seizing the wealth of other nations; although that might happen, the United States often has very high minded and even noble intentions when it invades, interferes, or helps another country.

The concept of an American Empire was promoted by President James K. Polk, who led the United States into the Mexican-American War of 1846. Eventually the United States annexed California and other western territories through the Treaty of Guadalupe Hidalgo and the Gadsden Purchase. In his book *The Rise and Fall of the Great Powers*, Yale historian Paul Kennedy wrote, "From the time the first settlers arrived in Virginia from England and started moving westward, this was an imperial nation, a conquering nation." Although this may be true, it is important to look at the intentions and philosophy behind this uniquely American style of imperialism. In the late nineteenth century, foreign territories such as Hawaii were sought by the United States in a push toward expansion. The Teller Amendment and the Platt Amendment were used to grant the United States the right to intervene in such territories if the United States believed that the government of a territory was unfit to rule itself. Was this paternalism, naked aggression, greed, pity, or wily bureaucratic maneuvering? Perhaps a little of everything? The anti-imperial imperialism of US foreign policy was beginning to take shape.

American exceptionalism is the theory that the United States is special and unique among all the nations of the world in terms of its political and religious institutions, history, and national purpose. The Puritan ideal expressed by Massachusetts Bay Colony founder John Winthrop defines the essence of American exceptionalism. The Puritans in New England believed they set an example of communal charity, affection, and unity to the world. Winthrop's famous 1630 sermon gave rise to the later widespread belief that the United States of America is God's chosen country because metaphorically it is a "Shining City upon a Hill."

To get an answer to the question of whether the United States is an imperialist country or not, it would be best to begin with the roots of US foreign policy.

TRADITIONAL FORCES IN US FOREIGN POLICY

1. Isolationism
2. Neutrality

3. The Monroe Doctrine (1823)
4. Expansionism (Manifest Destiny)

ISOLATIONISM

In 1796 President George Washington issued a warning in his farewell address:

> *The great rule of conduct for us in regard to foreign nations is in extending our commercial relations, to have with them as little political connection as possible … It is our true policy to steer clear of permanent alliances with any portion of the foreign world; so far, I mean, as we are now at liberty to do it; for let me not be understood as capable of patronizing infidelity to existing engagements. I hold the maxim no less applicable to public than to private affairs, that honesty is always the best policy. I repeat it, therefore, let those engagements be observed in their genuine sense. But, in my opinion, it is unnecessary and would be unwise to extend them.*

President Thomas Jefferson echoed Washington's warning in his March 4, 1801, inaugural address: "Peace, commerce, and honest friendship with all nations, entangling alliances with none." Since that time isolationism has been a determinant in the formulation of our foreign policy. Isolationist arguments today suggest the foolishness of spending billions of dollars helping others abroad while the American infrastructure is crumbling, Americans are out of work, and the education system is broken.

NEUTRALITY

It is always best to remain objective, especially in foreign affairs, but it is simply not human nature to do so. Human beings are emotional and naturally take sides. Yet, from an economic standpoint, neutrality is best. All American attempts at neutrality in our foreign policy have failed. Woodrow Wilson kept us out of World War I until his second term, when the United States entered the war "to make the world safe for democracy." Public reluctance to intervene in World War II lasted until the attack on Pearl Harbor. By examining our interpersonal relationships, we can see the difficulty of maintaining neutrality. At a personal level, when two of three best friends are fighting with each other, if the person stuck in between remains neutral, the other two will be upset. That neutrality is not comforting for a person in a fight. Human nature requires the seeking of allies and a clear determination of enemies. It comes down to the old adage: "If you're not with me, you're against me."

THE MONROE DOCTRINE

President James Monroe's 1823 annual message to Congress warned European powers not to interfere in the affairs of the Western Hemisphere. This warning became known as the Monroe Doctrine. The United States has always taken a particular interest in its closest neighbors in the Western Hemisphere. This interest has not always been well received by other countries in the Americas and on numerous occasions the Monroe Doctrine has been invoked. US Marines were sent into the Dominican Republic in 1904, Nicaragua in 1911, and Haiti in 1915. All of these incursions were made ostensibly to keep Europeans out of the Americas. Latin Americans saw this protectionism as simply a fig leaf for imperialism.

In 1962, the Monroe Doctrine was invoked symbolically when the United States responded to the Soviet Union building nuclear missile–launching sites in Cuba. The October 1962 Cuban Missile Crisis is the closest the world has come to nuclear war. With the support of the Organization of American States, President John F. Kennedy drew a naval and air quarantine around Cuba. After several tension-filled days, the Soviet Union agreed to withdraw its missiles and dismantle the sites. Subsequently, the United States dismantled several of its obsolete air and missile bases in Turkey. Cuba is still a flashpoint for both US foreign and domestic policy.

EXPANSIONISM (MANIFEST DESTINY)

Expansionism always fits in well with a business point of view. No successful business person would think that they have made enough money. Continual growth is expected. Theodore Roosevelt used a biological explanation for continual American expansion and growth—a cellular organism that is no longer growing is, by definition, dying. The same rationale that drove the United States to overrun the North American continent drove it overseas in search of new lands, markets, and opportunities—an internationalization of Manifest Destiny.

Probably the most interesting aspect of US foreign policy is its contradictory nature. Is the United States an expansionist imperial power? An isolationist country? A neutral business partner? A hemispheric meddler? The answer is yes, all of the above.

OVERVIEW: THE SPANISH-AMERICAN WAR

By 1898 the last remnants of the 1893 depression were gone. Many businesses had gone under and others consolidated into gigantic monopolies. Carnegie's steel company was sold to Charles Schwab and became the United States Steel Corporation, the first company capitalized at $1 billion. America had built up its power internally and had conquered the continent; now it set sights on the rest of the world.

FIGURE 3.1. USS *Maine*

FIGURE 3.2. Destruction of the USS *Maine*

The 1893 depression devastated the sugar-based economy of Cuba. Cuban patriots took advantage of the economic chaos to start a guerrilla uprising. The major promoters for American intervention in Cuba were not businessmen, but newspapers such as William Randolph Hearst's *New York Journal* and its rival, Joseph Pulitzer's *New York World*. Theodore Roosevelt, as assistant secretary of the Navy, also pushed for war because he felt it would invigorate the nation. Roosevelt sent the USS *Maine* to Havana harbor, where it exploded, killing 266 Americans. The explosion was probably internal or caused by a stray mine, but public opinion persuaded President McKinley to declare war on Spain. Because Spain also held the Philippines, McKinley decided to send an American fleet to Manila. He was concerned that Cuba and the Philippines might wind up in German hands. Admiral George Dewey entered Manila harbor and quickly blasted the Spanish fleet to pieces in just six hours. The United States annexed Hawaii during the Spanish-American War. Guam, Puerto Rico, and the Philippines were annexed as part of the Treaty of Paris that officially ended the war.

Not one to shy away from a fight, Theodore Roosevelt resigned as assistant secretary of the Navy and formed a volunteer cavalry regiment called the Rough Riders. This regiment was a cross section of American society. It had New York bluebloods, Midwesterners, Western outlaws, Southerners (including Confederate general Joe Wheeler), Mexicans, Indians, and African Americans. Roosevelt captured the thinking of many Americans when he said, "I should welcome almost any war for I think this country needs one." Fighting was very fierce and the Spanish army was equipped with German weapons. Roosevelt wound up leading the regiment in a charge up Kettle Hill overlooking Santiago. The war ended very quickly in an American victory. Hawaii became a territory, Puerto Rico a commonwealth, and Cuba a protectorate. The United States was now a world power in political as well as economic terms. Theodore Roosevelt became governor of New York and the Philippines were annexed because McKinley thought the "little brown brothers" were incapable of self-government and in danger of Japanese or German domination. The islands were of strategic importance to the United States as a gateway to the vast China market. US Secretary of State John Hay said, "It has been a splendid little war; begun with the highest motives, carried on with magnificent intelligence and spirit, favored by that fortune which loves the brave."

All was not well, however. The same Filipinos whom the United States had liberated became frustrated with a US policy that equated to occupation, so they began an insurgency that eventually led to another war—the Philippine War or the Philippine Insurrection.

UNDERLYING FACTORS IN THE SPANISH-AMERICAN WAR

ECONOMIC

The depression of 1893 frightened many Americans, none more so than those in big business and government. It was decided that expansion to foreign markets would cure the boom-and-bust cycle of business. Diversifying American investments would create more resiliency, smooth out the highs and lows of the business cycle, and insure continued prosperity and growth.

IDEOLOGICAL

US foreign policy has been and continues to be driven by the concept of Manifest Destiny. A feeling of superiority spurs American policymakers to push into foreign lands with almost missionary zeal. By 1898, Europeans were gobbling up territories around the world and Americans felt they needed to get in on the action. The United States ended up expanding to Alaska (1867), Midway Island, Puerto Rico, Guam, and Hawaii (all in 1898). The move across the Pacific was all part of a plan to provide stepping stones to Asia. We were lured by the Asian market, China specifically. There was a sense of urgency to act before all territories were taken.

PSYCHOLOGICAL

Americans felt a sense of insecurity at home. Much of this insecurity was caused by a dramatic rise in immigration. Most of the new immigrants after 1890 came from southern Europe and Russia. Strange people with strange accents, languages, and customs made many nativists nervous. The assimilation process was different for every immigrant group; some were slower than others. Many Americans also wanted to end the divisive legacy of the Civil War, where nearly 700,000 Americans had been killed. What better way to forget about the last war than to start a new one? Especially one where the North and South could fight together in a common cause?

These three underlying factors, interestingly enough, can be applied to any American war, not just the Spanish-American War.

PRE-WAR EVENTS

ANXIOUS PUBLIC MOOD IN THE 1890s

Alfred T. Mahan, a former naval officer, pushed for American imperialism in his 1890 book, *The Influence of Sea Power upon History*. Mahan's main argument is that modern industrial nations had to secure foreign markets to exchange goods and had to have a navy strong enough to protect trade routes. This book had a tremendous impact on US foreign policy and led to a crash program to build up the US Navy.

1893 DEPRESSION

At the start of the 1890s, the United States moved quickly into a new industrial age. At the World's Columbian Exposition in Chicago in 1893, millions came to see the innovations that powered American productivity: incandescent lights, efficient farming methods, modern railways, and a faster printing press. Only a few days after the Exposition opened, the nation was hit by a terrible financial crisis. Stock prices fell, businesses went bankrupt, and millions of Americans lost their jobs.

The Panic of 1893 was a serious economic depression. Similar to the Panic of 1873, it was largely caused by the overbuilding and shadow financing of railroads. This, of course, resulted in a series of bank failures. Compounding the collapse of the railroad bubble was a run on the gold supply. The Panic of 1893 was the worst economic depression the United States had ever experienced up to that time.

FLOOD OF NEW IMMIGRANTS

The Statue of Liberty opened in 1886 with its famous inscription: "Give us your tired, your poor, your huddled masses yearning to breathe free. The wretched refuse of your teeming shore." In spite of those words, a sudden influx of immigrants from southern Europe and Russia in the 1890s created anxiety among many in the United States, and not much welcoming spirit. During that time, over 2 million immigrants came from Italy and Austria and over 1.5 million came from Russia. They lived in ethnically separated neighborhoods in New York and Chicago. Many were Orthodox Christians or Jewish (from Eastern Europe) and they came from countries with little democracy. Many of these immigrants were illiterate. Many religious schools were established, as well as foreign-language newspapers, theaters, food stores, restaurants, parishes, and social clubs. Many Americans felt that the recent immigrants did not want to assimilate as rapidly as previous groups.

URBANIZATION

By 1890, 35 percent of Americans lived in urban areas. The rapid and largely unplanned growth of American cities led to unhealthy conditions and serious social problems not before seen in American history. One feature of the urban landscape was the spread of tenements, which were narrow, four-to-five story buildings that did not provide even the most common comforts or enough space for their tenants who were mostly ethnic minorities and immigrants. Tenements were the main housing available in slums and ghettos, the segregated communities into which blacks and immigrants were forced by poverty, prejudice, and even by law. These ghettos were plagued by disease, high infant mortality, and horrific levels of pollution, and were often the site of racial and ethnic conflict.

CLOSING OF THE FRONTIER

American historian Frederick Jackson Turner wrote, "The once vast American western frontier is closed. American energy will continually demand a wider field for its exercise ... The colonization of the Great West did indeed furnish a new field of opportunity. But never again will such gifts of free lands offer themselves. The frontier has gone, and with its going has closed the first period of American history." With the frontier gone there was nowhere to go to start over, as had been possible before. This created feelings of anxiety among the American people. Americans had to find some new outlet for their energy, their dynamic nature, and their sense of adventure. Consequently, American attention then focused overseas.

JINGOISM

Ultra nationalism that leaves reason behind is known as jingoism. Probably the first use of the term in the American press came in connection with the annexation of Hawaii in 1893, led by Americans who overthrew the Hawaiian constitutional monarchy and declared a republic. The term was also used in connection with the foreign policy of Theodore Roosevelt, who was frequently accused of jingoism. In an October 23, 1895, *New York Times* article, Roosevelt stated, "There is much talk about 'jingoism'. If by 'jingoism' they mean a policy in pursuance of which Americans will with resolution and common sense insist upon our rights being respected by foreign powers, then we are 'jingoes.'"

STRANGE BEHAVIOR

It is said that if one goes looking for trouble, one will find it. In the case of the United States in the 1890s, nothing could be more true. The country was spoiling for a fight.

On October 16, 1891, at the True Blue Saloon in Valparaiso, Chile, a bar fight broke out between American sailors and Chilean nationals. Two American sailors were killed, 17 wounded, and many arrested. Both sides blamed the other for initiating the violence. Some American sources suspected a setup of the American sailors. The incident ignited a diplomatic crisis that lasted for months and nearly led to war between the two countries, until a settlement was reached in early 1892.

After the incident, the Chilean government was not conceding and demanded that the US president come to Chile to issue an official apology and allow the American flag to be dipped in disgrace. US President Benjamin Harrison refused. Finally, on January 25, 1892, the Chilean administration, warned that the Americans were positioning themselves for war, gave up their arguments and conceded. In February 1892, a Chilean court sentenced three Chilean rioters, and offered to pay the United States $75,000 in reparations. The Harrison administration accepted, and war with Chile was averted.

NEW ORLEANS

Another near war incident occurred in New Orleans in 1891. Southern Italian immigration and Mafia criminality ignited tensions among nativists. Ethnic conflict erupted in New Orleans with the murder of Police Chief D.C. Hennessy and the lynching of 11 imprisoned Italians in 1891. The police chief, in the throes of death, apparently told a witness that Italians had shot him. Dozens of Italians were arrested, but a jury trial in 1891 ended without convictions. Outraged citizens then called for a meeting on Canal Street. After that meeting, a crowd gathered at Orleans Parish Prison, near the site of Municipal Auditorium, forced its way inside the prison, and lynched 11 Italian men, creating an international crisis. Three of the victims were Italian nationals and several of them had not yet faced trial. The lynch mob were never caught and were even defended by the mayor and the press.

Nationally, the lynching focused attention on anti-immigration laws. The events in New Orleans provoked a major international crisis and war-scare with Italy. The US government's refusal to pay reparations until 1892 led Italy to break off diplomatic relations. The incident also highlighted America's own defenselessness against Italy's navy (the world's third largest at that time). During the height of the crisis, US Secretary of State James "Jingo Jim" Blaine told the Italian government, "Lynching is not as bad as it sounds." The incident also served as example of the desperate desire for national reunification after the Civil War. North and South united in taking on foreign powers. Ultimately, war with Italy was averted when the US government paid reparations to the families of the Italian men who were lynched.

BRITISH GUIANA–VENEZUELA BORDER DISPUTE

The Venezuela Crisis of 1895 occurred over Venezuela's bitter dispute with England, about the territory which England claimed as part of British Guiana and Venezuela saw as Venezuelan territory. Invoking the Monroe Doctrine, US Secretary of State Richard Olney demanded that the British submit the boundary dispute to arbitration. The British response was that the Monroe Doctrine had no validity as international law. President Grover Cleveland was not happy with the British response so he asked Congress to set up a commission and support aggressive measures against Great Britain. Talk of war with Great Britain then began. Britain accepted the United States' demand for arbitration and did not challenge the Monroe Doctrine. A tribunal in Paris decided to give most of the disputed territory to British Guiana thereby averting any hostilities between the United States and Great Britain.

CUBAN REVOLUTION OF 1895

President McKinley did not want war, but the mood in the country was supporting conflict for ideological, economic, and psychological reasons. None of the international incidents in the early 1890s seemed to supply the requisite righteous cause that Americans could get behind. Then, in 1895, the idea of supporting Cuban independence began to take hold. McKinley saw an opportunity to invoke the Monroe Doctrine once again, and gain control of the Caribbean. Assistant Secretary of the Navy Theodore Roosevelt thought that a war with Spain over Cuba would make the United States a world power. There seemed to be a special connection between America and Cuba. In 1868, Cuban sugar planters, frustrated by increasing Spanish taxes, fought with Spain over their independence. They took over much of eastern Cuba, freeing the slaves and destroying Spanish sugar mills. The commander of the rebel army was General Máximo Gómez.

Throughout 1895, as Americans visited and invested in Cuba, Cubans moved to the United States to study and work. Cuban immigration started in Florida and then spread to New York City, Philadelphia, Boston, and Washington. A Cuban national identity was forming and spreading in Cuba and the United States. Americans became increasingly aware that Cubans were not content with the Spanish colonial system. At the same time, baseball became a national obsession in Cuba. The North American sport provided an alternative to traditional Spanish entertainment and further tied America and Cuba together. The revolution began to really pick up under the leadership of José Martí, a poet and journalist living in New York. He visited Cuban communities across the United States to promote and raise funds for Cuban independence. His ideas reshaped "Cuba Libre."

A new Spanish colonial governor, General Valeriano Weyler, was sent to Havana to stop General Gómez. Weyler was forced to deal with a rebel army that operated with the support of peasant farmers. Weyler built concentration camps in rural areas. Rebel sympathizers provided images of these camps to American newspapers. General Weyler became the perfect villain for Americans who were ready for a fight, and especially a fight based on a righteous cause. With Weyler being portrayed as a savage brute in the American press, the stage was set for US intervention.

YELLOW PRESS

"Weyler is a fiendish despot, a brute, a devastator of haciendas, pitiless, cold, an exterminator of men. There is nothing to prevent his carnal brain from inventing torture and infamies of bloody debauchery." This is from William Randolph Hearst's *New York Journal*, February 1896. The yellow press or yellow journalism is news reporting that puts profit ahead of objective journalism. Hearst, the son of a gold miner who struck it rich, was one of the most brilliant newspapermen in American history. Hearst promoted and pushed the Cuba story not only to sell newspapers and beat his rival Joseph Pulitzer at *The New York World*, he wanted to affect US foreign policy and use the Cuban independence movement as a way to bring America

FIGURE 3.3. William Randolph Hearst

together. The competition between the two newspaper moguls, in essence, promoted and provoked the war between the United States and Cuba. The February 17, 1898, edition of *The New York Journal* displayed this headline: "Destruction of the warship Maine was the work of an enemy." No one knew what actually caused the USS *Maine* to blow up, but that did not matter to Hearst, who wanted to push for war in order to sell newspapers.

CISNEROS INCIDENT

President McKinley read many newspapers every day. Like millions of Americans, he was moved by the story of Evangelina Cisneros, a convent-educated Cuban teenager, imprisoned by the Spanish in Havana. Although the whole truth may never be known, the Spanish claimed she was active in the rebellion and tried to murder a Spanish officer. Cisneros claimed that a Spanish officer made sexual advances; she turned him down and was punished for her non-compliance. Famous women around the world were asked by Hearst to send telegrams to the Spanish government in support of Ms. Cisneros. Julia Ward Howe, the author of "The Battle Hymn of the Republic," wrote a letter to the pope. President McKinley's mother joined the cause. All this continued to sell newspapers, but it did not get Cisneros released. She continued to be held by the Spanish in Cuba.

Finally, frustrated by the US government's slow reaction to events, William Randolph Hearst arranged an escape. One of his newspaper reporters bribed the Spanish guards and secured her release. They brought Cisneros out of Cuba and brought her to New York. She was featured at balls at the Waldorf, dinners at Delmonico, and brought to Washington in the company of William Randolph Hearst. She later went on to a career on the stage. American men had rescued one Cuban woman and the question that now faced the nation was: When would the United States free Cuba?

DUPUY DE LÔME LETTER

On January 24, 1898, President McKinley ordered the battleship *Maine* to Havana to protect American interests in Cuba. Spain's ambassador to Washington, Enrique Dupuy de Lôme, was unimpressed with McKinley. Cuban revolutionaries stole a letter from de Lôme. Part of the letter read, "McKinley is weak and catering to the rabble, and, besides a low politician who desires to leave a door open to the jingoes of his party." Hearst published it immediately with the headline "Greatest Insult Ever to America: Spanish Insult Our President." The newspaper insisted that war was the only solution.

REMEMBER THE *MAINE*

Americans generally need a dramatic incident to push them into war. By February 15, 1898, the USS *Maine* had been anchored for three weeks in Havana harbor without incident. But on that day the Maine suddenly exploded, killing 266 US sailors. The sailors were all buried at Arlington National Cemetery. McKinley's appointed naval committee investigated the destruction of the Maine, but most people had already made up their minds because of the yellow press. American newspapers blamed Spain. Joseph Pulitzer's *New York World* suggested that an army of American Indians under Buffalo Bill Cody would clear Spain out of Cuba in 60 days. Jesse James's brother Frank volunteered to lead a company of cowboys. Every day brought new editorials claiming that there was no other choice but to go to war to avenge the *Maine* and save the Cubans from cruel Spanish tyranny. The general public, the churches, big business, the press, and the government now realized that the time had come for war. The righteous cause for war had come at last.

The Declaration of War came on April 21, 1898, with a theatrical flourish. Northern congressmen rose up out of their seats to sing "The Battle Hymn of the Republic." Not to be outdone, the Southern congressmen responded with a stirring version of "Dixie." This spectacle demonstrates how the Civil War was still heavy in the minds of Americans and tied to the Spanish-American War. Americans wanted a new war to replace the painful memories of the Civil War. One war inevitably leads to another.

THE SPANISH-AMERICAN WAR ANALYSIS

Ostensibly a war to liberate the Cuban people, the Spanish-American War started in the Philippines. McKinley served as a 19-year-old sergeant during the Battle of Antietam in 1862.

He was the last American president to have served in the Civil War, and he was familiar with war. At one point he said, "I've been through one war. I've seen the bodies stacked like cord wood, and I don't want to go through that sort of thing again." McKinley's reluctance gradually gave way to overwhelming public pressure for war.

Dewey's Victory at Manila Bay on May 1, 1898, took all of six hours to complete. The war against Spain in Cuba took a bit longer. Spain had ruled the Philippines since the early 1500s. More than a thousand islands in the Philippines were inhabited, but the capital of Manila dominated culture and commerce. The Philippines shipped commodities like sugar, hemp, and tobacco to the Chinese market. Unlike Cuba, whose sugar industry created great wealth for Spain, the Philippines were not very profitable. Filipinos were forced to convert to Catholicism by Spanish missionaries who collected taxes on their land. Filipinos who called for reforms ended up in prison or were executed.

Filipinos finally became sick and tired of Spanish oppression and living as second-class citizens. In 1896 they got together to launch a major nationwide revolution against Spain. Emilio Aguinaldo, 27-year-old son of a wealthy landowner, took control of the revolutionary movement. With 200,000 troops fighting in Cuba, Spain could not afford a war in the Philippines as well. Americans knew that there was an insurgency in the Philippines, but there was only mild public support for the Filipino rebels. Just after midnight on May 1, 1898, Commodore Dewey's flagship *Olympia* entered Manila Bay. Dewey's nine ships, modernized to compete with the navies of Europe, decimated the Spanish fleet. By noon, the Spanish had surrendered their naval base in Manila Bay. Ten Spanish ships were destroyed. Only one American sailor was killed. The quick and decisive American victory in the Philippines made Dewey the most famous man in the United States.

The Filipinos had been led to believe that the Americans were their liberators, but when American soldiers arrived, they became suspicious of American motives. The Filipinos were portrayed by the American press as children. The Americans saw their mission as to educate the Filipinos for self-government.

Spain had at one time ruled over a global empire that included most of Central and South America, and a large portion of North America. In the 1890s, all that remained of Spain's empire was Cuba and Puerto Rico, and in the Pacific, the Philippines, Guam, and a few scattered islands. By the 1890s, Spain was weak and not very well thought of by Americans. Peace negotiations between the United States and Spain began in Paris on October 1, 1898. No Filipinos or Cubans were invited to attend. For President McKinley, the question was what to do with the Philippines. He had already been convinced that the United States needed the port of Manila in the Philippines to establish a US naval base in the western Pacific. General James Rusling documented a President McKinley speech from an 1899 meeting with a delegation of Methodist church leaders in *The Christian Advocate*, on January 22, 1903.

> *The truth is, I didn't want the Philippines and when they came to us as a gift from the gods, I did not know what to do with them ... sought counsel from all sides—Democrats*

as well as Republicans—but got little help. I am not ashamed to tell you, gentlemen, that I went down on my knees and prayed Almighty God for light and guidance. ... And one night late it came to me this way: (1) that we could not give them back to Spain—that would be cowardly and dishonorable; (2) that we could not turn them over to France or Germany—our commercial rivals in the Orient—that would be bad business and discreditable; (3) that we could not leave them to themselves—they were unfit for self-government—and they would soon have anarchy and misrule over there worse than Spain's was; and (4) that there was nothing left for us to do but to take them all, and to educate the Filipinos, and uplift and civilize and Christianize them, and by God's grace do the very best we could by them. ... And then I went to bed, and went to sleep and slept soundly, and the next morning I sent for the chief engineer of the War Department (our map-maker), and I told him to put the Philippines on the map of the United States (pointing to a large map on the wall of his office), and there they are, and there they will stay while I am President!

US foreign policy was self-serving, nationalistic, imperialist, and racist. McKinley offered Cuba limited self government and the Platt Amendment made Cuba a US protectorate. The United States could intervene in Cuba's affairs and establish a naval base at Guantánamo Bay.

PHILIPPINE WAR, 1899–1902

In August 1899, American commanders in Manila requested 60,000 reinforcements, bringing the total number of US forces in the Philippines to 126,000. Revolutionary leader Emilio Aguinaldo ordered his officers to begin a guerrilla war against the Americans. Problems began almost immediately. The American war against the Filipino insurgents was bloody, filled with atrocities and racism, and covered up by the American government (it is often compared to the American war in Vietnam). Letters sent home from American soldiers talked about "killing the Filipinos," whom they called "Indians," and filled with references to the Indian Wars of the American West.

The body count in the Philippines worried President McKinley. By 1900, 3,000 Americans and 15,000 Filipinos had been killed. US generals in Manila ordered the American press to censor any unfavorable news. American reporters claimed that the generals were not acting under orders from President McKinley regarding censorship. So, by the early part of 1900, a protected and shielded McKinley was in much better shape in spite of the number of casualties and the atrocities that were going on in the Philippine revolution. McKinley was re-nominated in 1900 and choose Theodore Roosevelt as his running mate.

Roosevelt was nominated not because he was governor of New York State, but because he was a recent war hero and, therefore, could add gravitas to the Republican ticket. One of the first acts of McKinley's new administration was to offer Cuba limited self-government. In the

Philippines, US troops had posed as prisoners of war to infiltrate rebel headquarters. Three weeks after President McKinley's March inauguration, they captured rebel leader Emilio Aguinaldo. President McKinley appointed William Howard Taft as civilian governor of the Philippines. Taft called the Filipinos his "little brown brothers." McKinley described Taft's mission as one of "benevolent assimilation." The American government quickly established schools for the Filipinos that used American methods of education and the English language. It was illegal to promote any type of anti-Americanism, whether it was written, spoken, or even a picture. Even flying the Philippine flag was banned.

On September 5, 1901, President McKinley visited the Pan-American Exposition in Buffalo, New York. He spoke about the nation's new role in the world. He had been warned by his secret service detail about the possibility of an assassination attempt. Anarchists made threats against McKinley and had already killed members of royal families in Europe. McKinley ignored the warnings and met the public face to face at the Buffalo exposition. Leon Czolgosz, an anarchist fired two shots from a revolver. One bullet was deflected by a button on the president's shirt. The second cut through his stomach. President William McKinley died eight days later from infection because his doctors were unable to find the bullet. Ironically, there was a new x-ray machine being displayed at the exposition that may have saved his life had someone thought to use it. Vice President Theodore Roosevelt was sworn in as president on September 14, 1901. Interestingly, he is the only US president to be sworn in without using a Bible.

FIGURE 3.4. US troops in action in the Philippine-American War

Meanwhile, the Philippine Insurrection continued. The American soldiers' attitude was captured in this song: "Oh, I'm only a common soldier in the blasted Philippines. They say I've got brown brothers here, but I don't know what it means. I like the word fraternity, but still I draw the line. Oh, he may be a brother of Big Bill Taft, but he ain't no brother of mine." In 1902, Filipino insurgents surrendered to the United States. The US foreign policy of anti-imperial imperialism had now been defined.

CONCLUSION: HOW HAS US FOREIGN POLICY CHANGED SINCE 1898?

The short answer to how much US foreign policy has changed is, very little. The same basic principles still apply: isolationism, neutrality, the Monroe Doctrine (although more widely applied), and expansion. Media coverage of the war in Iraq and Afghanistan rarely compares these modern wars with previous wars, almost as if each war exists in a vacuum and has no roots and predecessors. The fact is, one war leads to another. The roots of tomorrow's wars are being planted today. The same predicament that the United States had in the Philippines in 1899 is apparent today in Iraq and Afghanistan. The United States moves in to do some good and becomes imperialistic in its application of help to foreign countries. Compounding this historical blindness is the decline of American power. According to the cycles of great powers discussed in Paul Kennedy's *The Rise and Fall of the Great Powers*, the United States is experiencing imperial overstretch as it desperately tries to hang on to its power in a changing world. The Spanish-American War is a good comparison to what the United States is doing in Iraq and Afghanistan, but no one sees it or talks about it. Americans suffer from historical amnesia. At this point it might not make a difference, since the deed has been done and all the United States can do now is make a camouflaged retreat and try to save face.

US Marine Corps Major General Smedley Butler, who had fought in the Philippines, China, Central America, and World War I, wrote a book called *War Is a Racket*. He earned two Medals of Honor and his book is often quoted by members of the military. He wrote:

> *I spent thirty-three years and four months in active military service as a member of this country's most agile military force, the Marine Corps. I served in all commissioned ranks from Second Lieutenant to Major General. And during that period, I spent most of my time being a high class muscle-man for Big Business, for Wall Street, and for the Bankers. In short, I was a racketeer, a gangster for capitalism.*

TIMELINE

1895

The Cuban War for Independence takes place.

1896

August: Revolt begins in the Philippines.

1897

March 4: President McKinley is inaugurated.

April 16: Teddy Roosevelt is appointed assistant secretary of the navy.

December: McKinley asks Congress for aid to Cuba.

1898

February 9: The Dupuy de Lôme letter is published, igniting a scandal.

February 15: The battleship USS *Maine* blows up and sinks while anchored in Cuba's Havana harbor. Spain is blamed, causing war with the United States.

March 17: Senator Proctor exposes Spain's brutality in Cuba.

April 25: Congress declares war on Spain.

April 25 to August 12: The Spanish-American War takes place. As a result of the conflict, the United States acquires Puerto Rico, Guam, Cuba, and the Philippines.

May 1: Commodore Dewey defeats the Spanish at Manila Bay in the Philippines.

May 15: Theodore Roosevelt resigns as assistant secretary of the navy to form a volunteer cavalry regiment to fight in Cuba.

May 28: The Supreme Court rules that a child born of Chinese parents in the United States is an American citizen and cannot be deported under the Chinese Exclusion Act.

June 22: US troops land in Cuba.

July 1: US troops secure victory in San Juan Heights, Cuba.

July 7: President McKinley signs a resolution annexing Hawaii.

July 17: The Spanish surrender in Santiago, Cuba.

August 12: Spain signs the Peace Protocol.

December 10: The Treaty of Paris is signed by the United States and Spain.

1899

The Bayer Company introduces "aspirin," an acetylsalicylic acid designed to reduce pain.

US occupation of the Philippines after the Spanish-American War leads to the Philippine Insurrection, in which Filipino nationalists fight with American troops.

January: The US Senate debates the ratification of the Treaty of Paris.

February 6: The Treaty of Paris is ratified.

May 18 to July 29: Delegates from the United States and 25 other nations meet at The Hague to discuss the laws of warfare.

1901

March 4: McKinley is inaugurated for a second term and Roosevelt becomes vice president.

March 23: Emilio Aguinaldo is captured by US troops in the Philippines.

April 1: United States Steel, J. P. Morgan's holding company, is chartered by the state of New Jersey.

September 6: President William McKinley is shot by anarchist Leon Czolgosz. When McKinley dies eight days later Theodore Roosevelt is sworn in as president of the United States.

1902

July: The end of the Philippine-American War is officially declared.

CREDITS

1. Fig. 3.1. "USS Maine," http://commons.wikimedia.org/wiki/File:USS_Maine_h60255a.jpg. Copyright in the Public Domain.
2. Fig. 3.2. "Destruction of the USS Maine," http://www.loc.gov/pictures/item/2013646059/. Copyright in the Public Domain.
3. Fig. 3.3. "William Randolph Hearst," http://commons.wikimedia.org/wiki/File:William_Randolph_Hearst_cph_3a49373.jpg. Copyright in the Public Domain.
4. William *McKinley, The Christian Advocate.* Copyright in the Public Domain.
5. Fig. 3.4. "US Troops in Action in the Philippine War," http://commons.wikimedia.org/wiki/File:1899UStroops.jpg. Copyright in the Public Domain.

IT'S THE BIG CLUB...

BY DR. BRUCE OLAV SOLHEIM WITH ART BY GARY DUMM

DAD ALWAYS SAID THAT IT IS A PROBLEM IF YOU HAVE TOO LITTLE MONEY AND A PROBLEM IF YOU HAVE A LOT. I NEVER HAD THE SECOND PROBLEM.

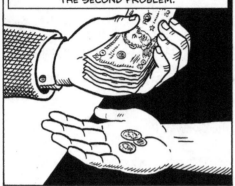

MY DAD WAS A CARPENTER AND BELONGED TO THE CARPENTERS UNION (PART OF THE AFL-CIO). MY MOM AND DAD WORKED VERY HARD FOR THEIR MONEY AND MADE IT TO THE MIDDLE CLASS. DAD WAS ALWAYS WORRIED THAT SOMEONE WOULD TAKE AWAY OUR HOME AND SAVINGS.

LIFE, LIBERTY, AND THE PURSUIT OF HAPPINESS: A PROMISE MADE IN THE DECLARATION OF INDEPENDENCE.

UNION

IWW

STRIKE

IN THE PAST PROGRESSIVES SUCCESSFULLY FOUGHT FOR UNIONS, A WORK WEEK OF ONLY 40 HOURS AND AGAINST CHILD LABOR.

I FIGURED I COULD MOVE BEYOND MIDDLE CLASS BY GOING TO COLLEGE. MY PARENTS EACH HAD 6TH GRADE EDUCATIONS. I EARNED MY PH.D., YET, I AM MIDDLE CLASS LIKE MY PARENTS. WHY?

WORKING CLASS WAGES ARE TAXED AT TWICE THE RATE OF WALL STREET INVESTOR CAPITAL GAINS. IT TAKES TWO OR THREE FAMILY MEMBERS TO EARN ENOUGH TO STAY MIDDLE CLASS TODAY. ALSO, WAGES HAVE NOT KEPT PACE WITH THE COST OF LIVING.

BUT AT LEAST THE BOSSES AREN'T ALLOWED TO MAKE CHILDREN WORK IN COAL MINES ANYMORE.

CHAPTER FOUR

THE PROGRESSIVE ERA

Objectives

1. Describe how the Progressive movement was organized.
2. Determine who the Progressives were.
3. Understand the impact of New Nationalism and New Freedom.
4. Determine how progressive the Progressive Era was.

Personal History

Many of my students feel that voting makes little difference. I hear that from my young students every presidential election cycle, especially after I explain the electoral college system to them and they watch and listen to partisan mudslinging. I am afraid that many people feel that way in America, and not just young students. Less than half of those who are eligible to vote actually cast ballots in America. How can we have a fair and just society and vibrant democracy if the citizens are not active? The answer is: we cannot. Corrupt government officials will line their pockets with special interest group and corporate money and conduct their business in Washington, D.C., and the state houses undeterred by a sleeping citizenry. The tools of justice are inherent in our constitution. We are a government of the people, for the people, and by the people. Justice only happens when citizens actively work hard to achieve good things. Bad things and injustice happens when good people do nothing. It is unfortunately the default. So, what can be done? Well, the Progressive Era offers a lesson in what can be done. American democratic processes give ordinary people the power to make changes if the system runs amok. I tell my students that studying history can help you understand and frame today's problems and perhaps provide some possible answers and solutions. The key, however, is that they must vote. It is their future more than mine, I tell them. I remind them that old people vote in great numbers. When I ran a voting precinct in 2004, I noticed how many older people showed up to vote and how few young people showed up. I even had one lady arrive in an ambulance to vote. I had to carry a portable voting machine out to her, because she was on a gurney and was hooked up to an IV line. That is dedication to voting.

Introduction

The Progressive era is one of the most important eras in American history, yet it is often downplayed or ignored. Working-class Americans had simply become sick and tired of being used and abused by the wealthy. The Progressive Era provides an example of how everyday people can empower themselves to make government more responsive. There are common themes that run throughout the Progressive Era:

1. End the abuse of power.
2. Utilize scientific techniques.
3. Replace corrupt power with reformed social institutions.

In 1900 there was too much power in the hands of too few people. As detailed in the first chapter, in 1890 the top 1 percent of Americans controlled more than half of the nation's wealth. This unequal distribution of wealth led to an unequal distribution of power in America. The Progressives realized that ending the abuse of power by the wealthy elite was an absolute necessity.

In the latter 1800s American cities had been haphazardly built to suit the needs of big business, and not to make life comfortable or safe for the working class and their families. The second theme of the Progressive Era was that Americans needed to use their ingenuity to create a better society. If American inventors could build incredible and marvelous machines, then why could they not build efficient cities and urban areas that would make life pleasant for all Americans?

The last theme, to replace corrupt social institutions with reformed ones, is simple: clean up government at all levels. An unequal distribution of wealth corrupted the political system to the point where the average worker was not represented in Washington, DC, or any statehouse in America. The table had to be leveled to allow for a fair chance for all to build their American dream.

THE PROCESS OF MAKING CHANGES

How did so many Americans come together and make significant changes in their society from 1900 to 1920? The process of change is fascinating and an integral part of this story of Progressivism. The key is the formation of coalitions. A coalition differs from an organization in that coalitions are not permanent, have no formal structure, and are dedicated to one narrowly defined goal. In other words, all of the energy expended in a coalition goes toward the end goal. Once the goal is achieved, there is no longer a need for the coalition, so it dissolves. An organization, as we all know, is permanent, has a formal structure and hierarchy or chain of command, and its primary mission is self-preservation. An organization wants to go on indefinitely. In fact, if it were not for coalitions, organizations would do nothing but concern themselves with self-preservation. Because of the pressure exerted on organizations by coalitions, organizations have to change and to act. Although coalitions can pressure any organization to change, they are most effective in getting governmental organizations, at all levels, to make changes. Coalitions simply make things happen. Ad hoc is a Latin phrase that is used to mean "for this special purpose." So, ad hoc shifting coalitions, the method of change during the Progressive Era, are basically groups of people who come together to achieve a particular goal, and upon achieving that goal dissolve and form new coalitions concerned with other issues. The coalitions shift in that regard. There has been too much emphasis on the organization in history, and not enough attention paid to the coalition. The coalition is where the real power of the people resides.

WHAT WAS PROGRESSIVISM?

Most historians portray the years 1900–1920 as a reform era, led by activist presidents who went after the monopolies and trusts, enacted child labor laws, offered consumer protection, and furthered the growth of democracy. A few recent historians have been less generous and downplay the effectiveness of the Progressive Era. They are quick to point out that most workers, immigrants, and farmers resented the Prohibitionists, child labor laws, and government bureaucrats. Trusts remained and poverty persisted. Reforms were often challenged by the Senate and the Supreme Court, and racism even intensified in the South. This may all be true, but the spirit of reform was there and Progressive Era presidents Theodore Roosevelt and Woodrow Wilson embraced it (as did Taft, to a lesser degree). America was made better by the Progressive Era, but there was much more work to be done.

Progressivism was not only a movement, it was a philosophy, a process, and a method to solving social problems. Young college-educated Progressives rejected the old self-help philosophy of the 1880s. When President McKinley was assassinated, Theodore Roosevelt was perfectly suited to leading this energetic group of social activists in a crusade of reform. Populism was based in nineteenth-century agrarian protest and was represented by farmers and Southerners who wanted to change the economic system. Progressives were generally middle-class reformers who were fed up with corruption and wanted to change the whole political system. Both groups were dedicated to reform and the result was an overlap of basic interests that allowed the two groups to work together, and accomplish more than they could have on their own. Had those with wealth and power been quicker to realize the power of reform, they could have pitted the two groups against each other, not unlike what happened with the Occupy Movement and the Tea Party since 2008 in America. Progressives lost support in the South when they advocated stronger federal government oversight, and in the urban working class when they pushed for Prohibition and breaking up the corrupt urban political machines, which many immigrants relied on.

WHO WERE THE PROGRESSIVES?

What drove people to want change? Did these people, representing different groups, classes, and social strata, want the same things for the same reasons? These are some important questions that require answers. What is clear is that if enough people want something to change, it will change. Let's examine some different groups of American people who wanted change during the Progressive Era, and why they wanted that change.

OLD URBAN MIDDLE CLASS

Before the rise of big business in America, small towns were run by the old middle-class merchants and artisans. These folks were respected for their important roles in the community and rose to positions of leadership. With the rise of corporations, the old middle class was left behind, and there to take their place in political office were the professional politicians who tend to be lawyers. Rather than being inspired by a sense of civic duty to a community they were closely tied to, corporate politicians sought to wield power and rise through the ranks as quickly as possible on the coattails of big business. The old middle-class reformers wanted bureaucratic reform, a cleanup of government, and a curtailment of corporate power.

THE WORKING CLASS

The greatest percentage of Americans at this time belonged to the working class. Hard working, poorly compensated, these folks were often immigrants in urban areas who wanted reform but did not have time to serve in leadership positions. With little union representation, no government protection for workers in workplaces, and especially no protection for children in the workplace, the working class put pressure on government to make significant improvements. The key was their numbers, and the fact that they had the most to gain and nothing to lose. Things could not have been worse for the workers, so they moved forward without fear. There is nothing more dangerous than someone with nothing to lose.

NEW URBAN UPPER CLASSES

Taking to heart the theme of utilizing scientific techniques to better American society, the new urban upper class saw an opportunity to build a better America. They figured the country had outgrown the leadership of the old middle class and needed to move on to a more powerful role for government. These college-educated folks were doctors, engineers, technicians, college professors, social workers, and the like. They did not need reform for themselves since they generally lived well, but they felt an obligation to the toiling masses who were suffering amidst the wealth generated by the American industrial dynamo.

OLD SMALL-TOWN AND FARM FOLK

In spite of the rise of cities and the dramatic movement of people from farms to cities, the majority of Americans in 1900 still lived in small towns and farms across the country. Some people call this the heartland. Small town and farm folk prided themselves on the tradition of Thomas Jefferson and his vision of a nation of yeoman farmers living in harmony, peace, and prosperity. But these farmers and small-town folk realized that cities were draining away their young people and many other talented people. To preserve the traditions of small towns and farm life, these folks sought to promote those small-town values in the urban areas. They saw urban areas as filled with sin, filth, poverty, despair, crime, social problems, and general wickedness. Many of the reforms, including Prohibition, arose from these small town and farm folks.

SMALL BUSINESS

It makes sense that small business would be opposed to the takeover of the political economy by big business. Corporations tended to move toward monopolies and trusts, and drove out any other competition. Small business favored empowering the government to dismantle the monopolies and trusts, and to reform government in the process. The goal was to go back to a time of free and open competition.

BIG BUSINESS

Compared to all the other groups previously mentioned, it seems as though big business is out of place. Why would big business want reform when they had it all? Corporations had a stranglehold on the political system, the courts, and the economy. The formation of monopolies and trusts ensured that they would not have to worry about competition, and union busting was easy enough with the support of the government. However, with the great numbers of other folks calling for reform, they would have been ill advised to ignore the Progressive movement. Their motivation thus became to co-opt the reforms. Using their control of political capital, they steered the reform movement in a friendlier direction. They gave up some so they could keep most of what they had. This makes sense because they had everything to lose. The worst possible scenario for big business was that the reform movement would lead to socialism or even communism, which would seize their capital assets and leave them out of the game.

So, as it turns out, everyone wanted reform for one reason or another. Though the popular perception of the Progressive Era is that of people versus the interests, common people taking back power from corporations, and restoration of democracy, with roots in the heartland and agrarian protest, it turned out that everyone embraced progressivism, often for their own reasons.

THEODORE ROOSEVELT AND NEW NATIONALISM

Roosevelt's concept of progressivism fits his larger-than-life personality. He believed in big business, big labor unions, and big government. The United States in 1900 had 76 million people, 45 states, and more and more women and children entering the workforce. Americans wanted to believe in the American Dream, but sharp class differences and lack of economic mobility made that rather difficult. About 10 percent were rich, 20 percent middle class, and the rest working class and poor. Inequality was growing in the 1890s. The 1893 depression wiped out thousands of companies and, as a result, big business became even bigger. As an example, J. P. Morgan ran 85 percent of the railroads in America.

Americans had never seen a president like Theodore Roosevelt. He was the youngest president ever to serve (age 42 when he assumed the presidency). Roosevelt was loud, hyperkinetic, a warrior, a cowboy, an author, and an eccentric genius. The leaders of the Republican Party were horrified by this outspoken maverick, who was constantly at odds with much of his own party. Theodore Roosevelt was born on October 27, 1858, in New York City. He was from an upper-class Republican family descended from steamboat pioneer Nicholas Roosevelt. He had a lifelong admiration for Abraham Lincoln. Theodore was a sickly boy who suffered with asthma. Combative and unrelenting, Roosevelt threw himself into vigorous physical activities. In 1880 he graduated from Harvard and in 1881 he was elected to the New York State Assembly.

Roosevelt was like other political leaders of his time—trained in the new social sciences. He was not appreciated by the old guard, Gilded Age political bosses. His life had some tragic turns. On the same day in 1884 his mother and his wife died. Overcome by grief, Roosevelt worked for two years as a cattle rancher in the Dakotas until a blizzard in 1886 wiped out his herd. He returned to New York and married his childhood sweetheart, Edith Carow, and raised several children. As New York City police commissioner, Roosevelt rooted out corruption. During a heat wave in 1896, Theodore provided huge blocks of ice to the poor who were dying in their unventilated tenement buildings. Roosevelt supported McKinley in 1896, and, as a reward, was appointed assistant secretary of the Navy.

In this role Roosevelt presided over the rapid buildup of the US Navy. When war with Spain was looming, he resigned to form the famous Rough Riders regiment, which he led into battle, becoming a war hero. Roosevelt used this political capital to run for governor of New York. Republican leaders saw Roosevelt as an irritant and had a plan to run him as vice president. The plan to bury Roosevelt in the vice presidency backfired when McKinley was assassinated. As Republican Party boss Mark Hanna said, "That damn cowboy is president." Roosevelt reveled in the presidency, which he called, the "bully pulpit." He was popular with the people and adept at handling the press as well as his fellow politicians.

When Roosevelt first addressed Congress on December 3, 1901, he let it be known that America was about to enter into a new era. Roosevelt spoke about trusts, which had become a major public policy concern. Many Americans were concerned that the ideal of free market competition had become a myth. Roosevelt accepted big business for what it was—the engine of the economy. Corporations were a big part of America's wealth and power. He considered himself a conservative, yet he spoke of "the public interest" in his address. He felt that big government was needed for the regulation of business. The Sherman Antitrust Act had been around for a while but had not been used against corporate power. J. P. Morgan was in the process of monopolizing all rail traffic in the Northwest through his Northern Securities Company when he was stopped in his tracks by the first federal antitrust suit, filed in March 1902. Two months later, 140,000 United Mine Workers went on strike. The miners were no better off than Southern sharecroppers. To attempt to resolve the strike, Roosevelt ordered representatives from labor and management to the White House. For the first time, an American president was treating labor as an equal partner to negotiations. The miners got shorter hours and better pay.

By 1903, Roosevelt's Square Deal domestic reform policy was taking shape. He created the Department of Commerce and Labor and then signed the Elkins Act in 1903, which amended the Interstate Commerce Act of 1887. The act authorized the Interstate Commerce Commission (ICC) to levy substantial fines on railroads that offered rebates, and on the shippers that accepted these rebates. The Elkins Act greatly boosted Roosevelt's popularity.

Like his boyhood hero Abraham Lincoln, Roosevelt was both conservative and liberal. The conservative in him recognized large corporations as the producers of the nation's wealth and power. The liberal in him realized that corporations needed to be regulated in the public interest. Roosevelt's nationalism reconciled these tendencies. He argued that what was good for America was good for business. This was a reversal of standard political thinking in America prior to his presidency. Roosevelt's nationalism fed his foreign policy as he endeavored to make America a world power. He recognized the dangers that both German and Japanese power would pose to American interests abroad. He knew that America would have to have a strong navy and be able to defend itself. To build and maintain such a fleet,

America would need corporate power and muscle, but, at the same time, could not afford to have domestic disharmony.

The Square Deal at home blended nicely with his Big Stick foreign policy. Roosevelt often quoted an African proverb: "Speak softly and carry a big stick and you will go far." Roosevelt deployed the US Navy to defend American interests in the Pacific and the Caribbean. A Roosevelt Corollary was added to the Monroe Doctrine. Roosevelt felt that the United States reserved the right to intervene in Latin America to protect American lives, property, and national strategic interests. He used this stance to take control of Panama and build the Panama Canal. Roosevelt won re-election easily in 1904, even though he had alienated many conservatives in his own party.

Compared to his contemporaries, Roosevelt was on the leading edge of civil rights. There was some movement regarding civil rights during the Progressive Era, but not as much as was expected. Booker T. Washington had taught African Americans his self-help philosophy in the 1890s and the first decade of the 1900s in response to Jim Crow segregation laws. Washington was misunderstood because publicly he opposed civil rights agitation. In private, however, he filed lawsuits to challenge Jim Crow laws. W.E.B. Du Bois founded the National Association for the Advancement of Colored People (NAACP) in 1909. The NAACP called for the enforcement of the Fourteenth and Fifteenth Amendments. Theodore Roosevelt invited Booker T. Washington to the White House, which enraged Southern whites, who rioted. In spite of Roosevelt's progressive thinking on racial issues (for his time), the federal government was not ready to overturn racial discrimination.

Roosevelt kept up progressive reforms in his second term. He called for an investigation into insurance companies in 1905 and signed the Hepburn Act, giving the ICC authority to regulate railroads, in 1906. One day after the passage of the Hepburn Act, the Pure Food and Drug and Meat Inspection Acts were enacted. In spite of these reforms and Roosevelt's leadership, labor, women, and minorities still struggled in an America that remained a plutocracy. The Supreme Court under Chief Justice Melville Fuller upheld the rights of corporations, affording corporations the same rights as people, citing the Fourteenth Amendment: "nor shall any State deprive any person of life, liberty, or property, without due process of law; nor deny to any person within its jurisdiction the equal protection of the laws." This ruling made more extensive reforms very difficult.

Roosevelt was not afraid to use his bully pulpit in the name of reform, conservation, and foreign policy. He issued executive orders when Congress rejected his creation of public parks and bird sanctuaries. He signed the Panama Canal Treaty and then presented it to Congress as a fait accompli. In 1907 Roosevelt sent the US Navy around the world to demonstrate American power, and he himself mediated disputes between Russia and Japan, and between France and Germany that may have postponed World War I.

In the fall of 1907, trust companies began to fail and the stock market dropped precipitously. There was a run on the banks and the US Treasury stepped in with a bailout. J. P. Morgan helped bail out the failing banks. The panic of 1907 did not result in depression because the stock market was not overvalued as it had been in 1893, or would be in 1929. Conservatives blamed the financial troubles on Roosevelt's Square Deal and his insistence on further regulating the economy. Theodore Roosevelt is one of the top four most popular presidents, and he could have run for another term in 1908. After he retired from the presidency, Roosevelt went on an expedition into the Amazon and contracted several illnesses. In the 1912 election, Roosevelt with his New Nationalism political platform was more radical than was his Progressive Square Deal. Roosevelt called for massive federal regulation of the trusts, banning child labor, and enforcing workplace safety, minimum wage laws, and the eight-hour work day. He later pushed for the United States' entry into World War I, but was devastated when his son Quentin died in battle in 1918. He was seen as the frontrunner for the Republican nomination in the 1920 election, but the heartbreak over the loss of his son and ill health took their toll, and he died in 1919.

Theodore Roosevelt created the modern presidency. He saw the office as one of leadership, not just stewardship. He governed as a warrior, leading the nation into the battlefield of world power. He took the first steps toward an active federal government in tackling economic problems. Roosevelt was a true maverick and many of his fellow Republicans did not share his Progressive views.

WILLIAM HOWARD TAFT

Recommended by his friend Theodore Roosevelt, Secretary of War William Howard Taft was chosen by the 1908 Republican convention as their candidate for president. Taft had been praised for his work as governor of the Philippines. Roosevelt hoped that Taft would continue with his work and follow in his footsteps. In the 1908 election, the Northern Democrats moved from rural Populism to pro-union Progressivism. Unions linked with the American Federation of Labor (AFL) continued to gain membership and power in the early 1900s. Factory workers still labored long hours in unsafe workplaces. More than 30,000 workers died and 500,000 were injured every year. Pro-business state legislators, US senators, and judges blocked pro-labor laws and issued injunctions against the right to strike. The Supreme Court even went as far as to use the Sherman Antitrust Act to bust unions.

Taft defeated the Democrat William Jennings Bryan in 1908 but he had a big problem—he was not Roosevelt. Taft weighed in at 325 pounds and lacked Roosevelt's charisma. He was not a warrior, he was an attorney who took a much stricter view of the US Constitution than did Roosevelt. Taft's conservative tone and rhetoric aggravated Progressives, despite the fact that he filed 90 antitrust lawsuits in his four years in office (twice as many as Roosevelt). In foreign policy, Taft expanded Roosevelt's interpretation of the Monroe Doctrine and replaced Roosevelt's Big Stick with something he called Dollar Diplomacy. Taft's take on foreign policy furthered the economic development of less-developed nations through American investment in their infrastructures. As it turned out, this was not popular in Mexico. American support of friendly dictators and investment in railroads, mines, and other Mexican resources had few benefits for the Mexican people.

In spite of Taft's conservatism, two important constitutional amendments passed during his presidency: the Sixteenth Amendment, which legalized a federal income tax, and the Seventeenth Amendment, which allowed the direct election of US senators. The Seventeenth Amendment was designed to weaken the grip big business had on state legislatures, the senatorial nomination and election system, and its subsequent influence over the US Senate.

While Roosevelt was quite progressive for his time, and Taft rather conservative, Eugene Debs was a true radical. Eugene Debs formed the Socialist Party in America along the same lines as the British Labour Party. Debs called for an eight-hour work day and public ownership of factories, banks, and railroads. The Socialist Party won 3 percent of the vote in the 1908 presidential election and did elect a number of mayors in the Midwest. A true Labor Party of socialist union members did not form in America like it had in England. The Knights of Labor might have done it, but did not remain a major force. The American Federation of Labor (AFL) became more conservative and shied away from socialism. They assumed that American workers wanted equal opportunity and not a confiscation of wealth from the elites. The Industrial Workers of the World (IWW, or Wobblies), who were founded in 1905, thought that Debs's Socialists were not radical enough. The IWW wanted all workers to belong to one big union that would overthrow all governments, corporations, religions, and nations in an all-out general strike. Wobblies frightened big business, politicians, and even most mainstream Americans.

ELECTION OF 1912

Theodore Roosevelt and his friend William Howard Taft both sought the 1912 Republican nomination. Roosevelt disagreed with Taft on issues of Progressivism. Their friendship broke apart, and Roosevelt tried but failed to block Taft's re-nomination. Roosevelt then created the Progressive "Bull Moose" Party, which called for progressive reforms. This new party split the Republican vote, allowing Democrat Woodrow Wilson to win the election and become president. Roosevelt and his New Nationalism political platform were more radical than his progressive Square Deal. Roosevelt called for massive federal regulation of the trusts, banning child labor, and enforcing workplace safety, minimum wage laws, and the eight-hour work day.

Table 4.1. Popular Vote in the 1912 American Presidential Election

	PARTY	PERCENTAGE
Woodrow Wilson	Democrat	43
Theodore Roosevelt	Bull Moose	28
William Taft	Republican	23
Eugene Debs	Socialist	6

WOODROW WILSON AND NEW FREEDOM

The split in the Republican Party allowed the Democrats to take the White House in 1912. Governor Woodrow Wilson of New Jersey was a transplanted Southerner from Staunton, Virginia. Wilson was a scholar and an idealist in the tradition of Thomas Jefferson and James Madison. He wrote seven books on government, including a history of the United States. Wilson's rise to power was rather sudden. In 1909 Wilson was running Princeton University, in 1911 he was governor of New Jersey, and in 1912 he was the Democratic nominee for president.

Wilson's Progressivism was part Grover Cleveland conservatism, part William Jennings Bryan populism, all mixed together with the democratic ideals of Thomas Jefferson and Andrew Jackson. Roosevelt wanted New Nationalism as his form of Progressivism that favored big government. Wilson's New Freedom Progressivism respected the free market and states' rights. Wilson believed in small government, small business, and small labor unions. Despite their differences, New Nationalism and New Freedom shared one thing in common: they both aimed for a balance of power, which is the key to Progressivism and a successful democracy.

FIGURE 4.1. Woodrow Wilson

Wilson was not an experienced politician. He had only served briefly as governor. To categorize the three progressive presidents, Roosevelt was the warrior, Taft the lawyer, and Wilson the professor. Wilson's style would have been better suited for the British parliament. Wilson was able to push through the Clayton Antitrust Act, which put an end to lawsuits against labor unions based on the Sherman Antitrust Act. He cut tariffs and even empowered the Internal Revenue Service to levy an income tax on millionaires. Wilson also felt the nation's banks needed more regulation, so he pushed for and signed the Federal Reserve Act in 1913 that chartered a new national banking system. The Federal Reserve was set up as a private institution with 12 branch banks. The president nominated the directors, who were approved by Congress. The Federal Reserve would set interest rates, set lending requirements for member banks, rescue failing banks, and stabilize the US money supply. Wilson also set up the Federal Trade Commission, made sure railroad workers had an eight-hour work day, and pushed for a ban on child labor.

Wilson was an idealist, whereas Roosevelt was a realist. This was especially true in foreign policy. Wilson also had a stubborn moralist streak in him that could rub people the wrong way in his conduct of foreign policy. World War I was a huge challenge for Wilson. He sympathized with Britain and France, as did most Americans, but sought to keep America out of the war. Most Americans agreed, trying to remain neutral but favoring the Allies. In spite of major technological advances at the outset, the war became a seemingly endless and brutal trench war, with each side bombarding the other and suffering mass casualties. Desperate to win, Germany employed a number of new weapons which the Allies also used: poison gas, flame throwers, airships, airplanes, howitzers, mortars, perfected machine guns, and the U-boat. The U-boat, or submarine, was the most disconcerting weapon for Wilson because it impacted international shipping and jeopardized American neutrality.

Roosevelt's Big Stick foreign policy was based on realism and nationalism. Wilson's foreign policy, liberal capitalist internationalism, was based on idealism, human rights, and international law. Wilson admired England and feared that Germany could dominate all of Europe. Neutrality was really not possible in World War I, as American factories produced munitions for the Allies and shipped them in US ships. Loans were made to both sides by American bankers, but most went to the Allies. Germany proclaimed a war zone around the British Isles and warned that German U-boats would sink any ship approaching England. Wilson relied on international law to protect US ships from German U-boats, but Germany did not cooperate. Unrestricted submarine warfare eventually brought the United States into the war.

Progressive reforms began to have an impact as workers' wages rose and a majority of Americans moved from farms to larger towns and cities. Industrialization, urbanization, and modernization pushed Americans forward into the future. By 1913 Henry Ford had invented the first assembly line and eventually his factories could produce a Model T in just one hour. Ford quickly dominated the new automobile industry. At the same time, cultural divisions emerged. Radicals were pushing for more reforms and intellectuals began to rebel against traditional Victorian values, consumerism, and the mindless pursuit of wealth. Margaret Sanger and others advocated feminism, attacked marriage, and encouraged sexual freedom, atheism, abortion rights, birth control, and euthanasia. As a sign of the times, two of the most popular revolutionary figures were Pancho Villa and Vladimir I. Lenin. Most Americans were rather conservative, despite the fact that secularization was spreading. Divorce, working women, and sex outside of marriage became more acceptable. Urban Protestant churches focused on fighting poverty and social injustice through what was called a New Social Gospel. American Catholics had their own version, as they supported labor unions and social action for the poor. This helped Catholic workingmen become liberal Democrats. In the heartland and the South there was a conservative backlash to Progressivism—this became known as Fundamentalism. Fundamentalists rejected evolution, stressed traditional values, guarded the sanctity of marriage, and adhered to the concept of biblical infallibility. The Ku Klux Klan also staged a comeback in the South and the Midwest.

In the 1916 election the Democrats became known as the progressives and the Republicans as the conservatives (still divided by the 1912 party split between Roosevelt and Taft). New Freedom replaced the Square Deal and turned out to be more sophisticated and comprehensive. The Federal Reserve, Underwood Tariff, Clayton Act, and the Federal Trade Commission had proven that Democrats were leading progressive reforms. Most Americans wanted to stay out of the Great War that began in 1914. Roosevelt was a constant thorn in Wilson's side. When Wilson didn't go to war immediately over the sinking of the *Lusitania*, Roosevelt called Wilson a coward. Ignoring Roosevelt on foreign policy, Wilson took many of Roosevelt's progressive ideas as his own. Wilson hoped to capture the Bull Moose progressives and progressive Republicans to win in 1916. He supported child labor laws and even advocated loans to farmers. When the railway workers threatened a nationwide strike, Wilson sided with the railway workers.

The 1916 election was very close, but Wilson won with 49 percent of the vote. The threat of war began to slow down progressive reforms. Yet two more monumental amendments, long brewing, were passed. The Eighteenth Amendment banned alcoholic beverages and the Nineteenth Amendment guaranteed women the right to vote.

Wilson remains a controversial figure. Hoping against hope to keep America out of war, after his election in 1916 the United States entered World War I and suffered tremendous losses over 18 months of fighting. In spite of his reforms, he turned a blind eye to civil rights and civil liberties. The Reform Era was coming to a close. The federal government played an active role in the nation's economy. Labor union membership increased dramatically, although management still held the upper hand.

SPECIFIC REFORMS DURING THE PROGRESSIVE ERA

SHERMAN ANTITRUST ACT (1890)

With only one dissenting vote, Congress passes the Sherman Antitrust Act, which prohibited business monopolies by holding them to be an unlawful restraint on interstate commerce. The act was the first attempt by the federal government to deal with monopolies.

PURE FOOD AND DRUG ACT (1906)

President Roosevelt signed a comprehensive Pure Food and Drug Act and the Meat Inspection Act in 1906. The acts passed after muckraking journalists like Upton Sinclair (in his book *The Jungle*) revealed unsanitary conditions in food production and exposed the existence of fraudulent medicines. The imposition of fines was authorized for any companies that endangered the health of consumers.

SIXTEENTH AMENDMENT (1913)

The Sixteenth Amendment was ratified, empowering Congress to levy federal income taxes in 1913. Progressives supported the income tax, because they though it was a fair method of collecting revenue, especially from the wealthy.

FIGURE 4.2. *The Jungle* by Upton Sinclair

FEDERAL CHILD LABOR LAW (1916)

The Keating–Owen Child Labor Act limited how many hours children were allowed to work, and banned interstate transport of goods produced by child labor. The act was far reaching and protected the more than two million American children who were employed in manufacturing.

FIGURE 4.3. Child labor in the United States, 1908, Gastonia, North Carolina

EIGHTEENTH AMENDMENT (1919)

America dried up in 1919 with the passage of Prohibition—the Eighteenth Amendment prohibited the sale and manufacture of alcoholic beverages. Temperance societies and many other Progressives were very supportive of this measure. Unfortunately, the unforeseen consequence of Prohibition was the rise of organized crime. The amendment dried up the legal supply of alcohol, but Americans continued to drink. Naturally, organized crime stepped in to provide the product illegally and at a much higher price.

NINETEENTH AMENDMENT (1920)

The Nineteenth Amendment was ratified on August 18, 1920. Women already had full voting rights in 15 states prior to its passage. Jeannette Rankin (R-Montana) had already been elected to Congress in 1916. Wyoming, Colorado, Utah, and Idaho all allowed women to vote prior to 1900.

FIGURE 4.4. Jeannette Rankin, first
woman elected to US Congress, 1916

There were 11 states that allowed women to vote only for president. With the passage of the
Nineteenth Amendment, women were guaranteed the right to vote throughout the entire
United States. Oddly enough, most of the original 13 colonies did not allow women to vote
until passage of the amendment.

DIRECT DEMOCRACY

The Seventeenth Amendment, allowing for the direct election of US senators, was ratified in
1913. US senators had previously been elected through state legislatures. Progressives were
instrumental in this change, believing it would eliminate corruption and lead to better public
representation.

REFERENDUM

Referendums originate in the state legislature and then they are put to a citizen vote. This was
not allowed prior to the Progressive Era. Legislators usually choose a referendum if they feel
the issue may be divisive or controversial.

INITIATIVE

The initiative originates with citizens who gather signatures from registered voters and submit
those signatures for verification to the state attorney general. The issue is then put on the
ballot for a citizen vote.

RECALL ELECTION

Any elected official at the state or local level can be removed from office before their term is up if enough registered voter signatures are gathered and a recall election scheduled. Hollywood actor Arnold Schwarzenegger became governor of California through this method in 2003.

CONCLUSION: HOW PROGRESSIVE WAS THE PROGRESSIVE ERA?

Although many Americans were helped through numerous improvements in society during the Progressive Era, there were blind spots. The years 1877 to 1920 saw the worst period of lynching in American history, worse than during the time of slavery. Blacks were usually the

FIGURE 4.5. Lynching in Duluth, 1920

target, but other ethnic minorities suffered as well. Emboldened by blatantly anti-Asian legislation, the San Francisco School Board segregated Japanese students into separate schools. President Roosevelt intervened, calling segregation "a wicked absurdity" in an address to Congress in December 1906. The School Board reversed its decision. In spite of this victory, racism and discrimination were widespread and very little was done to deal with it during the Progressive Era.

TIMELINE

1887

February 4: The Interstate Commerce Commission (ICC) is created to address price fixing in the railroad industry.

1889

September: Jane Addams establishes Hull House in Chicago as a "settlement house" for the needy.

1890

Jacob Riis publishes *How the Other Half Lives*, revealing the conditions in New York slums.

July 2: Congress passes the Sherman Antitrust Act.

1891

March 3: The Forest Reserve Act allows the government to protect forest land.

1896

November: Populist, anti-monopoly Democrat William Jennings Bryan loses the presidential election to Republican William McKinley.

1899

Florence Kelley, a founder of Chicago's Hull House, advocates better working conditions for women and children, health care, enforcement of child-labor laws, and a minimum wage.

1900

December 27: Temperance crusader Carry A. Nation destroys a hotel barroom in Wichita, Kansas, with a hatchet. She becomes a symbol of the Prohibition movement.

1901

William McKinley is assassinated; Theodore Roosevelt becomes president.

1902

March: President Roosevelt begins his "trust-busting" crusade.

May 12: Anthracite coal miners go on strike in Pennsylvania, protesting their working conditions.

June 17: Under the National Reclamation Act, the federal government sells public land to finance irrigation projects and to build dams.

1903

February 14: President Roosevelt asks Congress to authorize a Department of Commerce and Labor to help decrease tension between labor and management.

February 19: The Elkins Act becomes law thereby strengthening the Interstate Commerce Act.

1904

March 14: The Supreme Court upholds the Sherman Antitrust Act in *Northern Securities Co. v. United States.*

November 8: Roosevelt wins the 1904 presidential election. Progressives support Roosevelt's "Square Deal" programs.

1905

Wisconsin voters elect former governor Robert La Follette to the US Senate, responding to his Progressive platform.

April 17: The Supreme Court decides in *Lochner v. New York.* States are not allowed to restrict working hours in private businesses—a victory for big business.

1906

Writer Upton Sinclair publishes *The Jungle,* exposing unsanitary conditions in meat-packing plants.

June 29: President Roosevelt is influential in the passage of the Hepburn Act. Under the Hepburn Act, railroads cannot raise rates without prior approval by the Interstate Commerce Commission (ICC).

June 30: President Roosevelt signs the Pure Food and Drug Act and the Meat Inspection Act.

1907

A financial panic strikes the nation. Conservative Republicans blame Progressive reforms.

Theologian Walter Rauschenbusch articulates stance of the "Social Gospel" movement in his book *Christianity and the Social Crisis.* He connects reform movements with Christian ideals.

1908

February 24: The Supreme Court rules in *Muller v. Oregon* that a reduced 10-hour work day for women is constitutional. The ruling is a breakthrough for the reform movement.

November 3: Republican William Howard Taft is elected president.

1909

August 6: Payne-Aldrich Tariff, which reduces tariffs and imposes corporation tax, is signed by President William Howard Taft.

February 12: The National Association for the Advancement of Colored People (NAACP) is formed.

September 7: Sigmund Freud makes his first American appearance at Clark University in Worcester, Massachusetts.

1910

The word "Progressive" is commonly used as a description of the growing political movement that seeks to reform various aspects of American society and politics.

June 18: The Mann-Elkins Act empowers the ICC to regulate telephone and telegraph companies, strengthening the Hepburn Act.

1911

The Taft administration creates the Department of Labor.

March 25: The deaths of 146 workers in a fire at New York City's Triangle Shirtwaist Company raise awareness of urban work environments and inspire further reform efforts.

May 15: The Taft administration uses the Sherman Antitrust Act to act against the Standard Oil trust and the American Tobacco Company.

October: President Taft invokes the Sherman Antitrust Act in ordering that the government bring suit against US Steel.

1912

Roosevelt forms the Bull Moose Party, which proclaims it will put individuals' interests over those of corporations. The party's platform includes an endorsement of a woman's right to vote.

November: Democrat Woodrow Wilson wins the White House after Roosevelt splits the Republican vote.

1913

February 3: The Sixteenth Amendment is ratified.

April 8: The Seventeenth Amendment is ratified.

October: President Wilson pushes the Underwood-Simmons Tariff, which reduces protective tariffs.

December 23: Congress passes the Federal Reserve Act.

1914

September 26: Wilson approves the Federal Trade Commission to regulate businesses and investigate possible violations of antitrust laws.

October: President Wilson signs the Clayton Antitrust Act into law in order to supplement the Sherman Antitrust Act.

1915

March 4: Senator Robert La Follette sponsors the Seamen's Act, which regulates safety, living conditions, and food standards on merchant vessels and passenger ships.

July 17: The Federal Farm Loan Act allows farmers to borrow money at favorable rates of interest.

1916

September 1: The Keating–Owen Child Labor Act is passed. This act limited the working hours of children and outlawed the interstate sale of goods produced by child labor.

September 3: The Adamson Act establishes an eight-hour work day for railroad workers.

September 7: President Woodrow Wilson signs the Workingmen's Compensation Act, extending financial help to federal employees who are injured on the job.

November: The first woman is elected to Congress—Jeannette Rankin, a Republican from Montana and a lifelong pacifist.

November: Woodrow Wilson is successfully re-elected after campaigning with the slogan "He kept us out of war."

1917

April 2: President Wilson appears before a joint session of Congress to ask for a declaration of war against Germany and the Central Powers. The United States' entry into World War I requires massive mobilization of resources. As a result, the Progressive agenda, with its focus on domestic issues, loses much of its influence.

June 15: Congress passes the Espionage Act, which imposes a maximum fine of $10,000 and up to 20 years in prison for anyone who interferes with the draft or otherwise encourages disloyalty.

June 3: The Supreme Court declares the Keating–Owen Act (against child labor) unconstitutional.

1918

May 16: Congress passes the Sedition Act, an even more repressive measure than the Espionage Act.

November 11: Germany surrenders and the Allies win World War I. This comes to be known as Armistice Day.

1919

January 16: The Eighteenth Amendment is ratified, prohibiting the sale and manufacture of alcoholic beverages.

January 18: The Versailles peace conference opens. Woodrow Wilson becomes the first sitting president to leave the United States when he travels to Paris.

September 25: President Wilson suffers a stroke and spends the last 18 months of his presidency in a semi-invalid state.

1920

August 18: Nineteenth Amendment ratified.

For the first time, a majority of the American population now lives in cities.

CREDITS

1. Fig. 4.1. "Woodrow Wilson," http://www.loc.gov/pictures/item/2001696919/. Copyright in the Public Domain.
2. Fig. 4.2. "The Jungle by Upton Sinclair," http://commons.wikimedia.org/wiki/File:TheJungleSinclair.jpg. Copyright in the Public Domain.
3. Fig. 4.3. "Child Labor in the United States, 1908, Gastonia, NC," http://commons.wikimedia.org/wiki/File:Child_Labor_United_States_1908.jpg. Copyright in the Public Domain.
4. Fig. 4.4. "Jeannette Rankin," http://commons.wikimedia.org/wiki/File:Jeannette_Rankin_cph.3b13863.jpg. Copyright in the Public Domain.
5. Fig. 4.5. "Lynching," http://www.loc.gov/pictures/item/npc2007012927/. Copyright in the Public Domain.

GAS, GAS, GAS!

BY DR. BRUCE OLAV SOLHEIM WITH ART BY GARY DUMM

I ARRIVED AT FT. MCCLELLAN, AL. FOR MY ARMY BASIC TRAINING IN 1978.

DURING BASIC TRAINING, THE ARMY USED CS GAS (LIKE TEAR GAS) THAT BURNED MY EYES, NOSE, SINUSES, THROAT AND LUNGS. THE PAIN FELT LIKE A THOUSAND NEEDLES.

IN 1983 I BEGAN WORKING AT A SUPERMAX STATE PRISON IN OAK PARK HEIGHTS, MN. AS PART OF OUR TRAINING, THE WARDEN WANTED US TO BE GASSED IN A SOLITARY CONFINEMENT CELL.

SOLHEIM IS OUR FIRST VOLUNTEER.

I ENTERED THE CELL, AND SOMEONE PROMPTLY RIPPED OFF MY GAS MASK. WHEN I WOKE UP OUTSIDE, I COULDN'T STAND UP OR WALK FOR 30 MINUTES. THE WARDEN JUST SMILED.

CS (OR TEAR GAS) WAS THE LEAST HARMFUL GAS USED IN WORLD WAR I.

CHLORINE GAS, PHOSGENE, TOXIC SMOKE AND MUSTARD GAS WERE ALSO USED. MUSTARD GAS MAY HAVE BEEN THE MOST HORRIBLE.

MUSTARD GAS CREATED BLISTERS AND THIRD-DEGREE BURNS.

GASP!... COUGH!

IF YOU BREATHED IT IN, BLISTERS WOULD FORM AND FILL YOUR LUNGS WITH FLUID, AND YOU WOULD SLOWLY SUFFOCATE.

CHAPTER FIVE

WORLD WAR I

OBJECTIVES

1. Describe how World War I started.
2. Describe how World War I was the first modern war.
3. Determine the factors leading to the United States entering the war.
4. Understand the legacies of the war.

PERSONAL HISTORY

I went home to Seattle in 1999 to visit my father, who was in a Seattle-area nursing home. When my mom died in 1990, shortly after their 50th wedding anniversary, my father began deteriorating. By 1999 he was suffering from Alzheimer's and Parkinson's and his time on earth was growing short. My father and mother had worked very hard as immigrants in America. They lived under Nazi occupation in northern Norway during World War II. My dad was in a Nazi forced labor camp. I grew up with stories about World War II and always had a fascination with the military and with war. My own six years in the army had been during the Cold War, but I never saw combat.

One day while I was visiting my father in the nursing home, he pointed out a very old man sitting all by himself by the window. He was hunched over in a wheelchair.

"You should talk to him," my dad said. My dad was sometimes lucid, other times he did not know who I was. So I was not sure why he wanted me to talk to the man in the wheelchair. After I helped my dad get back to his room after our visit, I walked over to the elderly man in the wheelchair. I noticed that he had a very handsome medal around his neck. I said hello to him and he greeted me with a wave.

"Hello young man," he said as a nurse came by.

"He was in the First World War you know." I was impressed. I had never met a World War I veteran. He was looking out of the window again, not focusing on anyone else, a kind of mournful look.

"That's a very nice medal," I said. He looked at me.

"The French government gave it to me, it's the French Legion of Honor," he said with a smile.

"That's wonderful."

"They gave it to me in honor of my service in the Great War."

"World War I?"

"Yeah."

"That is quite an honor."

"Better late than never," he said.

"I'm very glad to have met you, sir." He smiled, and then a nurse came and wheeled him away. I wish I could remember his name. I remember that he was over 100 years old. Now, that generation is gone. The last American World War I veteran died in 2011. His name was Frank Buckles and he lived to be 110 years old. It is odd to think of it, but during my lifetime, more than likely, the last World War II veteran will die. We have to learn as much as we can from these brave veterans before they are gone. There has been much written in 2014 about the 100th anniversary of the Great War. Numerous articles deal with every aspect of the war: military, social, economic, political, and cultural. The Great War still affects us today, sometimes in unexpected ways.

I remember watching a 1998 movie with Ian McKellen called *Gods and Monsters*. The film was about the director of the original 1931 movie *Frankenstein*. The director's name was James Whale, a man who happened to be a veteran of World War I. The destruction caused by World War I and the false progress of the 1920s, followed by the hopelessness of the Great Depression, influenced Whale's adaptation of Mary Shelley's book *Frankenstein* (1818). Whale's monster was like a returning, mutilated, and misunderstood soldier. World War I veterans, like Frankenstein's monster, were forgotten and discarded men. First World War veterans were dispossessed citizens returning to a depressed economy. Whale's *Frankenstein* and *Bride of Frankenstein* are symbolic of the interwar years and the deterioration of the human community. The Frankenstein story took hold of popular culture in the twentieth century as machines became increasingly anthropomorphic, and humans more mechanical. At the root of the story is the idea that in order to fight monsters, you have to become a monster yourself. I remember the poignant scene in *Frankenstein* when the monster comes up to the little girl by the pond. There is also a scene in *Bride of Frankenstein* where the monster meets a blind man. The monster does not want to do harm, but does so anyway. Such is the fate of every combat veteran. They bring the war back home with them. Ultimately, in war, all soldiers have

FIGURE 5.1. *Frankenstein* movie poster (1931)

to come face to face with the darkness within themselves, and when they return home, the darkness comes along. This is not to blame the soldier; this is the nature of war. One war leads to another, in an endless cycle.

OVERVIEW OF WORLD WAR I

The underlying causes of World War I were political, territorial, and economic conflicts that had been brewing for decades among the European powers. A high state of military readiness, secret alliances, old-fashioned imperialism, and ultra nationalism also came into play. The inciting incident was the July Crisis of 1914, caused by the assassination of Archduke Franz Ferdinand and his wife Sophie. The assassin, Gavrilo Princip, was an ethnic Serb and Yugoslav nationalist and a member of the Black Hand Movement, a terrorist organization that wanted Serbia to be independent from the Austro-Hungarian Empire. Tensions were already high because of colonial territorial disputes and regional tensions in the Balkans. Austria-Hungary competed with Serbia and Russia for territory and influence in the region. The assassination was like a lit match in a room full of gun powder.

The Austro-Hungarians were concerned that the Serbs would unify the Slavs and threaten the Hungarian part of the empire. The Russians thought the Balkans should be under their control. After the assassination, Russia prepared its troops for war, which caused the Germans (allies of the Austro-Hungarian Empire) to declare war on both Russia and France. In 1914, the Germans did an end run through neutral Belgium and attacked France. England entered the war against the Germans because they saw an opportunity to eliminate the Germans, who were their rivals for naval superiority and sovereignty. Japan, Serbia, Portugal, Romania, Italy, and China joined the Allies (Britain, France, and Russia), while the old, weak Ottoman Empire joined the Central Powers (Germany and Austria-Hungary). A world war had begun.

The war escalated from its start through 1915 and 1916. Germany, Britain, and France mobilized their nations yet were still locked into a bloody stalemate in the trenches. None of these countries realized how modern weaponry had changed warfare and made their tactics obsolete. Tens of thousands died in battles at Verdun and the Somme. By 1916 Russia was near collapse. On the other side of the world, the Great War was good for the American economy. The United States became a creditor nation, as Americans bought millions of dollars of British overseas investments that were sold to pay for the war. The United States then turned around the loaned money to the British and the French.

In April 1915 the German Foreign Ministry ran a front-page announcement in the *New York Times* warning that American citizens sailing on the *Lusitania* would do so at their own risk. The Germans announced that their U-boats would sink any ship that approached Britain (even passenger ships). President Wilson argued that this was a violation of international law, which required warship commanders to warn the target ship. Then, on May 7, 1915, the British passenger liner *Lusitania* was sunk by a German submarine. The death toll: 1,195 passengers, including 128 Americans. The American public was outraged, and pressure mounted for Wilson to enter the war. Germany backed down and suspended unrestricted submarine warfare. Wilson was able to avoid war, at least temporarily. He campaigned for a second term on the slogan "He kept us out of war."

Wilson attempted to negotiate a peace between the Allies and the Central Powers, but with no success. By the end of 1916, Germany and Austria-Hungary had countered every Allied offensive in the west and taken over Serbia and Romania. Russia began to fall apart, which led to the downfall of the czar, the Communist revolution, and Russia backing out of the war. The Germans then announced the resumption of unrestricted submarine warfare. Germany also tried to persuade Mexico to attack the United States, but the Mexican government refused. Wilson was outraged, and in April 1917 sent Congress a declaration of war against Germany, which Congress approved with only 50 dissenting votes (including Jeannette Rankin [Republican-MT], who was the first woman elected to Congress). The United States then had to quickly mobilize an army and a navy.

THE UNITED STATES AT WAR

The assassination of the archduke of the Austro-Hungarian Empire and his wife by a Serbian nationalist was the inciting incident that brought Europe to war. The United States remained neutral and tried to trade with all sides, but this neutrality was not genuine, as Americans favored the British from the outset. The German strategy of unrestrictive submarine warfare brought the United States into the war more so than any other reason. The sinking of the *Lusitania* without warning meant that the Germans had breached the international laws known as the Cruiser Rules. Although the Germans had reasons for considering the *Lusitania* as a naval vessel, as the ship was carrying war munitions, this incident pushed US public opinion toward war. The British had already been doing an excellent job of spreading propaganda in the United States that demonized the Kaiser and Germany. For example, elementary school children in Ohio were asked to write essays on why they hated the Kaiser. Many of the essays were shocking in their level of hatred and violent imagery (e.g., cutting off all of his limbs).

President Wilson ran for re-election in 1916 on the campaign motto "He kept us out of war." Once he was safely re-elected, Wilson asked for a declaration of war in April 1917. It was well known that if Wilson was to ask for a declaration of war, the Russians could not be a fellow ally. It would be hard to justify Wilson's call to make the world safe for democracy if one of the allies was an absolute monarchy. In January 1917, the British deciphered a telegram from German foreign minister Arthur Zimmermann to the German minister to Mexico, offering United States territory to Mexico in return for joining the war on the German side. This message, known as the Zimmerman Telegram, helped draw the United States into the war. On April 6, 1917, Congress formally declared war on Germany and its allies.

American soldiers were called doughboys, but no one is quite certain why. It may have been because of the large donut shaped buttons on their uniforms. General John "Blackjack" Pershing was selected as the commander of the American Expeditionary Force. The Americans did not want US soldiers fighting under foreign commanders, so they did not call themselves an Allied power; they fought as an associate power. In 1917 the federal government did not know how to pay for the war without raising taxes, so they printed more money. The new Federal Reserve System made credit more available, and Wilson hoped that inflation would be more palatable than higher taxes. The federal debt rose from $1 billion in 1915 to $20 billion in 1920. In 1918 the deficit was bigger than the nation's prewar budget. Wilson finally raised taxes using the War Revenue Act of 1918. The Great War changed the role the federal government played in the American economy. Progressives pushed for taxing the rich, which eventually became public policy. In 1916, 75 percent of the money collected by the federal government came from tariffs, which in essence taxed the working class. By 1919, approximately 75 percent of the money collected by the federal government came from the income tax levied by the Internal Revenue Service.

FIGURE 5.2. American troops wearing gas masks

The War Industries Board set up by Wilson was run by businessman and entrepreneur Bernard Baruch. Baruch wanted to bring managed order to the economy, as J.P. Morgan had done in the 1880s. Baruch, like Theodore Roosevelt, saw government and business as partners. Many companies made enormous profits during the war and the American industrial base grew dramatically. During the war, a young Franklin D. Roosevelt, Theodore's fifth cousin, served as assistant secretary of the Navy. He observed the new federal agencies in operation. The Capital Issues Committee of the Federal Reserve, the War Industries Board, and the War Finance Corporation would later help inspire some of Franklin Roosevelt's New Deal programs. Wilson mobilized and manipulated public opinion. Social pressure and patriotism were used to secure enlistments, sell war bonds, encourage war production, and put down any dissent. Americans who refused to buy war bonds were seen as disloyal and Kaiser sympathizers. Most Americans, especially in the Northeast and the South, supported the war effort, but many Irish and German Americans did not. The Socialist Party and the Wobblies also opposed the war. They saw it as a war for capitalist profits. African Americans, eager to find jobs, began to leave the South for Northern urban areas. Anti-German hysteria grew, fueled by vigilante groups. Anything German or foreign was suspicious. Some German Americans even changed their names. Racism was at an all-time high as well, since Wilson was no friend of equality among the races. Censorship, propaganda, and suppression of dissent were widespread. The war effort revealed how much power the modern American president could wield.

The war reached a critical climax in 1917 and 1918. British shipping was being sent to the bottom of the Atlantic by German U-boats until the British and American navies finally organized a convoy system. By autumn 1917 the Allies had regained control of the Atlantic shipping lanes and American doughboys were on their way to France. The Americans arrived just as Germany launched its last offensive in March 1918. The Battle of Cantigny was the first battle between the American and German forces. In the Battle of Belleau Wood in June, the Germans ran into a brigade of 18,000 marines, who fought so ferociously that the Germans nicknamed them Devil Dogs. By August an American Expeditionary Force of 900,000 men was organized under General John J. Pershing's command, with Colonel George C. Marshall as operations officer. French and British commanders were incredulous. They felt that the American victory at Belleau Wood was a stroke of luck and more to do with Germans being in retreat already. Pershing's troops were put into position to take part in the Meuse-Argonne, which would end up being the biggest battle of the war. American forces lost 26,000 and had over 100,000 wounded in that battle.

If things were not bad enough, the Spanish Flu struck in 1918. The influenza or flu pandemic of 1918 to 1919, the deadliest in modern history, infected an estimated 500 million people worldwide—about one-third of the planet's population at the time—and killed an estimated 20 million to 50 million people. More than 25 percent of Americans became sick, and approximately 675,000 Americans died during the pandemic. The 1918 flu was first observed in Europe, the United States, and parts of Asia, before quickly spreading around the world. At the time, there were no effective drugs or vaccines to treat this deadly flu strain or prevent its spread. In the United States, people were told to wear masks and many public places were shut down. The Spanish Flu was so deadly because it invaded the lungs and caused pneumonia.

The 1918 flu struck many healthy young people, including many World War I soldiers. More US soldiers died from the 1918 flu than were killed in battle during the war. Forty percent of the US Navy was hit with the flu, while 36 percent of the Army became ill. Even President Wilson reportedly contracted the flu in early 1919 while negotiating the Treaty of Versailles. It is possible that it weakened him and affected the negotiations.

By November 1918 Germany had collapsed. The Great War was over. Wilson hoped for peace without victors; it did not turn out that way. He wanted every nation to have its own homeland, trade freely, and seek negotiated alternatives to war and aggression. He proposed a League of Nations that would mediate disputes. All of these are great ideas, but the Republicans regained control of Congress in the 1918 midterm elections and many Americans were fed up with high-minded moral crusades, international intervention, taxes, inflation, big government, social unrest, and war. In spite of that, Wilson's vision of liberal capitalist internationalism has influenced every US president since. Wilson took his ideas to the American people to seek ratification of the peace treaty, which included League of Nations membership, but Senate Republicans wanted to water down American membership in the League. Wilson decided to kill his League rather than change it. Had Wilson been more flexible, he might have struck a deal with the Republicans.

In his last two years Wilson was very sick and some say that his wife served in his capacity. The Progressive Era was coming to a close, and in a climate of fear the government started striking out at subversives, mainly Communists. Attorney General Palmer launched raids against those with Communist sympathies. Most were wrongly accused and big business took advantage of this hysteria by denouncing labor unions as pro-Communist.

THE FIRST MODERN WAR

The First World War featured tanks, airplanes, poison gas, machine guns, U-boats, the formation of international organizations, and the concept of total warfare. The nature of warfare changed both on land and at sea because of these new weapons and innovations.

TANKS

The nature of battle in World War I demanded new weapons. There was a need for armored self-propelled weapons that could navigate any kind of terrain—the tank. The armored car did not work on cross-country terrain and could not stand up to modern artillery. The tank was considered a solution to the stalemate of the trenches on the western front. It was designed to cross the killing zone (no man's land) between trench lines and break into enemy defenses. The tank was intended to withstand machine-gun fire, artillery, and easily pass through barbed wire. Compared to today's tanks (e.g., the American M1 Abrams), which can fire in any direction

FIGURE 5.3. English battle tank

with laser-guided computer accuracy while travelling at more than 60 miles per hour, World War I tanks were slow, not very maneuverable, and not very accurate, because they had not figured out how to mount a large gun in a fully articulated turret.

Civil engineer Lance de Mole (English) designed a tank in 1912. There were claims from other nations—Captain Levavasseur (French), Gunther Burstyn (Austrian), and Vasily Mendeleev (Russian)—in the decade before World War I, but none were built. After the start of the war, the British and French both began building tanks, but it was the British who first used tanks on the battlefield, on September 15, 1916. The French first used their tanks in April 1917. The Germans did not begin development of their own tank until after the Allies had deployed theirs, but the Germans did have anti-tank weapons that were quite effective. The German general staff were not big believers in tank warfare so the Germans only built 20 tanks. The first German tank battle appeared on April 24, 1918. The Germans would later develop very good tanks that they used in the Second World War to support their blitzkrieg approach to modern warfare.

AIRPLANES

World War I was the first time that aircraft were used on a large scale in warfare. Observation balloons (tethered to the ground) had already been used for artillery spotting. Germany used Zeppelins for reconnaissance over the North Sea and the Baltic, and to conduct strategic bombing raids over England and the eastern front. Airplanes were used mostly for reconnaissance at the start of the war. The bird's-eye perspective allowed pilots and passengers a full view of the battlefield, which could give strategic advantage to ground commanders. It did not take long for each side to realize the importance of the airplane and the necessity

FIGURE 5.4. German airplane

for denying the enemy reconnaissance capability. Machine guns were designed and fitted for the lightweight aircraft so that the pilot could engage the enemy pilot and shoot them down. Aerial combat, or the dog fight, was born.

By the end of the war, bomber aircraft had been developed. The Germans deployed the Gotha bomber, while the British had the Handley Page bomber. Aerial bombardment also gave opposing militaries the option of targeting civilians in cities and towns. Airplanes could target industrial centers and war production factories. No one was safe in modern total war.

POISON GAS

Although it did not kill as many soldiers as machine guns or artillery, poison gas was the most feared weapon in World War I. Poison gas was indiscriminate and could be used on opposing forces in trenches without risking your own soldiers in an assault. Death by machine gun or artillery blast could be instantaneous, whereas poison gas victims could be in agony for days or weeks. Crude gas masks were developed, but did not provide enough protection. The first recorded gas attack was by the French. In August 1914, the French used tear gas grenades on the Germans. Tear gas was meant to slow down the seemingly unstoppable German army. In other words, it was a more spur-of-the-moment, desperate attempt to halt the German advance. The Germans responded in October 1914, firing gas-filled shells at the French containing a chemical that caused violent sneezing fits. The gas was designed to incapacitate, not kill, the enemy.

The more deadly chlorine gas was used for the first time at the Second Battle of Ypres in April 1915. On April 22, the French noticed a yellow-green cloud moving toward them—chlorine gas was delivered from pressurized cylinders dug into the German front line. They thought that it was a smokescreen to disguise the movement of German troops. Once exposed, the French troops ran in terror, giving the Germans an opportunity to advance forward and break the deadlock. Eventually even more deadly gases were developed: phosgene and mustard gas. Phosgene would slowly embed itself into a soldier's lungs without any immediate coughing or warning sign. By the time a soldier realized he had been exposed, it was too late. The Germans first used mustard gas against the Russians in 1917. Mustard gas caused both internal and external blisters within a short amount of time. The blisters were more pronounced on mucus membranes and moist body tissue, but could still be produced on dry skin. Blisters would form in the sinuses, throat, and lungs, causing difficult and painful breathing or death. The main purpose of gas warfare was to strike terror into the hearts of the enemy and diminish morale. Because gas was meant to incapacitate and spread fear, the number of soldiers who died due to gas attack was relatively small compared to more conventional attacks.

MACHINE GUNS

Machine guns changed the way war was fought on the ground. Because of the high number of casualties caused by the ruthless effectiveness of the machine gun, opposing armies

FIGURE 5.5. British Vickers machine gun

changed their tactics and even had to change their uniforms. Gone were shiny buttons, helmets, and uniform decorations. Soldiers dug into trenches and remained hidden or camouflaged until they were ordered to go over the top into no man's land to attack enemy trenches. Standing shoulder to shoulder in ranks facing the enemy like in the Civil War no longer made sense for the soldiers of World War I. Commanders were slow to adapt to the new style of ground warfare. The standard tactic was the infantry charge. Machine guns, which could fire hundreds of rounds per minute, could mow down hundreds of soldiers very quickly. Crude machine guns had first been used in the American Civil War.

The British Vickers machine gun had a water-cooled jacket on its barrel to allow for the high rate of fire. An ammunition belt fed it bullets. It could shoot 450 rounds per minute. These early machine guns were crew served and quite heavy. They sometimes weighed over 100 pounds, without all of the attachments and supplies. Lighter machine guns were developed both for the battlefield and for aircraft after 1915. Larger machine guns were also developed as anti-aircraft weapons and armaments for naval ships.

U-BOATS

U-boat comes from the German word *Unterseeboot*, meaning "under sea boat." U-boats, also known as submarines, changed the nature of naval warfare. Submarines are very effective when deployed against naval warships, but they are most effective in destroying an enemy's commercial shipping. The primary targets of the U-boat campaigns in both world wars were the merchant convoys bringing supplies across the Atlantic and in the Mediterranean. Germany completed its first fully functional submarine in 1903. Russia bought submarines from Germany and used them in the Russo-Japanese War in 1904.

At the start of World War I, Germany had 29 U-boats. In February 1915, the Kaiser declared a war zone in the waters around the British Isles. U-boat captains were told that they could sink merchant ships, even neutral ones, without warning. Unrestricted submarine warfare led to the sinking of the *Lusitania* in 1915 and disrupted the Atlantic shipping trade of the neutral United States. Submarines are very vulnerable to attack when surfaced. The old rules of naval warfare that President Wilson asked for would not make sense for submarines. The idea of surfacing, warning the ship that it was to be sunk, and allowing time for the crew to get in lifeboats and move a safe distance away was not possible for submarines. They would be blown out of the water easily by surface ships. Also, there was no space on a submarine to put rescued sailors who were, according to the rules, supposed to be dropped off at the nearest neutral port. Submarines are stealth weapons that must attack without warning and remain submerged. The reality of submarine warfare clashed with Wilson's insistence on adhering to the outdated rules of naval warfare. After the United States' entry into the war, and after the introduction of escorted convoys, shipping losses declined. In the end, the German strategy failed to destroy Allied shipping. Of the 360 submarines that had been built by Germany, 178 were lost, but they had sunk more than 11 million tons of commercial shipping.

INTERNATIONAL ORGANIZATIONS

Originally conceived of by President Woodrow Wilson as part of his Fourteen Points, which were used as a blueprint for peace at the Paris Peace Conference that ended the First World War, the League of Nations was an intergovernmental organization founded in January 1920. It was the first international organization whose principal mission was to maintain world peace. Its primary goals were preventing war through collective security and disarmament, and settling international disputes through negotiation and arbitration. At its peak, the League had 58 members. As it turned out, the League was a paper tiger that had no teeth. It did not have an armed peacekeeping force, and the Great Powers were reluctant to enact or enforce sanctions imposed by the organization. The League was not able to prevent aggression by Imperial Japan and Nazi Germany in the 1930s. Wilson could not get the United States to join the League, so America was never a member. The League lasted for 26 years until it was replaced by the United Nations (UN), which was founded in April 1946. Some say that the League might have stopped the rise of Germany and Japan in World War II if the United States had been a member. We will never know for sure.

TOTAL WARFARE

During Civil War it was not uncommon for rich people to watch battles from hilltops and other safe vantage points while being served lunch. Rich people were nowhere near the battlefronts of the First World War. No longer were wars to be fought simply by one professional army or navy against another, but like all wars, it was a rich man's war and a poor man's fight. World War I was a total war, involving the governments, economies, and populations of belligerent nations to a degree never seen before. In total war the entire nation was called into service, rather than just its military. The use of submarines changed naval warfare and made civilian shipping a target. Aerial bombardment made it possible to attack the war-making industries of belligerent nations. All of this led to more civilian casualties. Governments passed laws that would not be tolerated during peacetime. Government agencies took control of economic production, nationalized factories, determined production targets, and allocated manpower and resources. Conscription was introduced to create huge armies, and ships, trains, even horses and livestock were commandeered for military use. Wartime governments implemented press censorship, curfews, and strict punishments for any violations, as they acted aggressively to protect national security. All sides used propaganda to stir anger and provoke action, raise public morale, and raise money through war bonds. World history had its first total war.

THE END OF THE WAR: ARMISTICE, THE FOURTEEN POINTS, AND THE TREATY OF VERSAILLES

By 1918 German citizens were demonstrating against the war. The British Navy blockade caused them to starve and the economy to collapse. Kaiser Wilhelm II abdicated on November 9, 1918, and shortly thereafter the leaders of both sides met at Compiègne, France. The war ended on the 11th hour of the 11th day of the 11th month in 1918. The armistice was an agreement signed by representatives of France, Great Britain, and Germany. It was an agreement to end fighting and served as a prelude to peace negotiations. Wilson arrived in Paris for the peace negotiations with his Fourteen Points as a model or blueprint for peace. It was his intention all along to fight in the war in order to have the opportunity to influence the peace settlement and get other nations to agree with his worldview. His Fourteen Points were first outlined in a speech he gave to Congress in January 1918. They became the basis for Germany and her allies agreeing to an armistice in November 1918, and later served as the foundation for the peace talks in France. The Fourteen Points were as follows:

1. No more secret agreements ("Open covenants openly arrived at").
2. Free navigation of all seas.
3. An end to all economic barriers between countries.
4. Countries to reduce weapon numbers.
5. All decisions regarding the colonies should be impartial.
6. The German army is to be removed from Russia. Russia should be left to develop its own political setup.
7. Belgium should be independent, as it was before the war.
8. France should be fully liberated and allowed to recover Alsace-Lorraine.
9. All Italians are to be allowed to live in Italy. Italy's borders are to be "along clearly recognizable lines of nationality."

10. Self-determination should be allowed for all those living in Austria-Hungary.
11. Self-determination and guarantees of independence should be allowed for the Balkan states.
12. The Turkish people should be governed by the Turkish government. Non-Turks in the old Turkish Empire should govern themselves.
13. An independent Poland should be created, which should have access to the sea.
14. A League of Nations should be set up to guarantee the political and territorial independence of all states.

In 1919, the Treaty of Versailles officially ended the war. The treaty was not what Wilson wanted. As part of the armistice, the Germans were ordered to give up their heavy weapons, airplanes, and all submarines. They were also asked to give up several warships and disarm the rest. Germany was blamed for the First World War and would have to pay reparations for the damage caused, estimated to total about $54 billion. Germany also had to surrender some of its territory to surrounding countries and its African colonies, and limit the size of its military. Born in Braunau, Austria, Hitler served during the war with the German army and was awarded the Iron Cross. He was severely wounded in a gas attack. Many have wondered what would have happened had Hitler not survived World War I. We will never know, but what is clear is that the way Germany was treated after World War I led directly to Hitler's rise to power and to World War II. Hitler conveniently used the humiliation of Germany by the Versailles Treaty as an example of the "stab in the back" perpetrated by the Jews.

The treaty also established the League of Nations, ostensibly to prevent future wars. The League of Nations helped Europe rebuild, and 53 nations had joined by 1923. But the US Senate refused to let the United States join the League of Nations without certain reservations and conditions, and as a result, President Wilson (who had established the League) killed any chances the United States joining. Wilson later suffered a physical collapse and spent the rest of his term hidden from view. By the time all was said and done, four empires—the Russian, the Ottoman, the German, and the Austro-Hungarian—had collapsed because of the war. Another empire, Great Britain, would later fall from its hegemonic position and was replaced by the United States after World War II.

LIBERAL CAPITALIST INTERNATIONALISM

Wilson's worldview can best be described as liberal capitalist internationalism. There were four basic tenets to his view:

1. Non-democratic societies cause war.
2. Socialism/Communism must be destroyed.

3. The United States is an exceptional nation.
4. The United States has a mission to reform the world.

The interesting thing is that US foreign policy today is still influenced by Wilson's liberal capitalist internationalism. The United States is trying to build democracies in the Middle East to combat the spread of terrorism. Instead of Communism being the enemy, now it is terrorism. The key is that America is conflict driven. Americans need an enemy to focus on. The United States considers itself an exceptional nation still and US government officials act accordingly in international affairs. The last tenet is also still in effect. America has taken up the task of destroying terrorism and promoting Western-style democracy. Most people would agree that democracy worldwide would be a good thing and might indeed reduce wars and conflicts. Two questions come to mind: How does the US government plan to carry out this mission? Is going to war to create peace a good idea?

Conclusion

The First World War caused nations to build roads, railways, hospitals, food processing facilities, warehouses, and other industrial and infrastructure improvements. The war gave a boost to the industrial economies of Europe. A single mile of trench required 900 miles of barbed wire, 1 million cubic feet of timber, and 360,000 square feet of corrugated iron. For Americans, World War I is not as big of a deal as the Civil War, World War II, or Vietnam. This is odd, because World War I is what allowed the United States to become a superpower. The war caused the collapse of four empires, and led to the rise of a fifth—the United States. The boundaries set after the war started much of the ethnic and nationalist tension that still exists today, including that between the Palestinians and the Israelis. It was a big war. Naval battles were fought in the north Atlantic and the south Pacific. Battles raged on three continents. The Americans fought to build a new world order and make the world safe for democracy. The war gave many people a noble purpose, at least at the beginning. The noble warriors who eagerly went to battle fought at a precise time when technology made it easier to kill them in combat. The machines forced the men into the trenches, their ruthless efficiency having little to do with heroism or brilliant command. The inexorable hail of bullets and shells was the only sure way to win the war. Casualties were reaching numbers never seen before. In just one day during the Battle of the Somme, the British suffered 57,000 casualties. At the end of the battle, the British had 420,000 casualties, the French 195,000, and the Germans 600,000. It was a total war where victory would go to the nation that could mobilize all of its national resources the best. Everyone had to chip in and sacrifice on the home front.

The segregated 369th Infantry Regiment were African-American soldiers who distinguished themselves during the war. They became known as the Harlem Hell Fighters. Unfortunately, they came home to face prejudice and discrimination.

At the end of the war German soldiers were still in position, undefeated. It was their government that had collapsed, not the army. This would give Hitler the ammunition for his campaign of hate and blame against the Jews. Wounded, broken soldiers came home to unemployment, and noticed that war profiteers had made themselves fat and rich on their blood sacrifice. The League of Nations, created with noble intentions, failed as the United States, the creator of the League, refused to join and because there was no mechanism for enforcement. By 1929, facing a worldwide depression, people realized that what they had fought for was not a noble purpose; it was greed and profiteering. The romance had long since been stripped away. Although Britain emerged victorious, it was severely weakened and lost its hegemonic status. The United States was there to pick up the mantle of world leadership. What became clear was that the British went to war to stop German hegemony. For Britain, victory smelled like defeat. The Dual Monarchy of the Hapsburg Empire had collapsed, the Russian Empire had collapsed, the Ottoman Empire had collapsed, and the British Empire was on the verge. World War I allowed the United States to assume a leadership role among the world democracies, but it also meant that Americans would shoulder the burden of the remnants of the old empires. World War I was the most direct cause of World War II. Over 65 million soldiers fought on three continents, and 9 million were killed. The haphazard carving up of the remnants of empires led to today's problems. One war leads to another, the dramatic impacts of war are felt generations after the last bullet flies and the last soldier is buried in his grave.

My father was born in 1915 (the year the *Lusitania* was sunk) and my mother in 1919 (the year the Treaty of Versailles was signed) in Northern Norway. Norway had dissolved its union with Sweden and was totally independent in 1905. The goal was to remain neutral and consolidate its newly found independence. Great Norwegian national pride came with Roald Amundsen being the first person to reach the South Pole in 1911. During the First World War the Norwegian merchant marine fleet was used to support the British and the Allies. Although officially neutral, the Norwegians realized that they had to pick a side at least in terms of ideology and commerce. Therefore, Norway became a neutral ally. Half the Norwegian fleet was sunk and 2,000 sailors were killed by the German U-boats in World War I. My grandfather served in the Norwegian merchant marines and the Norwegian Navy and survived the war. A tradition of military service continued in our family with my father, my brother, me, and my eldest son. Norway's attempt to remain neutral in World War II backfired when the Nazis invaded on April 9, 1940.

TIMELINE

1914

June 28: Austro-Hungarian archduke Franz Ferdinand and his wife, Sophie, are assassinated by Serbian nationalist Gavrilo Princip in Sarajevo, Bosnia.

July 28: Austria-Hungary declares war on Serbia.

August 1: Germany declares war on Russia.

August 3: Germany declares war on France.

August 4: The United Kingdom declares war on Germany, after Germany invades Belgium.

August 6: Austria-Hungary declares war on Russia, and Serbia declares war on Germany.

August 19: US President Woodrow Wilson announces that the United States will remain neutral.

August 26: The Battle of Tannenberg begins.

September 5: The First Battle of the Marne begins. Trench warfare begins as soldiers on both sides dig trenches to survive the onslaught of modern weaponry.

October 19: The Battle of Ypres begins.

November 3: The United Kingdom blockades Germany.

December 24: The unofficial Christmas truce is declared. Soldiers on both sides take time to sing Christmas carols and share a drink. When commanders discovered this unofficial truce, they began rotating troops on the frontlines.

1915

February 4: Germany declares a "war zone" around Great Britain, using U-boats to attack even neutral merchant vessels.

February 19: The Dardanelles Campaign begins.

April 22: The Second Battle of Ypres begins. It is during this battle that the Germans first use poison gas.

April 25: The Battle of Gallipoli begins.

May 7: The British ocean liner RMS *Lusitania* is sunk by German U-boat U-20.

September 5: Czar Nicholas II takes personal control over Russia's armies.

1916

February 21: The Battle of Verdun begins. It is the longest battle of World War I and one of the bloodiest.

May 31: The Battle of Jutland, the major naval battle of the war, begins.

July 1: The Battle of the Somme begins. It is the first time that tanks are used in battle.

1917

January 19: Germany sends the secret Zimmerman Telegram to Mexico in an effort to convince Mexico to join the war. The British intercept and decipher the coded message.

March 15: Russian czar Nicholas II abdicates.

April 6: The United States declares war on Germany.

July 31: The Battle of Passchendaele (also known as the Third Battle of Ypres) begins.

November 7: The Bolsheviks successfully overthrow the Russian government.

December 17: The armistice agreed upon between the new Russian government and the Central Powers goes into effect.

1918

January 8: US President Woodrow Wilson issues his Fourteen Points for a peace settlement.

March 3: Russia signs the Treaty of Brest-Litovsk, which is a peace treaty between Russia and the Central Powers.

March 21: Germany launches the Spring Offensive.

April 21: German flying ace Baron Manfred von Richthofen (the Red Baron) is shot down.

July 15: The Second Battle of the Marne begins.

November 9: German Kaiser Wilhelm II abdicates and flees Germany.

November 11: Germany signs the armistice at Compiègne, France. Fighting ends on the 11th hour of the 11th day of the 11th month.

1919

June 28: The Treaty of Versailles officially ends World War I.

CREDITS

1. Fig. 5.1. "Frankenstein Movie Poster (1931)," http://commons.wikimedia.org/wiki/File:Frankenstein_poster_1931.jpg. Copyright in the Public Domain.

2. Fig. 5.2. "American troops wearing gas masks," http://commons.wikimedia.org/wiki/File:American%27s_wearing_gas_masks_during_World_War_I.JPG. Copyright in the Public Domain.

3. Fig. 5.3. "English battle tank," http://commons.wikimedia.org/wiki/File:Schwerer_englischer_Gefechtstank_beim_Versuch,_ein_unentwiibares_Drahthindernis_zu_durchbrechen.jpg. Copyright in the Public Domain.

4. Fig. 5.4. "German Airplane," http://commons.wikimedia.org/wiki/File:Crashed_World_War_I_German_airplane.jpg. Copyright in the Public Domain.

5. Fig. 5.5. "British Vickers machine gun," http://commons.wikimedia.org/wiki/File:Vickers_machine_gun_crew_with_gas_masks.jpg. Copyright in the Public Domain.

SHOVE OFF!

BY DR. BRUCE OLAV SOLHEIM WITH ART BY GARY DUMM

YOU DON'T BELONG IN GRADUATE SCHOOL IF YOU'RE GOING TO WRITE LIKE THIS!

THAT WAS MY INTRODUCTION TO DR. BERNARD STERNSHER WHEN I STARTED MY DOCTORAL PROGRAM AT BOWLING GREEN STATE UNIVERSITY IN 1990. I SURVIVED HIS EDITING PEN, AND HE BECAME ONE OF MY MENTORS.

HE SERVED ON BOARD THE COAST GUARD CUTTER JACKSON THAT SANK WHILE THEY WERE CHASING A GERMAN U-BOAT IN A HURRICANE. HE WAS ONLY ONE OF 19 SURVIVORS OUT OF A CREW OF 41.

BERNIE WAS BRILLIANT, CANTANKEROUS, AND NOT VERY POLITICALLY CORRECT. HE WAS ALSO ONE OF THE MOST WELL KNOWN GREAT DEPRESSION HISTORIANS IN AMERICA. AN ATHEIST JEW, HE LOOKED LIKE MEL BROOKS AND WAS MARRIED TO A SOUTHERN BAPTIST LADY WITH WHOM HE FOUGHT CONSTANTLY.

SHE ASKED ME TO BELIEVE IN SOME JEW WHO DIED, THEN CAME BACK TO LIFE AND CRAWLED OUT FROM UNDER A ROCK...I TOLD HER TO SHOVE OFF!

DUST BOWL MIGRANTS...

...ON THEIR WAY TO CALIFORNIA DURING THE GREAT DEPRESSION.

FRANKLIN D. ROOSEVELT

THE ONLY THING WE HAVE TO FEAR, IS FEAR ITSELF...AND THAT CRAZY GUY IN BERLIN WITH THE MUSTACHE.

FREE SOUP

I AGREED WITH BERNIE'S ADMIRATION OF PRESIDENT FRANKLIN D. ROOSEVELT (FDR).

HE LED US THROUGH THE GREAT DEPRESSION AND WORLD WAR II. CAN YOU IMAGINE WHAT WOULD HAVE HAPPENED WITHOUT FDR? PREPARING FOR A GERMAN VICTORY, NAZI SUPPORTERS BUILT A COMPOUND FOR ADOLF HITLER IN PACIFIC PALISADES, CALIFORNIA.

HEIL ME, AMERIKA!

CHAPTER SIX

THE TWENTIES AND THE GREAT DEPRESSION

OBJECTIVES

1. Define the transitional nature of the 1920s and the roots of the Great Depression.
2. Describe how the stock market collapsed and how this relates to the Great Depression.
3. Understand the New Deal, its goals and programs, and its impact.
4. Understand the legacies of the Great Depression and the New Deal.

PERSONAL HISTORY

My mom was born in 1919, the year of the Black Sox scandal. Eight players on the Chicago White Sox took bribes from professional gamblers to throw the World Series against the Cincinnati Reds. One of the eight players was Shoeless Joe Jackson, probably one of the best players in the history of baseball. Joe was illiterate and supposedly did not really understand what was going on. As it turned out, Jackson played very well in the Series anyway, so there is no evidence that he deliberately played poorly. Having been born in northern Norway on a remote island, my mom probably had no idea that Shoeless Joe Jackson had been banned from baseball for life. In fact, she did not know anything about baseball until my parents immigrated to the United States in August 1948, the month and year that Babe Ruth died. My eldest brother Bjørn died during World War II, and my sister was born in Norway. My brother Alf was born in Seattle on August 16, 1949, exactly one year to the day after Babe Ruth died. My brother Alf and I loved baseball and were both pretty good players—my brother a catcher, me a pitcher. Our parents did not really understand baseball, but they dutifully attended our games as often as they could. Babe Ruth changed baseball. In 1920 Babe hit 54 homeruns, more than any other entire team in Major League Baseball. The era before Babe Ruth is known as the Dead Ball era of baseball. Babe Ruth said he patterned his swing after Shoeless Joe Jackson.

The Great Depression was a worldwide phenomenon. I always wondered why my mother saved twist ties, rubber bands, pennies, pieces of string, nearly everything. She had them neatly put away in jars, empty margarine tubs, or drawers. I have since learned that she lived through the Depression in Norway, just like folks here in America. When you have next to nothing, you learn to be very thrifty and resourceful. My parents were also lifelong members of the Democratic Party. They would occasionally vote for a progressive Republican like Governor Dan Evans of Washington or US Representative Joel Pritchard of the 1st congressional district in Seattle. My parents were union supporters and most union folks voted for Democrats, the party of big labor. The two American presidents my parents most admired were Franklin D. Roosevelt and John F. Kennedy.

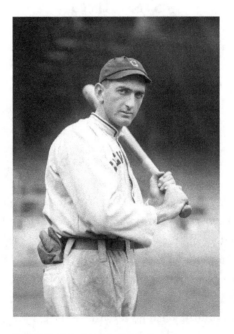

FIGURE 6.1. Shoeless Joe Jackson

A TALE OF TWO AMERICAS

The 1920s were an age of great social, cultural, and political change in America. For the first time in American history, more people lived in cities than on farms. The wealth of the nation doubled in the 1920s, and a consumer culture emerged in which people bought similar items, and sought the same leisure time entertainment. In spite of this image of the Roaring Twenties, there were still people living in small towns and farms who did not partake in this consumer culture, and were critical of it. Clear divisions grew between urban and rural culture in America Were the 1920s best characterized as the Roaring Twenties or something else? Rural America was not roaring. Farm families were living lives of quiet desperation. Certain individuals, events, and phenomena characterized the 1920s and help elucidate the complexities of that decade.

CHARLES LINDBERGH

Charles Lindbergh (1902–1974) was an American aviator who flew alone and nonstop across the Atlantic Ocean on May 20–21, 1927. In his aircraft the *Spirit of St. Louis,* he flew with only charts and a compass, often just above the surface of the ocean. The flight took 33.5 hours. He brought with him lots of coffee, sandwiches, and tons of courage. His daring accomplishment combined human bravery with the marvel of modern machines. This gave other Americans confidence that they belonged to a very special nation that could do anything. Lindbergh was a hero and role model for millions of Americans throughout the 1920s.

FLAPPERS

Flappers may be one of the most recognizable icons of the Roaring Twenties. Flappers were young women with short hair and short skirts who drank, smoked, spoke their minds, and ushered in a new sense of sexual freedom, liberating people from Victorian moral standards. The rise of the flapper coincided with the ratification of the women's suffrage amendment in 1920. The Nineteenth Amendment made it unconstitutional to deny women the vote. The new American woman was born.

BABE RUTH

George Herman Ruth was the first American sports celebrity. His likeness was everywhere, selling almost everything. He was also the first sports figure to make more money per year than the president of the United States. In 1930 Babe Ruth was asked if he knew that his annual salary of $80,000 was more than the beleaguered President Hoover's $75,000. "I know," he said, "but I had a better year than Hoover."

His life did not start out happily. Although Ruth was not an orphan, he did attend St. Mary's Industrial School for Orphans, Delinquent, Incorrigible and Wayward Boys in Baltimore, Maryland. His saloon keeper father did not know what to do with him. "Looking back on my boyhood, I honestly don't remember being aware of the difference between right and wrong," Ruth wrote in his autobiography. Ruth fell in love with baseball while at the school and signed a contract with the minor league Baltimore Orioles on Valentine's Day 1914.

Ruth first gained notoriety as a pitcher. He became one of the most dominant left-handed major league pitchers and won 24 games in 1917. Ruth helped Boston win three World Series championships. After being sold by Boston before the 1920 season, Ruth only pitched five games for the New York Yankees because they wanted him for his bat. Babe went on to become the best hitter in baseball history. His career homerun record lasted until Henry Aaron broke it in 1974. He is still probably the most recognizable sports figure worldwide. Ruth dreamt of being a big league manager, but it never happened.

PROHIBITION

The Eighteenth Amendment (1919) outlawed the sale and manufacture of alcohol. The unintended consequence of Prohibition was the rise of organized crime. Although the intentions were good, removing a legal supply and leaving a high demand literally invited organized crime to take over the alcohol business. Many people stockpiled liquor before the passage of the Eighteenth Amendment and the Volstead Act. It was not illegal to drink alcohol, but it was illegal to sell and manufacture it. To many middle-class white Americans, especially those living on farms and in small towns, Prohibition was a way to gain control over urban immigrants whom they considered to be unruly.

HENRY FORD

During the 1920s, many Americans had more expendable income and began to purchase more consumer, mass-produced items, such as ready-to-wear clothes, home appliances, and radios. By far the most important consumer product of the 1920s was the automobile. Henry Ford did not invent the automobile, but he did figure out how to mass produce them at a low enough cost that factory workers could afford them. The Ford Model T cost just $260 in 1924, and easy credit made cars affordable luxuries in the 1920s. In 1929 there was one car on the road for every five Americans. Meanwhile, as roads expanded, other businesses emerged to meet the needs of travelers (i.e., service stations and motels).

HOLLYWOOD

Americans flocked to the movies in the 1920s. Some estimates report that by the end of the 1920s nearly 75 percent of Americans went to the movies once a week. Hollywood expanded its filmmaking as worldwide demand increased. The 1920s was also the decade of the elaborate picture palaces. These were large urban theaters that could seat up to 2,000 guests and had orchestras and ornate furnishings. Many of these picture palaces were owned by the studios and used to premier their major films. Movie stars of the 1920s included Greta Garbo, Mary Pickford, Charlie Chaplin, Buster Keaton, Gloria Swanson, Douglas Fairbanks Sr., John Barrymore, Clara Bow, Harold Lloyd, and Laurel and Hardy. The first talking film was *The Jazz Singer* with Al Jolson. It came out in 1927.

AL CAPONE

Al "Scarface" Capone was an American gangster who came to power and prominence during the Prohibition era (1920–1933). He made his fortune from bootlegging and gained power through ruthless violence to build his criminal empire. At one point in the 1920s, Capone reportedly controlled an army of 1,000 gunmen and had half of Chicago's police force on his payroll. Alphonso Caponi was born on January 17, 1899, in Brooklyn, New York. He claimed he was forced into a life of crime by discrimination and the lack of opportunities he faced as an Italian American. Capone moved to Chicago and worked his way up through the Mob ranks. When his boss had to flee the country, Capone took over as boss. He protected his business interests, which also included gambling houses, by waging war on rival gangs. The federal government finally got Capone by convicting him for tax fraud. In October 1931 he was sentenced to 10 years of hard labor, which he served in a prison in Atlanta, and at Alcatraz. Released on parole in 1939, Capone spent the rest of his life at his estate in Florida, where he died in 1947.

FIGURE 6.2. Al Capone

THE HARLEM RENAISSANCE

The Harlem Renaissance was a literary, artistic, and intellectual movement that revealed black cultural identity to non-black patrons for the first time. Harlem was the cultural Mecca of America in the 1920s. One would visit Harlem to meet the best poets, writers, and painters, and listen to the finest music. Representing the movement were literary stars Langston Hughes and Zora Neale Hurston. The Harlem Renaissance served as a bridge between Reconstruction and the modern Civil Rights movement. For a brief, shining moment, racism could be put aside in favor of enjoying the arts together. The publishing industry sought out and published black writers. This literature focused on a realistic portrayal of black life in America. The movement was not political, it was artistic—but its influence was beyond art or artists. The Harlem Renaissance influenced future generations

FIGURE 6.3. Zora Neale Hurston

of black writers. Zora Neale Hurston arrived in New York City in 1925, when the Harlem Renaissance was at its peak. In 1926, a group of young black writers, including Hurston, Langston Hughes, and Wallace Thurman, produced a literary magazine that featured many of the young artists and writers of the Harlem Renaissance. In 1929, Hurston moved to Florida, where she wrote *Mules and Men*, published in 1935.

Unfortunately, not all Americans enjoyed or celebrated black culture. Social tensions did increase during the 1920s. The migration of African Americans from the South to the North, and the increasing visibility of black culture through music and the arts and literature, made some whites uncomfortable. There was a revival of the Ku Klux Klan in the 1920s. These social tensions broke along urban–rural, black–white, Catholic–Protestant, and gender lines.

THE GREAT GATSBY

The Great Gatsby is a novel written by F. Scott Fitzgerald, and is considered one of the greatest novels in American literature. The story follows a mysterious millionaire named Jay Gatsby who is living on Long Island and pursuing a beautiful young woman named Daisy. Daisy symbolizes the new American woman, the flapper. The themes of the book—decadence, idealism, resistance to change, social upheaval—provide a critical commentary on the American Dream. Fitzgerald was one of the discontented intellectuals who chose to live abroad because of their negative perception of America in the 1920s. By exploring why Fitzgerald and other brilliant Americans were discontented, one can gain a greater depth of understanding of the transformational 1920s.

THE DISCONTENT OF THE INTELLECTUALS

Why did so many gifted Americans of the early twentieth century reject their own civilization and its dominant values with eloquence and fervor? Nobody has been able to give a very profound or satisfying explanation, but many theories have been suggested. It could be that there is some truth to each of them.

THEY WERE DELUDED

The simplest suggestion is that they were deluded, immature, and ignorant. They swallowed whole the European criticisms of America that they had not themselves digested. They judged the entire American society on a one-sided esthetic criteria. Some of the discontented intellectuals were being superficial. Even if this is true, and we condemn H. L. Mencken and Ernest Hemingway, it does not explain why so many talented people were all deluded and went wrong all at once.

THEY WERE RIGHT

The best explanation may be that American society in the 1920s was the peak period of alienation, and exactly as unattractive as the intellectuals noted. Much of what was going on in America in the 1920s was deplorable. However, most Americans found their society highly satisfactory, and many Europeans tried hard to imitate it. Only a minority found life in the United States a failure. It is hard to criticize the general prosperity and world peace in the 1920s. The discontented intellectuals were allowed to express their views, which in itself is a good thing. To get to the heart of the question, other questions are required: In what terms was American society being judged? How did America compare to other societies at the time, and what did the discontented intellectuals expect of America, and why?

IT WAS THE WAR

Those who came of age during the First World War were called the Lost Generation by Gertrude Stein. Certainly World War I factored in to the discontent. The malaise that developed as a result of the horrible slaughter in the First World War was difficult to shake loose from. The United States did not succeed in its objectives in the war. Yet, discontent began before the war. Serious doubts about American society had been expressed in the nineteenth century by such noted intellectuals as Mark Twain, Edgar Allen Poe, Nathaniel Hawthorne, Herman Melville, and Walt Whitman. So it seems as though World War I was not the sole cause for intellectual alienation.

THE DECLINE OF CAPITALISM

Marxists note that alienation of the intellectuals is a predictable outcome in a declining capitalist society. Even if one accepts this assessment, it still does not answer the question, why did the alienation of the intellectuals reach its greatest extent during the period when American capitalism seemed to be flourishing as never before?

THE DECLINE OF THE OLD MIDDLE CLASS

Some have pointed out that many of the dissenting intellectuals belonged to the Anglo-Saxon Protestant, upper-middle class of New England and the older Midwest, and sensed the decline, within American society, of the class they represented and of its ideas. Much of this was due to the negative impact of big business in America.

MACHINE CIVILIZATION

Some have also noted that changes in the pace of living had happened faster than could be assimilated. The decline of the village, the rise of the automobile, movies, and other forms of mass entertainment had been causes of deep and unprecedented alterations in everybody's way of life. The social, moral, and intellectual lagged behind the economic forces. It was not just the speed of social change but the differential rate, with technology changing fastest and economic life adjusting, sometimes with difficulty, to technological change. Social life, moral and esthetic ideas were much harder to adapt. This explanation still holds true today in America, which may prove the explanation to be correct. But at what point and why did technological change become too rapid to assimilate?

LOSS OF FAITH

Some others believe that the underlying cause of intellectual alienation was loss of faith world-wide. The ideas of the eighteenth-century Enlightenment and of Protestant Christianity, ideas which had been basic to American civilization, had been attacked vigorously and effectively from many directions. Neither defense, adaptation, nor a search for new values had yet produced a consensus as stable as that which had been impaired. But why were the attacks, which had been going on for some time, felt so keenly in the 1920s? Many people were aware during the prewar Progressive Era that some difficult questions had been raised, to which no answers were forthcoming. But this was ignored, and the assumption was that they would be solved by the progress of knowledge and civilization. The war, however, made it harder to believe that everything was working for the best, and some people looked seriously for the first time at their own doubts and fears.

THE PURITAN HERITAGE

Most dissenting intellectuals focused their attacks on Puritanism. However, they owed much to the tradition of radical, essentially individualist Protestantism. Many of the dissenters were attacking their own Protestant, even Puritan, individualistic religion. While they lost their religion, they retained the emotions it inspired. Nothing else could account for some characteristics of American dissent: its hatred of materialism and complacency, its self-doubt and constant introspection, and above all its intense seriousness.

DEMOCRACY

Has democratic society always produced a tendency both toward uniformity and toward a resistance to uniformity? This was suggested earlier in American history during the Jacksonian era as documented in the book *Democracy in America* and at the beginning by Alexis de

Tocqueville. He thought Americans made a god of public opinion, and he feared the establishment of a tyranny in little things. Yet he also found many reasons to believe that Americans would resist these tendencies. If this is true, then the discontented intellectuals were far more a part of the civilization they were attacking than is generally thought. This does not mean that their complaints were trivial and unfounded; rather, it means, that one must study recent American dissent within the whole context of American history.

THE GREAT DEPRESSION

The Great Depression (1929–1939) was the deepest and longest economic depression in American history. It was also international in scope, related to many factors, not least of which the reparations payments forced on Germany after World War I and the disruption in worldwide balance of payments and banking. The stock market crash of October 1929 signaled the beginning of the Great Depression, but it actually began earlier, undetected. Over the next few years after the crash consumer spending dropped, investments were decreased, and industrial production dropped off abruptly, leading to massive layoffs and high unemployment. Financial failures followed the crash as more than half of the banks went bankrupt. President

FIGURE 6.4. Oklahoma migrant farm worker family

Herbert Hoover did not know what to do to combat the Depression, and what little he did do was not effective. Franklin D. Roosevelt was elected in 1932 with the promise of a New Deal for the American people. The New Deal did get America back on the road to recovery, and World War II brought America totally out of the Great Depression by 1939.

Stock prices had continued to rise throughout the 1920s, even though the economic reality did not reflect the confidence of the bull market. On October 24, 1929, the stock market finally collapsed as investors began dumping shares. That day became known as "Black Thursday." Millions of shares were suddenly worthless and investors who had bought stocks on margin (with borrowed money) were ruined financially. The gold standard, the world's fixed currency exchange, helped spread the Depression from the United States throughout the world, especially to Europe, where Germany was already in economic trouble. In spite of President Hoover's assertion that "prosperity is just around the corner," the crisis worsened. Unemployment climbed sharply and industrial production dropped by half. Bread lines, soup kitchens, and homeless men wandering from town to town and riding the rails became all too common. Farmers had been struggling since 1924 because of drought and falling food prices. Runs on the banks started in the fall of 1930, and by 1932 thousands of banks were closed.

CAUSES OF THE STOCK MARKET CRASH

There were numerous causes for the stock market crash. One problem was high productivity by American factories. Because businesses were flush with investor capital from a bull market, they invested in increasing production capability. There was also a concentration of profits in large corporations, and a concentration of income and savings in the upper-income classes. At the same time there was stagnant wages, or sticky wages, for the working class. High productivity and little disposable income for the masses meant a surplus developed. Farm prices had already dropped and then the price of surplus manufactured goods dropped. Consequently, there was a decline in mass purchasing power, a decline in sales of consumer durables, and a decline in home construction.

As a result of the concentrated profits and income, there was an over-investment in capital plant and equipment, an over-building of commercial and office structures, speculative excess in the mortgage bond industry leading to inflated real estate values, and an over-investment in securities based on naïve optimism and greed. Because the stock market continued to rise, there was a concealment of the real situation, like a person who looks good and feels good even when they are sick. Because the capital growth was not based on actual economic baseline conditions, the rising stock market was just a postponement of the inevitable reckoning. Nobody had ever seen the market behave that way, it was unprecedented and no one could predict what was going to happen. When investors realized that the market was too high and precarious, they began to sell. The selling led to panic and the panic led to chaos in the market. By the time they were done, the value of the market was gone.

The stock market crash did not cause the Great Depression; it aggravated previously deflated sectors of the economy. The best analogy would be a tired boxer staggering around the ring. The US economy was this tired boxer, guard down, legs sluggish. Then came the knockout blow. That is what the crash was—the knockout blow. The economy was exposed for all of its weaknesses—decline in sales of consumer durables, decline in home construction, falling farm prices, sick industries and regions. There was a very heavy weight of debt, corporate, home mortgage, and farm mortgage. All of these things were made worse by the vulnerability of the banking system. In 1929 there were lots of small, weak banks and only 33 percent belonged to the Federal Reserve system started by President Woodrow Wilson. There was also no government-backed deposit insurance, and banks had used their deposits to invest in speculative markets (25 percent in security loans, 10 percent in real estate loans), which meant more than one-third of investments were in risky ventures.

The Hoover administration and the federal government did some things that made the situation worse. They did not increase taxes, interest rates remained high, tariffs were raised, and the government favored concentration policies in the economy. The government should have dealt with the imbalance between farm and business income, and between wages and productivity. The benefits of the economy were not passed on to the working class, leaving their wages flat and sticky. The government also should have cleaned up and monitored the irresponsible practices in the securities market, helped relieve the weight of private debt, and fixed the structural weakness in the banking system.

Overall, the attitude of the bureaucracy of the US government and old ideas of what to do in a financial crisis prevented Hoover and other leaders from taking action. President Calvin Coolidge had said that "the business of America is business," and that "when you build a factory you build a cathedral." Businessmen thought they were doing the right thing and US government officials agreed. The trickle-down theory was popular at that time. It meant that corporations and the wealthy would create wealth, and the benefits would trickle down eventually to the working class. This did not happen, nor has it ever happened. In spite of the rising stock market from 1920 to 1929, farm prices were down 40 percent, productivity was up 55 percent, wages were up only 2–3 percent, and consumer prices were down 2-3 percent. These economic indicators spelled trouble for the US economy.

THE DEPRESSION BEGINS

Unemployment increased steadily after the stock market crash. By the election of 1932, unemployment estimates are as high as 40 percent. The psychological impact was tremendous for regular, working-class people. Even in the best of times there is residual unemployment, but by 1932 millions of American workers, who had always brought home a steady paycheck for their families, were unemployed and joined the ranks of those who were never employed. Many men could no longer face their families and abandoned them. Suicides were common. The unemployed needed hope, but received none. President Hoover's assurance that "prosperity was just around the corner" did not pay the bills for the unemployed. They were told that everything would be okay in the long run. "We don't eat in the long run, we eat every day," was the response from Harry Hopkins who became one of Roosevelt's closest advisers. Some people took things into their own hands and broke into food warehouses. Breadlines formed in every major city. Newspapers were called Hoover blankets and pants pockets turned inside out were called Hoover flags. Hoovervilles (homeless encampments) sprung up everywhere. Probably one of the saddest incidents during the early days of the Great Depression was what happened to the World War I veterans.

THE BONUS MARCHERS

In 1924, Congress enacted a law overriding a veto by President Calvin Coolidge, providing for a system of adjusted compensation in the form of a bond for World War I veterans based on length of service. World War I veterans each received a dollar for each day of domestic service, up to $500, and $1.25 for each day of overseas service, up to $625. The bond would accumulate compound interest that would amount to an average payment of $1,000 for each veteran, payable in 1945. In 1931 Congress approved veterans borrowing, overriding the veto of President Herbert Hoover, up to 50 percent of the face value of their bond. By 1932 the veterans were demanding immediate redemption of the bonds at face value. This full redemption of the bond came to be known as a bonus. Hoover and Congress refused the veterans' demands.

In May 1932 more than 20,000 World War I veterans arrived in Washington to press for their bonus. Known as the Bonus Expeditionary Force, the veterans continued to hold marches and rallies despite the fact that Hoover told them he would use troops to force an evacuation. On July 29, 1932, the US Army under the command of Douglas MacArthur pushed the World War I veterans out of Washington. When it was over, 1 veteran had been killed and about 50 veterans and Washington police had been injured. When Roosevelt became president, he offered veterans jobs through the Civilian Conservation Corps instead of paying the bonus.

RECONSTRUCTION FINANCE CORPORATION

By the end of 1931, the American economy was slipping so fast that President Hoover was forced to move away from laissez-faire economic policies and began to think that if the government could shore up banks and railroads, he could halt the rise of unemployment and get industry going again. Hoover's Reconstruction Finance Corporation (RFC) sought to assure the survival of large banks, railroads, farm mortgage associations, savings and loan associations, and life insurance companies.

Despite some initial success, the Reconstruction Finance Corporation failed to have an impact. Democrats argued that Hoover was bailing out the rich and not helping those in most need at the bottom. To many Americans it looked like a relief for big business and not for the people (similar to what happened in 2008 in America).

FRANKLIN D. ROOSEVELT

Franklin Delano Roosevelt (FDR) was born on January 30, 1882, in Hyde Park, New York. Growing up, FDR had a happy but sheltered childhood. His family was very wealthy and he had a privileged upbringing, with trips to Europe and private tutors. At age 14 he was sent to Groton, an exclusive prep school. He graduated from Groton in 1900, went to Harvard, and graduated in 1903. He then fell in love with his sixth cousin, Eleanor Roosevelt. They married in 1905, with President Theodore Roosevelt standing in for Eleanor's deceased father. The marriage was not a happy one, and Franklin's mother did not help (Roosevelt was a self-proclaimed mama's boy). Franklin and Eleanor had six children. In 1910 Franklin was elected to the New York State Legislature and in 1913 he was appointed assistant secretary of the Navy by President Woodrow Wilson.

In 1918 he had an affair with his wife's social secretary, Lucy Mercer. When Eleanor discovered the affair, she was devastated and told Franklin she wanted a divorce. Convinced by his mother, Roosevelt worked to save his relationship and promised Eleanor he would not happen again. Franklin and Eleanor became political rather than romantic partners

FIGURE 6.5. Franklin D. Roosevelt

from then on. In 1921 FDR contracted polio and was paralyzed. He permanently lost the use of his legs, but refused to let that end his political ambitions. With the help of Eleanor, he slowly regained his confidence, especially after starting a polio rehabilitation center in Warm Springs, Georgia. Roosevelt spoke at the 1924 Democratic Convention and heartily endorsed New York governor Alfred E. Smith. Franklin was always a clever politician, but he was missing the common touch. After his paralysis, he knew what it was like to suffer, like millions of other Americans, and that made him a better and more effective leader and communicator. His polio gave him the extra strength and courage he needed to be president of the United States during two of the worst crises in American history.

In 1928 Roosevelt was elected governor of New York, and survived financially when the stock market crashed in 1929. He provided relief and public works projects for the millions of unemployed in the state. His success as New York's governor made him a strong candidate for the presidency in 1932. He easily beat incumbent president Herbert Hoover.

THE NEW DEAL

President Hoover, a conservative Republican, believed that the US government should not directly intervene in the economy. His efforts to combat the Depression were too little and too late. He could never reconcile himself to the fact that the government would have to take drastic and unprecedented measures (e.g., create jobs and provide economic relief to the unemployed) in order to pull out of the Great Depression.

Americans elected Franklin D. Roosevelt in 1932, at a time when more than one-third of the country was out of work. Roosevelt's first order of business was to order a four-day bank holiday. Inspiring, calm, and confident, he told Americans that "the only thing we have to fear is fear itself." The government reviewed the banks and reopened the ones that were determined to be sound. Based on almost universal dislike of American banking, Roosevelt probably could have nationalized the banks with little protest. Roosevelt also began a series of public radio addresses known as "fireside chats." In his first 100 days in office, Roosevelt's administration passed legislation meant to stabilize industrial and agricultural production, create jobs, and stimulate recovery. He also reformed the financial system, creating the Federal Deposit Insurance Corporation (FDIC), which would protect savings deposits. He also established the Securities and Exchange Commission (SEC) to regulate the stock market and prevent abuses of the kind that led to the 1929 crash.

THE THREE "R'S"

Franklin Roosevelt's plan to get the United States out of the Great Depression, the New Deal, can best be described by the three "R's:" relief, recovery, and reform.

RELIEF

The first step in the New Deal was to provide immediate relief for the unemployed. Roosevelt did not want to create a dole or entitlement program, he wanted to provide jobs for unemployed Americans so they could restore their own dignity, pay their bills, feed their families, and get the economy going again. The Works Progress Administration (WPA) was instituted by presidential executive order under the Emergency Relief Appropriation Act of April 1935, to generate public jobs for the unemployed. By 1936 almost 3.5 million Americans were employed by the WPA. Roosevelt's secretary of commerce, Harry Hopkins, said, "Give a man a dole, and you save his body and destroy his spirit. Give him a job and you save both body and spirit." The WPA was supposed to prime the pump and get the economy going until private industry could employ people again. The WPA focused on infrastructure and cultural improvements: WPA workers constructed 651,087 miles of roads, streets, and highways; and built, repaired, or refurbished 124,031 bridges, 125,110 public buildings, 8,192 parks, and 853 air fields. In addition, workers cleaned slums, revived forests, and extended electrical power to rural locations. The WPA funded cultural projects like state histories, art murals on public buildings, and songs written about the Great Depression.

Administered by Harald Ickes, Roosevelt's secretary of the interior, the National Industrial Recovery Act of June 16, 1933, established the Public Works Administration (PWA). The PWA was dedicated to building America's infrastructure through large-scale projects meant to provide employment, stabilize purchasing power, improve public welfare, and contribute to a revival of American industry. Between July 1933 and March 1939, the PWA funded the construction of more than 34,000 projects, including airports, electricity-generating dams, aircraft carriers, and 70 percent of the new schools and one-third of the hospitals built during that time. Although Roosevelt was roundly criticized for the building of the PWA hydro-electric dams, those dams and the electricity they provided were desperately needed for the continuous production that took place during World War II.

The Civilian Conservation Corps (CCC) was a public work relief program that operated from 1933 to 1942 for unemployed, unmarried men from families who were eligible for relief. Originally meant for young men ages 18–23, it was eventually expanded to include young men ages 17–28. The CCC provided manual jobs for unskilled workers on public lands. These jobs were aimed at conservation and development of natural resources. More than 3 million young men worked for the CCC, which provided them with a $30 a month wage, shelter, food, and clothing. Most of their wage was sent home to their families ($25 of the $30).

The American public and FDR himself found the CCC the most popular of all the New Deal programs. CCC jobs improved the physical condition of the workers, heightened morale, and increased employability. The CCC also led to a greater appreciation of the nation's natural resources; and allowed more Americans to enjoy and have access to the outdoors and natural environment and work to protect lands belonging to the public trust.

FIGURE 6.6. Grand Coulee Dam in Washington State (PWA project)

During the time of the CCC, volunteers planted nearly 3 billion trees to help reforest America, constructed more than 800 parks nationwide, upgraded most state parks, updated forest fire-fighting methods, and built a network of service buildings and public roadways in remote areas.

RECOVERY

When President Franklin Delano Roosevelt took office in 1933, farmers faced the most severe economic situation and lowest agricultural prices since the 1890s. Roosevelt's solution was the establishment of the Agricultural Adjustment Administration (AAA). The Administration had to try to eliminate agricultural surpluses in order to stabilize prices. Wheat, cotton, field corn, hogs, rice, tobacco, and dairy products were designated as basic commodities in the original legislation. Subsequent amendments in 1934 and 1935 expanded the list of basic commodities to include rye, flax, barley, grain sorghums, cattle, peanuts, sugar beets, sugar-cane, and potatoes. The government also encouraged crop rotation and soil management, and promoted and funded irrigation projects, in addition to subsidizing farm prices. In 1935 the income generated by farms was 50 percent higher than it was in 1932, partly due to farm programs such as the AAA.

The National Industrial Recovery Act of 1933 (NIRA) was signed by Roosevelt on June 16, 1933. The new law created the National Recovery Administration (NRA). The NRA worked with businesses to come up with fair competition codes that were exempt from antitrust laws. The concept of the NRA was to get factories up and running, with government serving as an honest broker between labor unions and businesses. As factories began running again, union membership increased dramatically. Just before the NIRA was to expire, the Supreme Court declared it unconstitutional. The Court decided that the NIRA gave legislative power to the NRA and violated the Commerce Clause because it went beyond powers granted to the federal government. Roosevelt criticized the Supreme Court's action and said that they were "living in the horse and buggy era."

REFORM

The Securities and Exchange Commission (SEC) was a regulatory agency created as part of the New Deal with the primary mission of regulating the stock market. Moreover, the SEC protects investors; maintains fair, orderly, and efficient markets; and facilitates capital formation. The SEC also has enforcement authority, allowing it to bring civil enforcement actions (and assist criminal law enforcement agencies) against individuals or companies accused of fraud, or engaged in insider trading, among other violations. The SEC's goal was to gain public confidence and trust in the capital markets by requiring uniform standards for disclosure of information.

President Roosevelt appointed Joseph P. Kennedy, Sr., father of President John F. Kennedy, to serve as the first chairman of the SEC. When criticized for appointing Kennedy to the position, in spite of his rather untrustworthy reputation, Roosevelt said, "It takes a thief to catch a thief."

After the stock market crash and the beginning of the Great Depression, there were runs on the banks. Banks generally hold reserve funds in amounts equal to only a small fraction of their total deposits. Because there was no insurance coverage for the deposits at the time, bank customers who did not withdraw their deposits in time lost their money when the banks failed.

On June 16, 1933, President Roosevelt signed the Banking Act of 1933. This legislation established the Federal Deposit Insurance Corporation (FDIC). The FDIC also had the authority to regulate and supervise state non-member banks and extend federal oversight to all commercial banks for the first time.

The Great Depression hit the young and old the hardest. Poverty rates for senior citizens exceeded 50 percent. The stock market crash of 1929 had taken many older citizens' retirement savings, and bank failures did further damage. President Roosevelt signed the Social Security Act on August 14, 1935. The act was drafted by the president's Committee on Economic Security, under Secretary of Labor Frances Perkins (the first woman to serve in a cabinet position). Still to this day, Social Security provides benefits to retirees and the unemployed, and a lump-sum benefit at death. Payments to current retirees are financed by a payroll tax on current workers' wages, half taken directly as a payroll tax and half paid by the employer.

The New Deal saved America from total economic collapse. After showing early signs of recovery in the spring of 1933, the economy continued to improve throughout the next three years, with the gross domestic product growing at an average rate of 9 percent per year. Depression-era hardships gave rise to extremist political movements in various European countries, and even in Japan. The most notorious was Adolf Hitler's Nazi regime in Germany.

Hitler's aggression led to war in Europe in 1939 and then the WPA turned its attention to building up the military infrastructure of the United States, even though the country remained neutral. With Roosevelt's decision to support Britain and France in the struggle against Germany and the other Axis powers, defense manufacturing geared up, producing many private-sector jobs. The Japanese attack on Pearl Harbor in December 1941 led to an American declaration of war, and the nation's factories went back into full production mode. This expanding industrial production, as well as widespread conscription beginning in 1942, reduced the unemployment rate to below its pre-Depression level.

ASSESSMENT OF THE NEW DEAL

Franklin D. Roosevelt was elected four consecutive times. His popularity was without question. Yet, there were those who despised him. Many conservatives on the far right of the political spectrum felt that the New Deal and FDR's leadership was too much of a departure from the American tradition and was a dangerous flirtation with socialism or even communism. Those on the far left of the political spectrum pointed out that the New Deal only resulted in modest gains for the working class in terms of income distribution. These left-wing critics believed that the New Deal compromised too much and took the pressure off of big business and thereby inadvertently perpetuated an unfair socioeconomic system. In other words, they believed that FDR sold out to big business. Liberal centrists, those who would call themselves New Dealers, defended FDR's middle way. Liberal centrists believed the New Deal was about all they could get, whereas the radical left believed they could have done more. All sides agreed that the New Deal had a positive psychological effect. On balance, the New Deal did help millions of unemployed Americans and their families. Women made strides in politics, as evidenced by Frances Perkins's rise to the position of secretary of labor and the expansion of the role of the First Lady by Eleanor Roosevelt. Even though the New Deal jobs were unequally distributed, due to corrupt and resistant state governments, enough minorities were helped that there was a change in voting behavior. In order to truly assess the New Deal, we need to look at both the obstacles *to* change and the forces *for* change.

OBSTACLES TO CHANGE

TRADITIONAL IDEAS

In order to push the New Deal through Congress and get Americans to back the programs, FDR had to overcome tremendous obstacles. The first obstacle was the persistence of old habits and the tendency to cling to traditional ideas. Hoover had become a prisoner of this first obstacle. He could never accept the fact that the government needed to do more than it ever had before to fight the Depression. In every depression prior to the Great Depression, the American government did nothing. The concept was simple: just wait it out. It was difficult for members of the government and for the general public to try something completely new. It was even difficult for Roosevelt. FDR had to overcome his own traditional conception of the economy, class, and the role of government. He was, after all, a member of the privileged class, an old-money capitalist. After successfully implementing the New Deal, FDR was called a traitor to his class.

DURABILITY OF THE CLASS STRUCTURE

Another obstacle was the durability of the class structure. Americans do not like to talk about it, but the United States is divided by economic class. The myth is firmly in place: anyone can become rich if they just work hard enough. The sad truth is that whatever economic class an American is born in is likely to be the economic class they will die in. Because of the rags-to-riches myth, many Americans do not support any programs that would put more tax burden on the rich, or would more equally distribute income and wealth. The New Deal did redistribute wealth, and it was a tough fight for Roosevelt to get the measures through Congress and accepted by the American people.

POOR KNOWLEDGE OF ECONOMICS

The American public also lacked imagination when it came to applying alternative economic theories. They had been used to largely laissez-faire capitalism and were well aware that market fluctuations and down business cycles could lead to a depression. But previous depressions had been short-lived and America always pulled out in fine shape after. Roosevelt's basic concept of spending money the government did not have seemed alien to most Americans. Additionally, America also suffered from what could best be called economic schizophrenia. Are we rugged individualists who always make it on our own through true grit and determination, or are we a united group that pool and share resources and work together in concert?

ABSENCE OF COMPETENT BANKERS

Yet another obstacle for Roosevelt and his New Deal was the absence of competent banking personnel. During the four-day banking holiday at the beginning of FDR's first term, the government had to determine which banks were sound and could reopen. This capability was limited by the fact that many banks were headed by incompetents. The government needed to work with banks and businesses hand in hand during the first 100 days of the New Deal, something unprecedented in American history.

THE SUPREME COURT

The New Deal faced a constant threat from the Supreme Court, which tended to be very conservative, pro-business, and resistant to change in general. FDR and the Supreme Court locked horns many times over the New Deal. The Supreme Court did strike down the National Recovery Administration, and limited plans for other programs. This fact, coupled with the Republican backlash and reactionary state governments, formed significant threats to the success of the New Deal. Some governors refused to accept the New Deal; others took the government money and did not implement the work programs, or gave the money to political cronies.

ORGANIZATION OF CONGRESS

Older people tend not to support change, especially radical change. Congress is led by the most senior members, who have the most seniority. All committees are headed by such senior members. The New Deal legislation had to get through committee before it could go to the floor for debate or a vote. Selling the New Deal to the more senior members of Congress in these chairman positions was not easy and served as a major obstacle for FDR. Related to this issue of seniority in Congress were the political parties, which tended to put off difficult issues in favor of more watered-down legislation.

APATHY

It did not help FDR and his New Deal that the media tended to support more traditional ideas. Gathering public support for novel measures requires some media support. This was in short supply for Roosevelt. Public ignorance and apathy exacerbated the problem. A great number of potential voters just did not (and still do not) have the capacity to understand complex issues. They tended to follow the crowd and became susceptible to manipulation. The poor, who benefited most from the New Deal, did not vote, creating a self-imposed political powerlessness and disadvantage.

RESTORATIVE IMPULSE

The last obstacle was the tendency for people to stick with what they know, even if what they know is not working. This is known as the restorative impulse. An analogy would be a person walking on a ledge between two buildings. If the person slips and is dangling by their fingertips from the ledge, their instinct is to pull themselves back up to the ledge they slipped off of. They would not instinctively throw themselves over to the other side. Many people have said that this helps explain why some people remain in bad relationships. As the old saying goes, "Better the devil you know than the devil you don't know."

FORCES FOR CHANGE

FDR'S LEADERSHIP

In spite of seemingly insurmountable obstacles, the New Deal did get pushed through, brought America back from the brink, and started the country on the road to recovery. There were some powerful forces that worked in Roosevelt's favor. Probably the most important was FDR's leadership. Roosevelt had supreme confidence and calm in a time of great worry and panic. He was willing to experiment and try things out to see what would work. He was not a deep thinker like Theodore Roosevelt—many people have described Franklin as having a fly-paper intellect. He was a quick learner and remembered many things that he would use to his political advantage. He relied on his so-called Brain Trust for the deep thinking. The Brain Trust consisted of different groups of policy advisers taken from Columbia University and Harvard University who helped FDR formulate the New Deal. Roosevelt was the consummate politician and knew how to make deals and maneuver in and around Congress. He was extremely charismatic and a superb public speaker. He made all Americans feel like he was taking to them like a neighbor over a backyard fence. His ability to talk about complex issues and put them in simple and easily understood terms created a sense of comfort among the people facing the crisis of the Great Depression and the burden of understanding how the New Deal and its novel programs would work. There is a reason that FDR was elected four times in a row: his leadership was needed by the American people, and they spoke through their votes. Few, if any, other politicians could have done what Roosevelt did for America.

PROGRESSIVE BLOC IN CONGRESS

If FDR could get his New Deal legislation out of committee and onto the floor, there was a good chance it would pass. Many Progressives were elected from 1900 to 1920, and were generally supportive of the New Deal. Certainly the most successful third party in the immediate post–World War I era was the Progressive Party, led by Senator Robert M. La Follette of Wisconsin. There was a rise in left-wing political activity in the United States after World War I. The Workers' Party (the Communists), the Socialist Party, and the Farmer-Labor Party, all developed and grew in the 1920s.

La Follette called for more government ownership of the means of production, tax reform, agricultural reform, and judicial reform. The Socialists, Farmer-Labor Party, and a number of labor organizations supported La Follette and broadened the movement into what was called the Progressive Party. The Progressive Party fell apart after the election defeat in 1924, but made a comeback in the 1930s on the state level in Wisconsin, where La Follette's sons, Robert Jr. and Philip, built a successful movement that lasted until the end of World War II.

THIRD PARTY SOCIALIST MOVEMENT

The strong socialist movement in Wisconsin, especially in Milwaukee, served as a force for change for FDR and his New Deal. The Socialist Democratic Party got Emil Seidel elected as mayor of Milwaukee in 1910. Then Victor Berger, founding member of the Social Democratic Party of America, was also elected in 1910, becoming the first Socialist ever elected to the US House of Representatives. He was convicted of violating the Espionage Act in 1919 and did not take his seat in the House of Representatives. The Supreme Court overturned the verdict and Berger was then elected to three successive terms in the 1920s. In the fall 1920 election, the Socialist Party of Wisconsin elected three state senators and another nine of its members to the Wisconsin Assembly. The Socialist Democratic Party of Wisconsin was the center of what was called "Sewer Socialism." The Sewer Socialists fought to clean up what they saw as "the dirty and polluted legacy of the Industrial Revolution," working in neighborhoods and industrial areas to establish better sanitation systems, municipal water and power, and better education systems.

RADICAL INTELLECTUALS

Left-wing politics today in America has its origins in the radical movement of the 1930s. The radicals of the 1930s had a dislike for capitalism and an attachment to revolutionary socialism. The historical determinism of the 1930s radicals, believing that events are historically predetermined, is not as popular today as it was in the 1930s. Anti-capitalist intellectuals, from the stock market crash to Hitler's rise to power and Roosevelt's inauguration, moved substantially to the left. These radical intellectuals proposed that American capitalism did not deserve to survive and were disappointed that New Deal reforms did not extend much beyond 1937. Although they were not happy with the New Deal, they felt it was a move in the right direction. Little did they know that socialist-leaning intellectuals from the 1930s would later be persecuted by Senator Joseph McCarthy in the early 1950s as part of his hysterical anti-Communist crusade.

RADICAL FRINGE

Another force for change that translated to support for the New Deal was the radical fringe figures in American life and politics. These popular figures of the time made FDR and his New Deal seem tame in comparison.

Huey Long was governor of Louisiana from 1928 to 1932, and was elected to the US Senate in 1930. Although officially a Democrat, Huey Long was really a radical populist. Long was very popular with poor people. He championed the poor against the rich and powerful. Long was a poor farm boy from northern Louisiana who, as a high-school dropout, taught himself law and got a law degree in only one year of study. His colorful, controversial, charismatic

FIGURE 6.7. Huey Long

style endeared him to his constituency, but frightened mainstream politicians. His nickname "Kingfish" came from his saying: "I'm a small fish here in Washington. But I'm the Kingfish to the folks down in Louisiana." Huey Long was a bitter enemy of Wall Street, bankers, and big business. He saw FDR as being in league with these powerful forces. FDR considered Huey Long to be one of the most dangerous men in America because of Long's radical programs and dictatorial control of Louisiana.

Long laid out his plan for America and his goal to become president of the United States. This plan was known as Share the Wealth, and it called for the government to confiscate the wealth of the nation's rich and powerful. Under Share the Wealth, every family in the nation would be guaranteed an annual income of $5,000, so they could all have a home, a job, a radio, and an automobile. He also proposed limiting private fortunes to $50 million, legacies to $5 million, and annual incomes to $1 million. Everyone over age 60 would receive an old-age pension. His slogan was "Every Man a King." Long was shot a month after announcing that he would run for president. On September 8, 1935, Dr. Carl Weiss fired a handgun at Long from four feet away, hitting him in the abdomen. Long's bodyguards returned fire, killing Weiss. Long was rushed to the hospital but died two days later. He was only 42 years old.

Father Charles Coughlin was a Catholic priest, originally from Canada, who lived in Detroit, Michigan. He began broadcasting his sermons in 1926, and by the early 1930s they had shifted from theology to economics and politics. Coughlin had a well-developed theory of what he called "Social Justice," based on certain monetary reforms. Coughlin was initially a big supporter of FDR and his New Deal, but then turned on him and became one of Roosevelt's harshest critics. His program of Social Justice was a very radical challenge to capitalism and to the New Deal. Roosevelt's early monetary policies made Father Coughlin view him as the savior of the nation. But when FDR did not push for enough radical reforms, Coughlin turned against him. Father Coughlin's influence on Depression-era America was widespread—millions of Americans listened to his weekly radio broadcast. Father Coughlin's Social Justice program promised a guaranteed income, nationalizing industry, taxing the wealthy to redistribute income, federal protection for labor unions, and decreasing individual property rights in favor of public property rights. His sermons also included attacks on prominent Jewish figures, and in the late 1930s he supported some of the policies of Adolf Hitler and Benito Mussolini. These views convinced many people that Coughlin was anti-Semitic. His broadcasts became increasingly controversial and by 1940 his superiors in the Catholic Church and the Roosevelt administration forced him to stop. He then returned to his work as a parish priest.

During the Depression Governor Floyd B. Olson was a hero in Minnesota. Olson was a popular leader with a knack for inspiring hope during tough times. Floyd Bjørnstjerne Olson was the son of poor Scandinavian immigrants who settled in north Minneapolis. In 1919 he was appointed assistant attorney for Hennepin County and went on to become county attorney. Olson was elected governor of Minnesota in 1930 as a member of the Farmer-Labor Party. Olson was a tough-talking politician who had appealed to the rural and urban poor. He often spoke of the "failure of government and the social system to function in the interests of the common happiness of the people." As governor, Olson used emergency powers to bring about economic and social change. Governor Olson's Farmer-Labor Party, a coalition

FIGURE 6.8. Upton Sinclair

of farmers, workers, socialists, isolationists, and progressives, advocated a fairer distribution of income and social justice. Some of his reforms included the state's first income tax, a tax on chain stores, bank reorganization, municipally owned liquor stores, ratification of the federal amendment prohibiting child labor, large appropriations for relief, a two-year halt to farm foreclosures, a pension system, incentives for cooperative businesses, government support in labor disputes, limiting working hours, establishing state forests, and state protection for wilderness areas. He was a supporter of FDR and the New Deal, even though his party would have preferred more aggressive programs. He died in office at age 44.

Upton Sinclair (1878–1968), who lived in Monrovia, California, was a novelist and social crusader who pioneered the kind of journalism known as "muckraking." He exposed the unsanitary conditions in the meat-packing industry in his best-known novel *The Jungle*, which was influential in obtaining passage of the Pure Food and Drug Act. Sinclair received a Pulitzer Prize for a later novel about Hitler's rise to power. He ran for governor of California as a Socialist. He was demonized in the press, and the Democratic establishment tried to stop his candidacy. His platform was called End Poverty in California (EPIC).

The goal of EPIC was to turn over factories and agricultural land to workers to be run as cooperatives. Sinclair argued that traditional relief programs financially benefited the political machines, rather than the poor. Sinclair believed that farm and industrial cooperatives were the best solution for the unemployed. These cooperatives would be voluntary, democratic, and jointly owned enterprises created to meet economic and social needs of the more than 750,000 unemployed and underemployed Californians during the Depression. Supporters of EPIC called for public welfare and hoped to build a new society that ended mass poverty through peaceful means. Sinclair believed that EPIC was not radical; he insisted that it was based on the American values of self-reliance, initiative, and equality. Despite the severe backlash by the mainstream political establishment, Upton Sinclair was very nearly elected governor of California in 1934. Had it been a two-man race, or had Sinclair not been such an honest intellectual instead of a politician, he could have won and EPIC would have influenced the New Deal as a model.

William Dudley Pelley (1885–1965) was an American fascist born in Lynn, Massachusetts. As leader of the pro-Nazi Silver Shirts, Pelley preached anti-Semitism, nationalism, and mysticism. Pelley was already publishing at age 19, and covered the Russian Revolution and subsequent Civil War as a writer for the *Saturday Evening Post*. Pelley moved to California after he returned to the United States and worked as a novelist, screenwriter, and magazine publisher. In 1928 he underwent a spiritual transformation in the form of an out-of-body experience that he called "seven minutes in eternity." Pelley moved to Asheville, North Carolina, where he formed his unorthodox views mixing Christianity, mysticism, and fascism. Pelley founded Galahad Press and used it to publish the *New Liberator* magazine. He called for a "Christian Commonwealth," a new kind of government that blended elements of his unique brand of fascism, socialism, and theocracy. The Christian Commonwealth would not have paper money, bankers, or big cities. Jews were also to be excluded and would be isolated in walled-off areas.

FIGURE 6.9. William Dudley Pelley

Adolf Hitler's rise to power in Germany had a dramatic impact on Pelley. When Hitler took control in Germany, Pelley estalished the Silver Legion of America, also known as the Silver Shirts. The Silver Shirts were modeled on the Nazi Brown Shirts. His Silver Shirts came under scrutiny as President Roosevelt asked the Justice Department to investigate Pelley on charges of sedition and insurrection. Pelley was arrested in April 1942, tried, and found guilty on 11 charges. He was sentenced to 15 years in a federal prison in Indiana. Pelley was released in 1952 and lived for the remainder of his years in Noblesville, Indiana. There, he developed an elaborate religious philosophy called "Soulcraft," based on his belief in UFOs and extraterrestrials. He died on June 30, 1965.

New Deal Achievements

Fulfilling Theodore Roosevelt's progressive New Nationalism plan of big government, FDR forever enlarged the federal government with the New Deal. The government took on functions that it never had before. The idea of providing for the public welfare, a social safety net, a national retirement system, and unemployment insurance were unheard of prior to the New Deal.

The New Deal did not discriminate against minorities, although FDR could have done more to support them. There was discrimination at the state and local level where New Deal funds were used to create jobs. Eleanor was more progressive in terms of civil rights than Franklin and pushed him to go farther. The New Deal did reach enough ethnic minorities so as to change voting patterns. The first woman to serve in a presidential cabinet was FDR's secretary of labor, Frances J. Perkins.

Federal government intervention saved many American homes and farms. This was unprecedented; it endeared Roosevelt to the working class and caused suspicion and hatred among the wealthiest Americans, who considered FDR a traitor to his economic and social class. FDR was pro-union and the federal government stood on the side of labor, causing the New Deal Democratic Party to emerge as the party of the labor unions in the following decades.

When FDR took office, seven out of eight farm homes did not have electricity. By 1940, seven out of eight American farms had electricity. The PWA building of hydroelectric dams and infrastructure improvements was considered a waste and careless tampering with the economy by New Deal critics. As it turned out, not only was rural America improved by such massive infrastructure projects, but the power was needed to run American defense plants and factories around the clock during World War II.

FIGURE 6.10. Unemployed man during the Great Depression

The New Deal shored up a very weak and decentralized banking system. In 1933 Roosevelt introduced a New Deal concept of providing deposit insurance for individual depositors in an effort to re-establish trust in American banking. The Federal Deposit Insurance Corporation (FDIC) was established in 1933 and not a single American has lost their money through bank failure since. The creation of the FDIC gave consumers confidence in the banks again. Some on the left may have criticized FDR for not going far enough and letting the banks and big business off the hook for the Great Depression and stock market crash, but Roosevelt's middle way seemed to satisfy the great majority of Americans.

The New Deal also strengthened the stock market and investment banks by establishing the Securities and Exchange Commission. Investors were being protected by an agency of the federal government that would protect honest investing and monitor the stock market for the benefit of all. Roosevelt realized that the young and the old were hardest hit by the Depression. A great number of elderly Americans were living in poverty. The New Deal established a national retirement system through the Social Security Act. America was the last modern industrialized country to establish a national retirement system.

The New Deal not only introduced the concept of public welfare, but also improved public facilities and the nation's infrastructure, and even offered cultural improvements, all the while providing jobs for the unemployed, kick-starting the economy, and bringing America out of the Great Depression. The New Deal coalition of Progressive Democrats and Republicans lasted until the mid-to-late 1970s. Voting patterns changed as a result. For instance, prior to the New Deal, African Americans voted for the Republicans (the party of Lincoln), but they switched allegiance after the New Deal. Although it may be true that World War II production brought us totally out of the Great Depression, the New Deal saved America, got things going again, and offered hope for the poor, unemployed, and disenfranchised. Ronald Reagan would emerge in the early 1980s and also have a huge impact on American society by launching the Conservative Revolution reversing many of the New Deal achievements.

CONCLUSION

I have always been fascinated by the 1930s and the Great Depression. I often wonder how I would have fared under such conditions. My parents were still very young and living in Norway in the 1930s, when times were very hard. They had no electricity, they had outdoor toilets, they burned peat for heat, and they ate mainly fish and potatoes.

My dad would go to sea for long stretches of time though, first in the Norwegian Navy and then in the merchant marines. He told me that he was in Chicago in the 1930s as a young sailor. He said life was pretty hard, and he could tell that things were not going well in America. My dad and another Norwegian sailor went on shore in Chicago and proceeded to the nearest bar. Soon after they sat down with their beers, an American man came up to them and started talking to my dad's friend. After a few moments, my dad's friend punched the American man in the face and told my dad to run. They left their beers and ran out of the bar and down the street. A few blocks later, they finally slowed down and stood in an alleyway.

"What did he say?" my dad asked.

"I don't know, but just in case it was bad, I hit him," his friend said. Lack of communication can lead to conflict.

President Franklin D. Roosevelt was a great communicator. He restored American confidence and assuaged our fears. He guided us through two of the worst crises in American history: the Great Depression and World War II. We were lucky; we could have chosen our president unwisely.

Besides passing on his wealth of knowledge on the Great Depression and American historiography, the most important thing Dr. Sternsher taught me was his definition of history: History is forces for change and against change, over time. I have shared that definition with my students over the past 25 years. Bernie died in 2011.

TIMELINE

1920

January 1: The population of the United States is over 100 million.

January 10: The League of Nations is established with the ratification of the Treaty of Versailles. Nine days later the United States Senate votes against joining the League.

February 3: The first performance of Eugene O'Neill's play *Beyond the Horizon* is held. The play would go on to win a Pulitzer Prize.

August 18: The Nineteenth Amendment is ratified, granting universal women's suffrage.

September 17: The American Professional Football League is formed in 1920, with Jim Thorpe as its president and 11 teams. It becomes the National Football League in 1922.

November 2: Warren G. Harding is elected president in a landslide victory over Democratic candidate James M. Cox and his vice presidential running mate Franklin D. Roosevelt. This was the first election in which women had the right to vote.

1921

May 19: A national quota system on the amount of incoming immigrants is established by the US Congress in the Emergency Quota Act.

September 7–8: The first Miss America pageant is held in Atlantic City, New Jersey.

November 12: The Washington Naval Conference convenes in Washington, D.C.

CHAPTER 5

1922

February 6: The Washington Naval Conference ends. The United Kingdom, France, Italy, Japan, and the United States agree limit naval construction, outlaw poison gas, restrict submarine attacks on merchant fleets, and respect China's sovereignty.

May 5: Construction begins on Yankee Stadium in New York City—the House that Ruth Built.

May 30: The Lincoln Memorial is dedicated in Washington, DC.

1923

March 2: *Time* magazine is published for the first time.

April 4: Warner Brothers Pictures is incorporated.

August 2: President Warren G. Harding dies and is succeeded by his vice president, Calvin Coolidge.

1924

January 25: The first Winter Olympic Games are held in France.

February 14: The IBM corporation is founded.

May 10: J. Edgar Hoover is appointed as director of the Federal Bureau of Investigation (FBI).

June 2: All Indians are declared citizens.

November 4: Calvin Coolidge wins his first election as president.

1925

January 5: Nellie Tayloe Ross becomes the first woman governor in US history in the state of Wyoming.

June 13: Radiovision is born. The precursor to television is demonstrated by Charles Francis Jenkins.

July 10: The Scopes Monkey Trial begins. John T. Scopes had violated Tennessee law by teaching Charles Darwin's theory of evolution at a high school in Dayton, Tennessee, which violated Tennessee law.

November 28: The Grand Ole Opry transmits its first radio broadcast.

1926

March 16: Robert H. Goddard demonstrates the viability of the first liquid-fueled rockets.

May 9: Floyd Bennett and Richard Evelyn Byrd fly to the North Pole.

May 20: The Air Commerce Act is passed, which helps the airline industry.

May 31: The Sesquicentennial Exposition opens in Philadelphia to celebrate the 150th birthday of the United States.

November 15: The NBC Radio Network is formed.

1927

March 5: The civil war in China leads to 1,000 US Marines being deployed to protect the property of US interests.

April 22 to May 5: The Great Mississippi Flood occurs, affecting over 700,000 people.

May 20: Charles Lindbergh leaves New York on the first nonstop transatlantic flight in history.

October 4: Work on the sculpture at Mount Rushmore begins.

October 6: The first talking movie, *The Jazz Singer* starring Al Jolson, opens in New York City.

1928

May 15: Mickey and Minnie Mouse appear for the first time on film in the animated short film *Plane Crazy*.

June 17: Amelia Earhart becomes the first woman to fly over the Atlantic Ocean.

November 6: Herbert Hoover is elected president of the United States.

December 21: Congress approves the construction of Boulder Dam (later named Hoover Dam).

1929

January 15: Future civil rights leader Martin Luther King, Jr., is born in his grandfather's house in Atlanta, Georgia.

February 14: Al Capone's henchmen kill seven rivals and citizens in the St. Valentine's Day Massacre in Chicago.

October 25: The Teapot Dome scandal is finally over when Albert B. Fall, the former secretary of the interior, is convicted of accepting a $100,000 bribe for leasing the Elk Hills naval oil reserve.

October 29: Postwar prosperity ends in the 1929 stock market crash.

1930

January 22: Excavation work on the Empire State Building begins.

February 18: American astronomer Clyde Tombaugh discovers the planet Pluto at the Lowell Observatory in Flagstaff, Arizona. He also reported seeing UFOs.

April 1: The population in the 1930 census reaches 123,202,624.

June 17: The Smoot–Hawley Tariff Act is signed by President Herbert Hoover and has a negative effect on world trade.

December 2: President Herbert Hoover asks Congress to pass a $150 million public works project to increase employment and stimulate economic activity.

1931

March 3: "The Star-Spangled Banner," by Francis Scott Key, is approved by President Hoover and Congress as the national anthem.

March 17: The state of Nevada legalizes gambling.

May 1: Construction is completed on the Empire State Building in New York City and it opens for business.

October 4: Cartoonist Chester Gould creates the Dick Tracy comic strip.

1932

January 22: With unemployment reaching 12 million American workers, Hoover establishes the Reconstruction Finance Corporation to stimulate business and banking.

January 23: Carlsbad Caverns National Park installs high-speed elevators that descend 75 stories in one minute.

March 1: The infant son of Charles Lindbergh and Anne Morrow Lindbergh is kidnapped and later killed.

August 23: The highest continuous paved road in the United States is opened to the public in the Rocky Mountain National Park, Colorado.

November 8: Franklin D. Roosevelt defeats incumbent President Hoover in the presidential election.

1933

March 4: Roosevelt's inauguration speech is highlighted by his phrase "We have nothing to fear, but fear itself."

March 9 to June 16: Many New Deal programs are passed by Congress in a special 100-day session to address the Great Depression.

April 19: The gold standard is dropped.

March 31: The Civilian Conservation Corps (CCC) is authorized.

May 27: The Century of Progress World's Fair opens in Chicago, Illinois.

November 11: In a series of dust storms in America, top soil is stripped from farmland, rendering the land useless.

December 5: The Twenty-First Amendment to the US Constitution is passed, ending Prohibition.

1934

March 22: The Master's golf tournament is held for the first time at Augusta National Golf Club in Augusta, Georgia, founded by golfer Bobby Jones.

June 6: The US Securities and Exchange Commission (SEC) is established.

August 15: The United States pulls its troops from Haiti.

December 29: Japan renounces the Washington Naval Treaty of 1922 and the London Naval Treaty of 1930.

1935

June 2: The greatest hitter in the history of baseball, Babe Ruth, retires from Major League Baseball.

August 14: The Social Security Act is passed by Congress.

August 21: The Historic Sites Act is passed to preserve historic sites, including National Historic Landmarks.

September 30: Hoover Dam is dedicated by President Roosevelt.

October 10: *Porgy and Bess*, the opera by George Gershwin, opens in New York City.

1936

May 12: The Santa Fe Railroad starts the all-Pullman Super Chief passenger train service between Chicago, Illinois, and Los Angeles, California.

May 30: *Gone with the Wind* is published by Margaret Mitchell.

August 1: The Summer Olympic Games open in Berlin, Germany. The star of the games is Jesse Owens, a black American who won four gold medals.

November 3: Franklin D. Roosevelt wins his second presidential term.

1937

February 16: At DuPont labs, Wallace H. Carothers patents the polymer.

March 26: William Henry Hastie is appointed to the bench, becoming the first African American to become a federal judge.

May 6: At Lakehurst, New Jersey, the German airship *Hindenburg* bursts into flames while mooring.

May 28: The Golden Gate Bridge opens for pedestrians and vehicles.

August 14: The Appalachian Trail is completed.

1938

May 17: The Naval Expansion Act passes.

June 25: The national minimum wage is signed into law within the federal legislation known as the Fair Labor Standards Act.

July 3: The final reunion of the Blue and the Gray is held commemorating the 75th anniversary of the Civil War Battle of Gettysburg in Gettysburg, Pennsylvania.

July 18: Equipped with a bad compass, Wrong Way Douglas Corrigan lands in Ireland after taking off from New York.

October 30: A nationwide panic ensues when Orson Welles broadcasts his *War of the Worlds* radio drama.

1939

January 5: President Roosevelt asks Congress for a defense budget increase.

April 30: The New York World's Fair opens for its two-year run.

June 12: The Baseball Hall of Fame opens in Cooperstown, New York. The first inductees included Ty Cobb, Babe Ruth, Honus Wagner, Christy Mathewson, and Walter Johnson.

August 2: Albert Einstein notifies President Roosevelt of the possibility of an A-bomb which leads to the Manhattan Project.

September 5: The United States declares its neutrality in the European war.

CREDITS

1. Fig. 6.1. "Shoeless Joe Jackson," http://commons.wikimedia.org/wiki/File:Joe_Jackson_1913.jpg. Copyright in the Public Domain.
2. Fig. 6.2. "Al Capone," http://commons.wikimedia.org/wiki/File:Al_Capone_in_1930.jpg. Copyright in the Public Domain.
3. Fig. 6.3. "Zora Neale Hurston," http://commons.wikimedia.org/wiki/File:Zora_Neale_Hurston_NYWTS.jpg. Copyright in the Public Domain.
4. Fig. 6.4. Dorthea Lange, "Oklahoma migrant farm worker family," http://www.loc.gov/rr/print/list/128_migm.html. Copyright in the Public Domain.
5. Fig.6.5. Elias Goldensky, "Franklin D. Roosevelt," http://commons.wikimedia.org/wiki/File:FDR_in_1933.jpg. Copyright in the Public Domain.
6. Fig. 6.6. "Grand Coulee Dam in Washington State (PWA project)," http://commons.wikimedia.org/wiki/File:Grand_Coulee_Dam_no_forebay.jpg. Copyright in the Public Domain.
7. Fig. 6.7. "Huey Long," http://commons.wikimedia.org/wiki/File:HueyPLongGesture.jpg. Copyright in the Public Domain.
8. Fig. 6.8. George Grantham Bain, "Upton Sinclair," http://www.loc.gov/pictures/item/ggb2004006238/. Copyright in the Public Domain.
9. Fig. 6.9. Harris & Ewing , "William Dudley Pelley," http://commons.wikimedia.org/wiki/File:WilliamDudleyPelley.jpg. Copyright in the Public Domain.
10. Fig. 6.10. Dorthea Lange, "Unemployed Man During the Great Depression," http://commons.wikimedia.org/wiki/File:Destitute_man_vacant_store.gif. Copyright in the Public Domain.

WALLY

BY DR. BRUCE OLAV SOLHEIM WITH ART BY GARY DUMM

THE GERMANS INVADED NORWAY ON APRIL 9, 1940. MY MOM AND DAD, MARRIED JUST A FEW MONTHS BEFORE, WERE TRAPPED.

THE NAZIS TOOK OVER, BUT THERE WAS ARMED RESISTANCE...

MY UNCLE THORVALD WAS A WAR HERO NAVAL CONVOY COMMANDER WORKING WITH THE BRITISH AND MY AUNT WALBORG (WALLY) WAS A NAZI GESTAPO AGENT.

UNCLE THORVALD   AUNT WALLY

DAD WAS FORCED TO WORK FOR THE NAZIS. MOM STAYED AT HOME WITH MY GRANDPARENTS AND MY OTHER AUNT AND UNCLE.

A YEAR LATER, A NAZI COLONEL ARRIVED AND MOVED INTO THEIR LITTLE FARMHOUSE, TAKING OVER THE LIVING ROOM AS HIS OFFICE AND QUARTERS. MY ELDEST BROTHER DIED AT AGE TWO. THE NAZIS TOOK ALL OF THE MEDICINE.

WALLY HELPED CAPTURE OR KILL NINE MEMBERS OF THE RESISTANCE. AFTER THE WAR, SHE WAS SENTENCED TO DEATH AS A WAR CRIMINAL. UNCLE THORVALD WAS ABLE TO GET HER SENTENCE COMMUTED TO LIFE. SHE WAS RELEASED AFTER NINE YEARS.

I WROTE A PLAY INSPIRED BY MY FAMILY HISTORY...

THE EPIPHANY

MY MOM, DAD, AND SISTER (BORN 1943), IMMIGRATED TO AMERICA IN 1948. NORWAY WAS IN BAD SHAPE AFTER THE WAR. MY DAD WAS ALSO TIRED OF HEARING ABOUT HIS NAZI SISTER. I WOULD PROBABLY BE A FISHERMAN IN NORWAY IF IT WERE NOT FOR WALLY, MY NAZI AUNT.

CHAPTER SEVEN

WORLD WAR II

OBJECTIVES

1. Understand the factors that led to the coming of another world war.
2. Understand the factors that led to the Japanese attack on Pearl Harbor.
3. Compare and contrast the two theaters of battle in World War II.
4. Understand the legacies of World War II.

PERSONAL HISTORY

My parents were married in January 1940 and lived in a cozy farmhouse on a remote island called Andøya in northern Norway. On April 9, 1940, the Nazis invaded Norway. I grew up with stories about the Nazi occupation and how hard life was during the war, and have always been fascinated with that time period. Over the years I met and became friends with several World War II veterans. My mom died in 1990, my dad in 1999, and all of my World War II veteran friends have passed away as well.

My dad was in Tromsø, Norway, when the German battleship *Tirpitz* was sunk by the British. He said that they could hear the screams of the German sailors trapped in the overturned ship. Another time he was working on the north end of our home island when he saw a German officer pull up to the guard gate in a staff car. The guard asked for identification papers. The officer told him to get out of the way and stop bothering him. The staff car moved forward and the guard opened fire on the German officer, killing him. During the war my eldest brother got pneumonia. The Germans had taken all of the medicine. My parents could not get any medicine for my brother, so he died. My parents left Norway and came to America in 1948. After my mom died and my dad developed dementia, he would often go back in time in his mind and say that the Nazis were coming, and become very upset and agitated. It was then that it really hit me how affected my parents were by the war.

THE ROOTS OF WAR: THE FIRST WORLD WAR

The German army was not defeated on the battlefield during World War I—the German government collapsed after Kaiser Wilhelm abdicated. The subsequent Treaty of Versailles was very harsh toward the Germans. Not only did they lose territory and have their military stripped down, they were forced to pay $54 billion in war reparations. As a result, the German economy was destroyed, unemployment was rampant, and humiliated and angry German soldiers began to look for someone who could restore German pride. The Great Depression did not only affect the United States, it was a worldwide crisis. The Depression hit Germany very hard, and also hit Japan. Adolf Hitler emerged, offering simple solutions to complex problems and rallying German support, harnessing their anger, and blaming the Jews. Hitler came to power legitimately, and then seized control as dictator. At nearly the same time, the military seized control of Japan under General Hideki Tojo. Luckily, Franklin D. Roosevelt, a democrat, not a dictator, came to the rescue of the United States during the crisis.

FRACTURING OF THE WORLD ORDER

THE RISE OF IMPERIAL JAPAN

The Russo-Japanese War, won by Japan, was fought over control of Korea and parts of Manchuria from 1904 to 1905. It was the first time an Asian power defeated a European power, and greatly enhanced Japan's international standing as a world power. As a result of Russia's defeat, Japan was eventually able to annex Korea in 1910. Japan entered World War I in 1914 and spread its influence in China and the Pacific while the European powers were distracted. In 1918 Japan sent troops to Siberia to support the United States' efforts to halt a Communist victory in the Russian Revolution.

Japan invaded and easily conquered Manchuria in 1931. It successfully set up a puppet government called Manchukuo. Japan created a similar puppet state in Inner Mongolia called Mengjiang. These carefully orchestrated moves improved Japan's access to natural resources as it prepared for an assault on China. Japan then invaded China in 1937, creating a three-way war between Japan, the Nationalist Chinese under Chiang Kai-shek, and the Communist Chinese under Mao Zedong. By the end of 1937 the large city of Nanking surrendered to Japanese troops, who then massacred as many as 300,000 people. This came to be known as the Rape of Nanking.

FIGURE 7.1. Hideki Tojo

Japan occupied French Indochina in 1940 and continued its war against China. As a result, the United States placed an embargo on Japan. This embargo denied the Japanese crucial war materials, including scrap metal and oil. The Japanese had to either comply with American demands or drive farther into European colonies, such as the Dutch East Indies, in order to secure their own source of oil. Then, in September 1940, Japan signed the Tripartite Pact with Nazi Germany and Italy. This union became known as the Axis powers. Because of America's continuing embargo and interference with their strategy, the Japanese government began planning an attack on the US Seventh Fleet at Pearl Harbor.

THE RISE OF NAZI GERMANY

Adolf Hitler had attempted a rise to power prematurely with the Munich Beer Hall Putsch in 1923. He was imprisoned, and during his time in prison wrote his book *Mein Kampf*. When he was released he assumed control of the National Socialist (Nazi) Party and organized his Brown Shirts (Sturmabteilung or SA). The Nazis advocated extreme German nationalism, pan-Germanism, and anti-Semitism. By 1933 the Nazis had enough electoral power to become the majority party in the German Reichstag (parliament). Hitler was appointed chancellor and then the SA set fire to the Reichstag (blaming it on the Communists) and used that incident as a pretext for suspending the constitution and allowing Hitler to assume dictatorial powers. Hitler's friend, Benito Mussolini, had already seized power in Italy in the late 1920s and turned it into a fascist state. Italy invaded Ethiopia in 1935 in an attempt to provide popular support for Mussolini and Italy's military during the Depression, and to expand Italy's hold on the Mediterranean. In 1935 the Saarland, a coal-producing area governed by the League of Nations after World War I, voted to rejoin Germany. A year later Hitler, who had refurbished, re-equipped, and built up the German military in violation of the Versailles Treaty, had his troops re-enter the industrial Rhineland that Germany had lost after World War I.

The Spanish Civil War started in 1936 when General Francisco Franco's Nationalists took on the democratically elected government of Spain. Germany helped Franco, who was eventually victorious. Germany used the Spanish Civil War as a dress rehearsal for World War II and many techniques were tried out, such as blitzkrieg (a lightning fast form of warfare using armor and close air support, and targeting and terrorizing civilians). After 1939 France was then surrounded by three Fascist dictators: Francisco Franco in Spain, Benito Mussolini in Italy, and Adolf Hitler in Germany.

In March 1938 Hitler rolled his tanks into Austria (the country of his birth). The Anschluss (union) took less than 24 hours and was accomplished without resistance. Another crisis emerged in 1938 when Hitler demanded that the western portion of Czechoslovakia (the Sudetenland) be given back to Germany, because some ethnic Germans lived there. The Czechs refused to give in. Hitler gambled that France and England would not be prepared to go to war over this matter. British prime minister Neville Chamberlain secured an agreement with Hitler that gave Germany the Sudetenland in exchange for a promise that Hitler would not take any more territory. Hitler, of course, abrogated the Munich Agreement not long after,

FIGURE 7.2. Adolf Hitler and Benito Mussolini

prompting one of the big lessons from World War II: aggressors cannot be appeased; they must be stopped at all costs.

Having successfully expanded German territory, Hitler turned his attention toward Poland. Since England and France did not attempt to stop him in his reoccupation of the Rhineland and Czechoslovakia, he felt emboldened. Hitler signed a non-aggression pact with Soviet dictator Joseph Stalin in August 1939. Under the terms of the agreement, the Soviet Union would get the eastern half of Poland, and Germany the western half. On September 1, 1939, Hitler's blitzkrieg attack on Poland began—and with that, World War II in Europe had also begun. Up to this point, the United States had done nothing to stop him.

AMERICA'S RESPONSE

The United States was slow to respond to both Japan and Germany. The main reason for this inaction was the Great Depression. Americans had become isolationists because they felt that the crisis at home was greater than any crisis abroad. Additionally, some disturbing investigations had revealed that the public had been manipulated when America entered World War I. This fed the isolationism and was reflected in opinion polls that overwhelmingly supported staying out of the war.

ISOLATIONISM

In 1934, the Senate Munitions Committee met because of reports that defense manufacturers and bankers had influenced the American decision to enter World War I in 1917. Many feared that defense manufacturers, popularly known as Merchants of Death, would once again push the United States into the coming war in Europe and the Pacific. Republican senator Gerald P. Nye of North Dakota led a special seven-person committee. For nearly two years Nye held hearings and found some evidence of conspiracy, although there was no legal action taken. The negative publicity inspired the Neutrality Acts of the 1930s. Public opinion polls revealed that Americans were overwhelmingly opposed to involvement in wars overseas. We know now that many US companies and organizations were helping to build Nazi Germany (i.e., Ford, IBM, GM, the Rockefeller Foundation, and GE).

NEUTRALITY ACTS, 1935–1937

In 1935 the first Neutrality Act was passed, in spite of President Roosevelt's opposition. The 1935 act prohibited the export of arms, ammunition, and implements of war from the United States to belligerent nations (nations that were at war). Congress renewed the act in 1936 and added that Americans could not make any loans to belligerent nations.

The Neutrality Act of 1937 made it illegal for American citizens to travel on belligerent ships, and American merchant ships were not allowed to transport arms to belligerent nations, even if those arms were produced in a country other than the United States. This act also clarified that civil wars would also fall under the terms of the act. FDR was able to get a special provision written into the act: belligerent nations were allowed, at the discretion of the president, to acquire nonmilitary items on a cash and carry basis. Foreign ships would have to come to America, load, pay cash, and then return to their country of origin.

The Neutrality Act of 1939 lifted the arms embargo and allowed trade with belligerent nations on a cash and carry basis. American banks were still not allowed to make loans and American ships could not transport goods to belligerent ports. Overall, the neutrality acts accommodated the isolationists in America and gave Roosevelt only limited flexibility to interact with the world. He was essentially handcuffed.

INTERVENTIONISM (FOUR STEPS TO WAR)

Roosevelt knew that America would have to go to war eventually, but needed to convince Americans that it was right to do so. Public opinion was not in favor of intervention until after the attack on Pearl Harbor. FDR chose to move forward in smaller steps, in preparation for a war he saw as inevitable.

DESTROYERS FOR BASES, 1940

In September 1940 Roosevelt signed the Destroyers-for-Bases Agreement with British prime minister Winston Churchill. The United States gave Great Britain 50 naval destroyers in exchange for the use of naval and air bases in various British possessions. Roosevelt wanted to help England and was impressed, as were many Americans, with Great Britain's success against the Germans in the Battle of Britain. In spite of that success, Prime Minister Winston Churchill knew that Britain would need American help to win the war. FDR was criticized for signing this executive agreement without involving Congress. Many accused him of violating the Neutrality Acts. Roosevelt simply told them that he was not selling weapons of war, he was bartering with a neighbor.

LEND-LEASE ACT, MARCH 1941

President Roosevelt proposed the Lend-Lease Act in December 1940 because the British were no longer able to pay for wartime supplies. The act allowed the United States to lend or lease military hardware and arrange for alternative payments or consideration later on. The United States went on to contract lend-lease agreements with another 30 countries. The Lend-Lease Act would not only help allies defeat Germany, it would also allow the American

FIGURE 7.3. Franklin D. Roosevelt signs Lend-Lease Act

public and industry to prepare for war and swing public opinion toward intervention while also preparing the US military. The Lend-Lease Act also had provisions that basically built the foundation for a new world order. When FDR was criticized for providing weapons to Great Britain and other allies in what was called a violation of the Neutrality Acts, Roosevelt asked his critics, "Would you not lend your neighbor a garden hose if their house was on fire?"

ATLANTIC CHARTER, AUGUST 1941

President Roosevelt and Prime Minster Churchill met off the coast of Newfoundland in August 1941 for what was called the Atlantic Charter Conference. The two leaders wanted to lay out plans to defeat Germany and even work out how the postwar world would look. The resulting Atlantic Charter included agreement on common principles, such as limits on the expansion of territory, liberalization of international trade, freedom of the seas, and rights to self-determination.

Although the meeting was largely successful in terms of drafting these principles, neither Roosevelt nor Churchill got exactly what they wanted. FDR wanted the Atlantic Charter to move US public opinion toward intervention. It did not. Churchill expected Roosevelt to bring America into the war. This did not happen. The Charter did solidify US–British connections and determination to defeat the Axis powers, as well as establishing FDR's vision for a postwar world, and inspiring many Third World colonial peoples to push for independence after the war.

BATTLE OF THE ATLANTIC, FALL 1941

Although the United States was officially neutral, American forces did clash with both German and Japanese forces prior to the Pearl Harbor attack. The earliest encounter was in

April 1941, when the USS *Niblack* attacked a Nazi U-boat off the coast of Iceland. The USS *Kearny* was attacked in October 1941 by U-boats while escorting a convoy, but made it back to port. The US Coast Guard had destroyed an unmanned German weather station located on Greenland just prior to the attack on the *Kearny*. Five weeks before Pearl Harbor, a German U-boat torpedoed and sank the American destroyer USS *Reuben James* in the north Atlantic. The American ship was escorting a convoy when it was attacked. Roosevelt had positioned the American Navy in the Atlantic and put them in harm's way as a bold move and last step prior to all out war with Germany. Had the dramatic event on December 7, 1941, not occurred, FDR might have faced dire political consequences at home.

Pearl Harbor

The Japanese attack on the US 7th Fleet at Pearl Harbor on December 7, 1941, not only pushed America into World War II, it set off a series of events that continue to impact American society today. How could it have happened?

UNITED STATES–JAPAN RIVALRY
(OPEN DOOR VS. CO-PROSPERITY SPHERE)

Between 1937 and 1941 the conflict between Japan and China ultimately pushed the United States into World War II. Roosevelt and his policy advisers were concerned about Japanese incursions into northern China and the rise of Japanese militarism. Americans were friendly with China and had maintained an Open Door policy to China in terms of trade. In spite of that, America did not want to go to war with Japan over China. Making matters worse was the internal turmoil in China between the Nationalists and Communists. A tentative truce had developed between Japan and the United States by 1940. Both countries wanted to be the number one power in the Pacific region. Japan called its vision the Co-prosperity Sphere. This translated as: whatever is good for Japan is good for Asia. Added to that was a movement toward excluding non-Asians. This clashed with the US Open Door policy that called for free and open trade with China, Asia, and the Pacific—with the United States at the forefront, of course. In 1940 and 1941 FDR offered aid and credits to the Chinese government to purchase war supplies and increased the United States' restrictions on Japan. This, in effect, forced Japan to act.

EMBARGOES AND JAPANESE DEPENDENCY

The Japanese military depended on the United States for oil, steel, iron, and other industrial commodities. In 1940 Japan broke its commerce treaty with the United States, and FDR used that to restrict the flow of supplies used by the Japanese military. FDR hoped that this restriction would serve as leverage to stop Japan's aggression in China. Combined with credits and aid to China, this strategy eventually led to an embargo. Japan wanted desperately to free itself from dependence on American war materials, so it used its Asia Co-prosperity Sphere concept to secure Asian sources for oil, steel, iron, and other commodities.

To make matters worse, and move Japan closer to war with the United States, Japan joined the Tripartite Pact with Germany and Italy in September 1940. Japan then signed a non-aggression pact with Russia and an agreement with Vichy France in regard to Southeast Asia. Japanese forces then moved into Indochina and begin a southern push. Japan, enduring shortages for its military due to the US embargo, refused to retreat from China as the Americans demanded, and concluded that it was left with no choice other than to attack the United States and disable its fleet. The Great Depression had deeply impacted the United States, Germany, and Japan. The civilian government slowly gave in to the military in Japan. When General Hideki Tojo became prime minister of Japan in 1941, it was only a matter of time before Japan would strike the United States.

DECEMBER 7, 1941: A DATE WHICH WILL LIVE IN INFAMY

It is certainly true that American leaders made a series of blunders that made it possible for the Japanese to attack Pearl Harbor successfully, but the Japanese should be given credit for both the audacity of their plan and the immediate results. A US Army radar site on Oahu picked up the incoming Japanese planes, and the Navy sighted and attacked a foreign

FIGURE 7.4. American ships burning at Pearl Harbor

submarine by the entrance to Pearl Harbor on December 7, 1941. American code breakers had broken the Japanese diplomatic code as well. In spite of those warnings, Americans were caught off guard.

Japan's strategy was to expand south into Southeast Asia and the Dutch East Indies, while protecting its home islands from an expected attack by the US Pacific Fleet. By destroying or disabling the US Pacific Fleet in Pearl Harbor, Japan would be unchallenged throughout Asia and the Pacific and could feel more secure that its home islands were safe. Japan figured that by the time the United States built up and replaced the ships it would lose, Japan would be too entrenched and the United States would negotiate rather than fight. Japan's leaders also believed that the attack would demoralize Americans.

The main reason the Japanese carrier task force managed to sail halfway across the Pacific undetected was Japan's radio denial-and-deception actions. This clever deception made American signal intelligence believe that Japan was still on the defensive, and disguised the movement of the carrier task force headed for Hawaii. No one believed that Japan would attack US territory—Japan and Hawaii were 4,000 miles apart. To attack Pearl Harbor the Japanese carriers would have to travel this distance undetected and get within striking range (about 200 miles). US strategists thought that Japan might attack, but they figured it would be an attack on some European colony or maybe the Philippines. Consequently, Pearl Harbor was not well prepared. On December 7, 1941, Japanese planes filled the sky over Pearl Harbor. A high-altitude Japanese bomber hit the USS *Arizona* and penetrated the decks to reach the forward gun powder magazine. The ship exploded and sank with more than 1,000 men trapped. The USS *Tennessee* was moored just in front of the *Arizona* and James Wire, a Pearl Harbor survivor, reported that the blast from the *Arizona* raised his ship several feet out of the water and knocked everyone off of their feet. When the attacks were over, every US battleship had been hit. The *Arizona* and the *Utah* were destroyed; the *Oklahoma, California, West Virginia, Maryland, Pennsylvania,* and *Tennessee* were all hit, but were later salvaged and repaired. The Japanese hit or destroyed 18 ships and more than 300 airplanes. Airfields and dry docks were also destroyed. Nearly 2,500 Americans were killed and another 1,000 were wounded.

The Japanese did not destroy the Pacific Fleet; they merely put US battleships out of commission, ships that were no longer the most important naval asset. The aircraft carrier had become the most important naval ship, and the American carriers were not in Pearl Harbor. The USS *Saratoga* was loading aircraft in San Diego and preparing to set sail for Pearl Harbor. The USS *Lexington* was heading to Midway Island, and the USS *Enterprise* was at Wake Island. The Japanese also failed to hit the oil storage depots, repair shops, shipyards, and submarine docks. The US Navy got back up to speed quicker than anyone could have imagined.

In his speech the next day before a joint session of Congress, FDR said, "Yesterday, December 7, 1941—a date which will live in infamy—the United States of America was suddenly and deliberately attacked by naval and air forces of the Empire of Japan." These are probably the most famous words uttered by an American president. Pearl Harbor changed

American public opinion overnight. Congress approved FDR's declaration of war with only one dissenting vote. Congresswoman Jeanette Rankin, a Republican from Montana, voted no. Angry crowds threatened her afterward and she had to be escorted from the building by Capitol police. Rankin had also voted no to the United States entering World War I, but this time she stood alone. She was a lifelong pacifist and was also the first woman elected to Congress, in 1916. Three days later, Germany and Italy declared war on the United States, because of its participation in the Tripartite Pact. Japan made some mistakes on December 7, 1941. First of all, the attack was not supposed to be without warning. The Japanese embassy in Washington, D.C., was supposed to deliver a message at least 45 minutes prior to the attack. This created a righteous anger among the American people. Second, Japan did not get to the carriers. Those same aircraft carriers were later used in the US victory at Midway. Japan underestimated American capabilities to fight a two-front war. It figured that America would be demoralized, and by the time the United States rebuilt the ships that were destroyed at Pearl Harbor, Japan would be too entrenched in the Pacific and the United States would have to negotiate. Last, but not least, the Japanese did not destroy the fuel depots at Pearl Harbor. All of the fuel for the entire fleet was stored in above-ground tanks.

CONSPIRACY THEORY

Some hold that Roosevelt allowed the Japanese to attack Pearl Harbor in order to gain public approval for getting into the war, and to stop any investigations into his engaging in the Battle of the Atlantic without authorization from Congress. If this is so, then everyone from FDR down to the private who was on the radar set in Oahu would have to have been in on the conspiracy. Conspiracy theorists say that the US carriers were out to sea to save them from destruction. In reality, the three carriers were on missions. Conspiracy theorists also point out that the airplanes on the airfields surrounding Pearl Harbor were all lined up in neat rows, making it easy for the Japanese to destroy them on the ground. The rational explanation was that General Walter Short had been advised that saboteurs were likely to blow up the aircraft, so he had them guarded and lined up in tightly packed rows to enhance physical security on the ground. The incoming Japanese aircraft were also picked up on radar, a relatively new invention at the time, but no warning was given. However, the radar operators and the officers in charge assumed the aircraft were American. No one figured that the Japanese could get close enough to attack. To make matters more confusing, some B-17 bombers were returning to Pearl Harbor at the exact same time as the Japanese attack. Americans had broken the Japanese diplomatic code and could actually decipher it faster than the Japanese embassy in Washington, D.C. In spite of that, the exact point of attack was not known, only that negotiations had broken off and the diplomats were to return to Japan. The warning to Pearl Harbor was sent by telegram instead of radio because of radio interference that day. The message arrived too late.

THE UNITED STATES AT WAR

Officially, World War II in Europe started with Hitler's invasion of Poland in September 1939. World War II in Asia could be traced back to 1933, when Japan invaded Manchuria, or 1937, when open warfare broke out between China and Japan. From an American perspective, World War II started with Pearl Harbor. World War II involved most of the nations of the world divided into two sides: the Axis powers (primarily Germany, Italy, and Japan) and the Allies (primarily the United States, Russia, Great Britain, and China). With an estimated 55 million people killed, World War II was the deadliest war in world history.

The United States began to turn the tide against Japan with its victory at Midway in June 1942, and by attacking the Japanese in the Solomon Islands and Guadalcanal in February 1943. American and Allied forces achieved a series of victories over the German Afrika Korps in North Africa by early 1943. On the eastern front, by the end of 1942, the German advance into Russia was halted. In July 1943 American and Allied troops landed in Sicily and hit the mainland of Italy shortly thereafter (known as Operation Torch). Mussolini was removed from power and the Germans seized the northern half of Italy, where they held out until 1945. Stalin was not happy with the decision of the Allies to attack Italy. He wanted instead for the Americans to cross the English Channel and attack Hitler's Fortress Europe in France, to give the Russian forces some relief along the eastern front. Meanwhile, in the Pacific, America conducted primarily a naval war, island hopping closer and closer to Japan. Allied forces

FIGURE 7.5. D-Day invasion

eventually achieved naval and air supremacy in the Pacific, conducting an island-hopping campaign and sustaining high casualties. In 1944, US forces liberated the Philippines and began sustained air attacks on Japan.

D-Day, codenamed Operation Overlord, began on June 6, 1944. More than 156,000 American, British, and Canadian forces landed on the beaches of Normandy. The Germans had heavily fortified the entire coastline and the D-Day forces met tremendous resistance. D-Day was the largest amphibious assault in history. The Germans were not sure where the D-Day forces would land and General George S. Patton was part of the deception plan. The Allies used Patton and a fake army group as a decoy to make the Germans think he was landing in Pas de Calais (the shortest distance across the channel). Although successful, there were 2,499 American D-Day fatalities and 1,915 from the other Allied nations. Allied forces liberated northern France by August 1944 and would conquer Germany the following spring. The landings at Normandy were essentially the beginning of the end of the war in Europe. On September 11, 1944, the first American troops entered Germany, one month after Russian troops crossed the eastern border. In mid-December the Germans launched a deadly but futile counterattack known as the Battle of the Bulge. Allied air forces attacked Nazi industrial plants, crippling the German war machine.

In early 1945 American forces had heavy losses during the invasions of Iwo Jima (February) and Okinawa (April). Enduring heavy casualties and suicidal Japanese air attacks, known as Kamikaze attacks, American forces took Okinawa in June 1945. In Europe, American troops crossed the Rhine River in March 1945. By April 1945 the Soviet army had surrounded Berlin. Hitler ordered children and old men to defend his bunker position. He committed suicide on April 30, 1945. On May 7, 1945, Germany surrendered unconditionally.

On August 6, 1945, an American B-29 bomber called the *Enola Gay* dropped an atomic bomb on the Japanese city of Hiroshima. General Eisenhower and General MacArthur both felt that the Japanese were already beaten and deemed the atomic bombing unnecessary. The atomic scientists, including Manhattan Project director J. Robert Oppenheimer and Albert Einstein, had suggested using the weapon on a deserted island instead of on a Japanese city. In spite of this, Truman went through with it. Nagasaki was bombed three days after Hiroshima. The atomic bombing of Hiroshima and Nagasaki killed approximately 120,000 people with many more dying later of radiation sickness. The Soviet Union invaded Manchuria after declaring war on Japan August 8, 1945. Japan formally surrendered on September 2.

THE HOME FRONT

World War II transformed America. There was a total mobilization of the country to fight the war in Europe and the Pacific. America went from 30 to 40 percent unemployment in 1932 to a shortage of workers in 1942. Consequently, those who had been denied jobs prior to the war found work during the war years.

Similar to World War I, there was rationing of critical commodities and foodstuffs. In the spring of 1942, government rationing limited the amount of clothing, gas, and food that Americans could buy. Many Americans planted victory gardens as an alternative to rationing. By 1945, victory gardens produced about 40 percent of all vegetables consumed in America.

Individuals and communities collected scrap metal, aluminum cans, and rubber, to be recycled and used as raw material in war production. The government also sold war bonds to help pay for the war.

America had to fight a two-front war. There were not enough workers, especially after millions of men enlisted or were drafted into the military. Consequently, women were hired for jobs as welders, electricians, and riveters in defense plants. Ethnic minorities were also given opportunities. For women and ethnic minorities who had been discriminated against in the past, the war was a giant leap forward in terms of social and economic change. Women made up more than half of the defense workers by the end of the war. In spite of segregation in the military and at home, some black airmen were given an opportunity to fly. The Tuskegee Airmen proved their worth in the war effort and had the best record of any bomber escort unit during the entire war.

After Pearl Harbor, panic spread quickly in America and many people were afraid that a Japanese attack on the US mainland was imminent. In February 1942, responding to pressure from the public, government, and military, President Roosevelt signed Executive Order 9066, which evacuated all Japanese Americans who resided on the West Coast of the United States. Nearly 120,000 Japanese Americans (men, women, and children) were sent to relocation camps, later called internment camps. More than two-thirds of those imprisoned were American citizens. None of them had done anything wrong. The military called them an enemy race.

Mr. Eddie Inouye from San Gabriel, California, was sent to Rohwer, Arkansas, along with his sister and his mother. His father was sent to a different camp. Eddie was in the same camp as George Takei (Mr. Sulu from the original *Star Trek* TV series). The Japanese Americans were kept in these internment camps for the duration of the war. Eddie only got out one time, when his teacher got special permission to bring him home to her house for Thanksgiving dinner. German prisoners of war in a nearby camp were allowed weekend passes. Other Japanese Americans were allowed to enlist in the military and fought bravely in a segregated unit in Italy. They became the most highly decorated unit of their size in US Army history. Eddie's uncle, Daniel Inouye (later becoming the first senator from Hawaii) was in the 442nd and earned a Medal of Honor. Eddie later joined the US Army himself and fought in Korea, earning a Silver Star for valor in combat.

Many professional baseball players went into the service during World War II. Hall of Fame players Bob Feller, Hank Greenberg, Joe DiMaggio, and Ted Williams all joined. Two major league players died in the war and 120 minor league players were killed. Even Hollywood was active during the war. Many movie stars joined up in special units and some actually fought in the war. Clark Gable was a tail-gunner and Jimmy Stewart was a bomber pilot; they both flew missions over Germany. Bob Hope entertained the troops around the world and famous directors made films for the military, like Frank Capra's *Why We Fight* series of films. There were also cartoons that depicted the enemy in a negative way and served as propaganda.

The New Deal saved America from ruin, but World War II pulled America totally out of the Great Depression. Military spending started in 1940 as millions of Americans went to work creating weapons of war. Economist John Maynard Keynes believed that sometimes governments need to spend in order to end a depression, until the private sector can pick up again. Mobilization of the nation's industries required big adjustments for the government and big business. Businesses that had not supported Roosevelt's New Deal now came on board with the buildup for the war as partners. FDR had many organizations set up to ensure the nation dedicated itself to war production: the National Defense Advisory Commission, Office of Production Management, War Production Board, and Office of War Mobilization. Roosevelt's system worked. The war brought prosperity, but it also stimulated the growth of big business and created what President Eisenhower would later call a military–industrial complex. The demographics of the country changed and new opportunities emerged. FDR strengthened the role of the president beyond even his cousin Theodore's wildest dreams. By the end of the war, the United States was ready to take on its role as leader of the free world.

FIGURE 7.6. Ted Williams being sworn in to the military in World War II

COMPARING THE TWO THEATERS OF BATTLE

World War II is actually two wars. They started at different times and ended at different times. However, there are some comparisons. There were dramatic turning points in both theaters in 1942. The American victory at Midway ended the expansion of the Japanese empire. The Russian defense at Stalingrad signaled the end of German expansion in Europe. The Axis powers were on the defensive for the rest of World War II. Another comparison is that both Nazi Germany and Imperial Japan had authoritarian governments. In other words, the United States was not fighting democracies. Although it should be pointed out that Communist Russia was not a democracy, either. Another point of comparison was that racism was rampant throughout the war. It is easy to point fingers at Nazi Germany, whose ideology was based on a racial hierarchy, but the United States also had problems. The internment of Japanese Americans in February 1942 was a gross violation of civil rights. US military units were segregated by race and there were race riots in America during the war. Japan's Co-prosperity Sphere was actually just a fig leaf for Japanese domination of all other nationalities and races. Imperial Japan's treatment of the Chinese, Koreans, and other Asians was terrible. This was in addition to the deplorable treatment of European and American prisoners of war. Lastly, submarines were used effectively in both theaters of war. German U-boats sank nearly 3,000 ships in the Atlantic. And in the Pacific, US submarines took a toll on the Japanese shipping intended to resupply Japan's island empire.

CONTRASTING THE TWO THEATERS OF BATTLE

Besides the fact that the war in the Pacific and the war in Europe started and ended at different times, there are other major differences between the two theaters of war. Both Japan and Germany, in spite of their both being Axis powers, had independent strategies. They did not consult with each other or coordinate their plans. In fact, had both been successful, their two positions would have made conflict between them inevitable. Another difference was that the US role in the Pacific theater was much greater than in Europe. The United States is primarily responsible for the defeat of Japan in World War II. In the European theater, the United States was one of the major combatants, but Russia was the country most responsible for the defeat of Germany. Another difference was that the war in the Pacific was primarily a naval war, where US forces captured Japanese island positions one by one on their way to Tokyo. Brutal battles for these Pacific islands inflicted heavy casualties on both sides. The closer the United States got to Japan, the more fierce the fighting became. In Europe, the war was fought primarily as a land war, with the exception of the battles in the Atlantic.

Another difference between the two theaters of battle was what the Nazis called the Final Solution. The Holocaust was systematically orchestrated by the Nazi regime and resulted in the persecution and murder of six million Jews. The Nazis believed that the Jews were racially inferior. Also on the list of inferior races and groups were Gypsies, the disabled, Poles, Russians and other Slavic peoples, Communists, socialists, Jehovah's Witnesses, and homosexuals. Hitler rose to power by harnessing the anger and the frustration of the German people in the depression that followed their defeat in World War I. Hitler found that blaming the Jews gave him an easy (although false) rationale for seizing power. The Jews and others were sent to concentration camps and either worked to death or murdered in gas chambers or by firing squads. American soldiers who liberated the camps were horrified at what they saw. There were only 150,000 Jews who survived the Nazi death camps.

Finally, atomic weapons were used in the Pacific against Japan, and not in Europe against the Germans. The United States is the only nation to ever use nuclear weapons in war. Ever since the atomic bombing of Japan, people have debated the necessity of using those weapons to end the war. Truman had many different reasons for using the atomic bombs: send a signal to the Russians, end the war quickly, revenge for Pearl Harbor, saving lives, and scientific curiosity. The Russians were going to take territory in Asia like they did in Europe. If the war ended quickly, the Russians would have to stop their advance into Asia. So ending the war quickly was directly related to denying Russians more territory. It is hard to separate revenge from racism in the decision. Prior to World War II, racist policies toward Asians were not uncommon in America. After Pearl Harbor, Japanese Americans were evacuated from the West Coast and put in camps. No German Americans and Italian Americans were systematically rounded up and imprisoned. Also, in opinion polls that were conducted among young men joining the US military, it was clear that American soldiers hated the Japanese twice as much as the Germans. Estimates were that had the United States invaded the Japanese home islands, more than one million people would have died. No one is sure if that number would

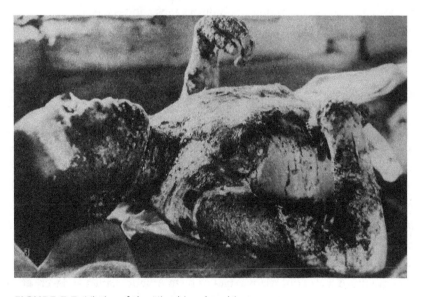

FIGURE 7.7. Victim of the Hiroshima bombing

have been correct. Based on the ferocity of the fighting in Okinawa, it seemed likely. Revenge for Pearl Harbor factors into that, but so too does racism that was inherent before. Would Americans have used atomic weapons against the German people? No one knows for sure.

There were alternatives other than an all-out invasion. Continued negotiations might have brought about results. The United States' insistence on unconditional surrender bogged down surrender negotiations prior to the bombings. Then, after the bombs, the United States allowed Japan to have conditional surrender conditions anyway (they were allowed to keep the emperor and make him immune to punishment for war crimes).

The cities of Hiroshima and Nagasaki were chosen because they contained different types of targets. They both had civilian populations, businesses, war industry, and military and other infrastructures. In retrospect, it would have been better to choose targets that did not include civilians. If that had been done, there would be no debate. The Japanese knew that they were beaten; it was only a matter of time. The bombings pushed them over the edge. Some people say that the second bomb was overkill and not necessary. Because Japan did not surrender after the Hiroshima bomb, the United States dropped the second bomb. It is clear that three days was not enough time. Had the United States waited a week or two, the Japanese would have surrendered. Most World War II veterans and those alive at the home front will say that there was no choice in using the bombs—the Japanese had done horrible things, attacked the homeland, and started the war. When that generation is gone, public opinion will probably change.

CONCLUSION

There are many things that changed in America due to World War II. Women and minorities were allowed to find good-paying war industry jobs and taste economic independence. Minorities had fought in World War II overseas and came home to prejudice and discrimination. Enough was enough. No one wanted to go back to the way things were before the war. Fighting to liberate millions of people only to face unfair treatment at home was not tolerated. Racism at home seemed a little too similar to Hitler's evil racial hierarchy in Europe. Economic independence and World War II service helped give rise to the modern civil rights movement. Atomic bombs ended World War II and began the atomic age and a new war—the Cold War. We still deal with the threat of nuclear weapons and their proliferation today. Another legacy is the Holocaust. Had there been no Holocaust, there may be no modern Israel today. Hitler's attempt to eradicate Jews from the world actually stimulated a movement for Jews in Diaspora to return to the holy land and ensure their survival.

My parents came to America in 1948 because postwar Norway was very bleak. Much of northern Norway had been burnt to the ground by the defeated Germans. My parents had lost their first-born son because of the hardships during the war. They wanted a new start, in the land of opportunity. A few of our relatives had come to America earlier and were encouraging my parents to come. When I think that my mom and dad and sister left everything behind to come to a foreign country without any money, no language ability, just hopes and dreams of a new life, it makes me so proud of them. That takes guts. My sister remembers my mom crying after they arrived, but only when my father was at work. My mom missed her mom, her family, and her homeland. Many years later after my father retired as a carpenter he told my mom that they should move back to Norway. She said no.

"My mother is dead and we have made America our home. We can visit Norway, but this is my home now." So, World War II led to my being born in America.

I often wonder how I would have fared under such conditions. My parents were still very young and living in Norway in the 1930s, when times were very hard. They had no electricity, they had outdoor toilets, they burned peat for heat, and they ate mainly fish and potatoes.

My dad would go to sea for long stretches of time though, first in the Norwegian Navy and then in the merchant marines. He told me that he was in Chicago in the 1930s as a young sailor. He said life was pretty hard, and he could tell that things were not going well in America. My dad and another Norwegian sailor went on shore in Chicago and proceeded to the nearest bar. Soon after they sat down with their beers, an American man came up to them and started talking to my dad's friend. After a few moments, my dad's friend punched the American man in the face and told my dad to run. They left their beers and ran out of the bar and down the street. A few blocks later, they finally slowed down and stood in an alleyway.

"What did he say?" my dad asked.

"I don't know, but just in case it was bad, I hit him," his friend said. Lack of communication can lead to conflict.

President Franklin D. Roosevelt was a great communicator. He restored American confidence and assuaged our fears. He guided us through two of the worst crises in American history: the Great Depression and World War II. We were lucky; we could have chosen our president unwisely.

TIMELINE

1931

September 18: Japan invades Manchuria.

1932

May: Japan withdraws from the League of Nations.

May 15: Japanese prime minister Tsuyoshi assassinated by military officers.

1933

January 30: Adolf Hitler becomes chancellor of Germany.

1936

October 25: Nazi Germany and fascist Italy form the Rome–Berlin Axis Treaty.

November 25: Nazi Germany and Imperial Japan sign the Anti-Comintern Pact.

1937

July 7: The Japanese launch an attack on Nanking, China.

1938

March 12: Hitler annexes Austria into Germany. This is also called the Anschluss.

November: Japan declares New Order for East Asia.

1939

July: The United States announces withdrawal from its commercial treaty with Japan.

August 23: Germany and the Soviet Union sign a non-aggression pact.

September: The Battle of the Atlantic begins.

September 1: Germany invades Poland.

September 3: France and Great Britain declare war on Germany.

1940

April 9: Germany invades Denmark and Norway.

May 10 to June 22: Germany uses blitzkrieg to take over much of Western Europe, including the Netherlands, Belgium, and northern France.

May 30: Winston Churchill becomes leader of the British government.

June 10: Italy enters the war as a member of the Axis powers.

June 22: France surrenders to Germany.

July 10: The Battle of Britain begins.

September: Japan invades Indochina.

September 16: The United States begins its first peacetime draft.

September 22: Germany, Italy, and Japan sign the Tripartite Pact, creating the Axis powers.

1941

March 11: President Franklin D. Roosevelt signs the Lend-Lease bill.

April: American volunteer pilots, named Flying Tigers, strike Japanese forces in Burma.

May 27: The German battleship *Bismarck* is sunk.

June 22: Germany invades the Soviet Union in Operation Barbarossa.

August: The United States initiates a complete oil embargo on Japan.

August 9: The Atlantic Charter Conference begins.

December 7: Japan attacks Pearl Harbor.

December 8: The United States declares war on Japan.

December 11: Germany and Italy declare war on the United States.

1942

January 20: The Wannsee Conference takes place (Final Solution planned).

February 19: FDR issues Executive Order 9066, which allows the internment of Japanese Americans.

April 18: The Doolittle Raid on Japan takes place.

June 3: The Battle of Midway begins.

June 4: The US Navy defeats the Japanese navy at the Battle of Midway.

July 10: The Allies invade and take the island of Sicily.

August 2: The Guadalcanal Campaign begins.

August 21: The Battle of Stalingrad begins.

November 8: The Allies invade North Africa (Operation Torch).

1943

January 14: The Casablanca Conference begins.

February 2: The Germans surrender at Stalingrad.

April 19: The Warsaw Ghetto Uprising begins.

September 3: Italy surrenders to the Allies, but Mussolini escapes.

November 28: The Tehran Conference begins.

1944

June 6: The D-Day invasion occurs.

June 19: The Battle of the Philippine Sea begins.

July 20: An assassination attempt against Hitler fails.

August 25: Paris is liberated.

October 23: The Battle of Leyte Gulf begins.

December 16: The Battle of the Bulge begins. Germany's last-ditch effort fails.

1945

February 4: The Yalta Conference begins.

February 13: The Allies begin bombing Dresden.

February 19: The Battle of Iwo Jima begins.

March 22: General Patton's Third Army crosses the Rhine.

April 1: The Battle of Okinawa begins.

April 12: US president Franklin D. Roosevelt dies. Vice President Harry S. Truman becomes president.

April 16: The Battle of Berlin begins.

April 28: Mussolini is hanged by Italian partisans.

April 30: Adolf Hitler commits suicide.

May 7: Germany surrenders to the Allies.

July 17: The Potsdam Conference begins.

August 6: The United States drops the atomic bomb on Hiroshima.

August 9: Another atomic bomb is dropped on Nagasaki.

August 15: Japan surrenders conditionally.

CREDITS

1. Fig. 7.1. "Hideki Tojo," http://commons.wikimedia.org/wiki/File:Hideki_Tojo_posing_cropped.jpg. Copyright in the Public Domain.

2. Fig. 7.2. "Adolf Hitler and Benito Mussolini," http://commons.wikimedia.org/wiki/ File:HitlerMussolini1934Venice.jpg. Copyright in the Public Domain.

3. Fig. 7.3. "Franklin Roosevelt signs Lend-Lease Bill," http://commons.wikimedia.org/wiki/ File:President_Franklin_D._Roosevelt-1941.jpg. Copyright in the Public Domain.

4. Fig. 7.4. "American Ships Burning at Pearl Harbor," http://commons.wikimedia.org/wiki/File:Burning_ships_at_Pearl_Harbor.jpg. Copyright in the Public Domain.

5. Fig. 7.5. "D-Day Invasion," http://commons.wikimedia.org/wiki/File:Omaha_Beach_Landing_Craft_Approaches.jpg. Copyright in the Public Domain.

6. Fig. 7.6. "Ted Williams Being Sworn In To The Military in World War II," http://commons.wikimedia.org/wiki/File:Ted_Williams_swearing_into_the_Navy_1942.jpg. Copyright in the Public Domain.

7. Fig. 7.7. "Victim of the Hiroshima Bombing," http://commons.wikimedia.org/wiki/File:Victim_of_Hiroshima_atomic_bombing_3.jpg. Copyright in the Public Domain.

COLD WAR KIDS

BY DR. BRUCE OLAV SOLHEIM WITH ART BY GARY DUMM

IN ORDER TO TEACH US HOW TO SURVIVE AN ATOMIC BOMB'S BLAST, WE HAD DUCK AND COVER DRILLS FAIRLY OFTEN IN ELEMENTARY SCHOOL IN THE 1960S.

FALLOUT SHELTER

I REMEMBER THE WAILING SIREN AND MRS. PAGE MY THIRD GRADE TEACHER AS SHE DREW THE CURTAINS CLOSED IN OUR CLASSROOM AND I THOUGHT ABOUT THE WORLD BLOWING UP IN AN INSTANT.

DUCK AND COVER CHILDREN... AND DON'T LOOK AT THE BRIGHT LIGHT, YOU'LL GO BLIND!

AFTER A WHILE, WE STOPPED DOING THE DUCK AND COVER DRILLS. NOBODY EXPLAINED WHY. FAST FORWARD TO 1992, AND I WAS VISITING MY NAZI AUNT IN OSLO, NORWAY. I WAS CONDUCTING DOCTORAL RESEARCH IN THE NORWEGIAN ARCHIVES AND LIBRARIES.

I FELL ASLEEP IN A SMALL ROOM WITH A LARGE WINDOW THAT WAS PROPPED OPEN. IN THE MORNING THE WIND BLEW IN, AND THE WINDOW CRASHED INTO THE WINDOW SILL MAKING A BIG BOOMING SOUND. AT THE SAME TIME, THE CURTAINS BLEW OPEN AND THE MORNING SUN SHINED DIRECTLY INTO MY EYES.

I THOUGHT OF MRS. PAGE: "DUCK AND COVER...DON'T LOOK AT THE BRIGHT LIGHT, YOU'LL GO BLIND." FOR ONE MINUTE I THOUGHT THAT A NUCLEAR WAR HAD STARTED AND THE WORLD WAS BEING BLOWN UP. THEN I REALIZED WHAT HAD HAPPENED AND I BEGAN TO THINK THAT MY DUCK AND COVER TRAINING HAD IMPACTED ME ON A SUB-CONSCIOUS LEVEL.

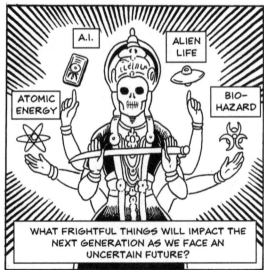

A.I.

ALIEN LIFE

ATOMIC ENERGY

BIO-HAZARD

WHAT FRIGHTFUL THINGS WILL IMPACT THE NEXT GENERATION AS WE FACE AN UNCERTAIN FUTURE?

CHAPTER EIGHT

THE COLD WAR

OBJECTIVES

1. Discover the nature and impact of nuclear weapons.
2. Determine the source of the ideological conflict between the Soviet Union and the United States.
3. Trace the development of the US policy of containment.
4. Understand the legacies of the Cold War.

PERSONAL HISTORY

I grew up in Kenmore, Washington, just north of Seattle. Our house, which my dad built, was on a hill with a beautiful view of Mt. Rainier and the Cascade range. I felt like the luckiest boy in the world. I had woods surrounding our house that I could play in, and my dad built me an A-frame tree house. It was an idyllic life for a young boy. However, in the middle of this dream-like childhood was a nightmare. Just above our house, higher on the hill at the very top, was a Nike missile site. Because Seattle was home to the Boeing Aircraft Company, and many other defense-related industries and military installations, the government set up a ring of defenses manned by the US Army. The base above our house, designated S-03, was built in 1957 and decommissioned in 1964. The Nike missiles, named after the Greek goddess of victory, were part of the US national defense system from 1954 to the 1970s, with nearly 300 sites nationwide holding supersonic surface-to-air missiles, ready to launch. These Nike missiles, both nuclear and non-nuclear, were designed to destroy incoming Soviet bombers. The development of long-range intercontinental ballistic missiles (ICBM) made the Nike missiles obsolete. The unofficial motto of the unit was "If it flies, it dies." We used to watch the army trucks and jeeps drive by our house on the way up to the Nike site. One day my brother got hit by an army jeep. My mother rushed out of the house to check on him. He had been thrown into the ditch, but was okay. My mom said that she had had enough of war, having lived through the Nazi occupation of Norway in World War II.

THE COLD WAR DEFINED

The Cold War is distinguished from other wars in that the two primary combatants never engaged each other directly on the field of battle. The United States and the Soviet Union engaged in wars, but never against each other directly. They often fought against armies equipped by the other side, and sometimes both used proxy armies to fight their Cold War battles for them. Millions of people died during the Cold War, but never through direct confrontation between the superpowers. The main reason for this is that both sides realized that a conventional war could turn into a nuclear one. After 1949, the Soviet Union also had nuclear weapons. Instead, both sides fought an ideological war and recruited other nations to their side.

In order to understand this ideological war, the differences between communism and democratic capitalism need to be sorted out. Communism began with Karl Marx and the publication of *The Communist Manifesto* in 1848. Marx had witnessed the ugly beginnings of the industrial revolution, especially in England, and developed his utopian ideas in response to the repression of the working classes by wealthy and powerful industrialists. Communism comes about when the workers free themselves, take over, and strip the rich of their power, rank, and money. At that point, everything would belong to the people; nobody would be rich, nobody would be poor. Peace and harmony would exist on earth. The problem with the application of communism is that it describes a utopian ideal. No application of communism in real life has come close to what Marx described. Democratic capitalism (combined here because communism is both a political and an economic system) is what has developed in the United States. Capitalism, free enterprise, the free market, all describe a system where business is allowed to follow the basic principles of supply and demand, unencumbered by government interference. The government has a backseat role to play. However, since the United States operates under a democratic system of government, the economy does come under some government jurisdiction. It would help to look at specific aspects of both Russian and American societies during the Cold War.

In terms of the economy, the Communist system is centralized and all means of production are controlled by the government. In other words, if you were the manager of a factory in the Soviet Union, you would be told by the government how many products to make every year and at what price. In a capitalist system, the means of production are privately owned. If you own a factory, you determine how many products you will make and set your own price. You make these decisions based upon the market conditions. Basically, there is no private property in a Communist country—everything is owned by the government—whereas in a capitalist country, one can have private property, assuming one has the money to afford it.

In terms of politics, in the Soviet Union there was only one party, the Communist party. Political dissent was not allowed. In the United States, democratic principles allow for multiple parties, even though two are dominant. Political dissent is allowed and expected. This difference had a direct impact on the people living under these two systems.

Personal freedom is one of the most important things a person can have. In Communist societies personal freedom is either not allowed or is seriously impinged upon. Freedom of speech, of assembly, of religion, and of movement are not guaranteed in a Communist society. Democratic societies pride themselves on their level of freedom. But such freedom can make a country less secure, so in wartime the level of freedom can fluctuate.

When comparing communism to capitalism it should be pointed out that capitalist countries, like the United States, have problems. Greed and corruption have impacted Americans throughout history, sometimes more so than others. However, the system of democracy allows for corrections and growth. The bottom line is: What kind of a country do you want to live in? Do you want to live in a country where people are willing to risk their lives to get in? Or do you want to live in a country where people are risking their lives to get out?

Socialism is very misunderstood. Simply put, socialism is the middle way between capitalism and communism. In socialist countries, like Canada, Norway, and Sweden, the government owns some means of production, usually key industries like energy. These countries are social democracies, so they still have democratic systems of government and personal freedom for their people.

THE CUBAN MISSILE CRISIS, 1962

The closest the world has come to nuclear war was the Cuban Missile Crisis in October 1962. On October 14 a U-2 spy plane photographed Soviet SS-4 medium-range nuclear missiles in Cuba. Each missile was capable of delivering a 1-megaton warhead. The Soviets did not want a nuclear exchange with the United States. They had far fewer missiles and warheads. The Soviet strategy was to deter an attack on the Soviet Union and prevent an invasion of Cuba. Soviet premier Nikita Khrushchev equated Soviet missiles in Cuba with US missiles on their border with Turkey. Some Kennedy advisers suggested a strike on Cuba, followed by an invasion. Others suggested a blockade, because the missiles were not totally operational and needed more parts to be shipped in from Russia. As it turned out, the United States privately agreed to remove its missiles from Turkey and promised not to invade Cuba in exchange for the Soviet Union removing its missiles from Cuba (negotiated by Attorney General Robert F. Kennedy). Any number of things could have gone wrong in October 1962 that could have caused a nuclear war. Humiliated by the event, Khrushchev only lasted another year and the Soviet Union went into a crash program of building nuclear missiles.

Nukes 101

Since nuclear weapons are what ended World War II, it would seem natural that they would figure into all the wars after. Many people do not understand nuclear weapons and their capabilities. They are just afraid of them, and with good reason. The atomic bombs dropped on Japan to end the war in the Pacific were fission weapons, the power released by splitting the atom. Today's weapons are fusion weapons, the power released by fusing atoms together, specifically hydrogen (hydrogen or H-bombs). There are different classifications of nuclear weapons. The largest are called intercontinental ballistic missiles (ICBM). These missiles have a global reach and usually contain multiple warheads in each missile. Warning time would be approximately 30 minutes if launched from maximum distance. The next type of missile is the

FIGURE 8.1. Titan II intercontinental ballistic missile

TABLE 8.1. Nuclear Nations

COUNTRY	FIRST TEST	ESTIMATED WARHEADS
United States	1945	7,650
Russia	1949	8,420
United Kingdom	1952	225
France	1960	300
China	1964	240
India	1974	80–100
Pakistan	1998	90–110
North Korea	2006	Fewer than 10
Israel	No confirmed test	80
Iran	No confirmed test	0

Sources: Federation of American Scientists, CIA World Factbook, Nuclear Threat Initiative, U.S. Census Bureau.

intermediate-range ballistic missile (IRBM). These missiles are hemispheric weapons, meaning they can reach anywhere on their half of the world from where they are launched. They house a single warhead, and warning time is just 15 minutes. Short-range ballistic missiles (SRBM) are regional weapons, housing a single warhead, and would only give the intended target a 5- to 10-minute warning. There are also battlefield nukes that are fired from a 155mm howitzer cannon. The smallest nuclear weapons are briefcase or backpack nukes. Such small weapons would probably be used as suicide weapons and could pack quite a lethal punch. Dirty bombs are not real nuclear weapons. They are conventional bombs containing radioactive material.

Just how destructive are nuclear bombs? A 1-megaton bomb could destroy 80 square miles (the size of most good-sized cities). The nuclear detonation produces a blinding light; a blast wave that can generate winds up to 700 miles per hour; thermal energy that begins as hot as the interior of the sun and spreads out, burning everything; and radioactive fallout that causes radiation disease and is deadly to humans. It also creates an electromagnetic pulse that destroys most electronics. With thousands and thousands of these warheads in existence, human beings have the capacity to destroy the world many times over. The Table 8.1 below lists all of the world's nuclear power nations.

COLD WAR OVERVIEW

World War II was the most destructive war the world has ever known. The changes in the international system after the war were also very dramatic. Germany lost more territory after World War II than in World War I. Japan also lost all of the territory it had gained since 1905. The end of the war created power vacuums in Europe, Asia, and Africa. Massive colonial changes were underway. The British Empire had declined and was losing its grip on India and its African colonies. Leadership passed to the United States.

America's empire would be different from the British Empire. The American empire had an informal hierarchical structure. Nations within the United States' sphere of influence had important economic, military, and political ties. America's strength was based on four fundamental aspects:

1. vast economic superiority,
2. substantial military power,
3. a broad, bipartisan foreign policy base at home, and
4. international ideological support.

In 1945, Soviet industrial production may have been only 25 percent of it was for the United States. The United States produced almost as much as the rest of the world combined. From 1940 to 1950 the United States made 82 percent of the major inventions, discoveries, and innovations. And, although America had 6 percent of the world's population, Americans consumed 46 percent of the electrical power in the world. The United States also controlled 59 percent of the world's total oil reserves. In 1950 America produced 40 percent of the world's gross national product. By 1960 this had fallen to 30 percent. The US economy bolstered its military capabilities and strength.

Until 1949, the United States had a monopoly on the atomic bomb, and continued to have many more atomic weapons than the Soviet Union until the late 1960s. The United States had the strongest and most modern air force and navy. In 1960, America accounted for 51 percent of total military spending in the world, yet had only 13 percent of the total military force in uniform.

World War II brought about a change in American attitudes. Isolationism, although still a contributing factor in the formulation of US foreign policy, was largely a thing of the past. Bipartisan foreign policy developed as never before. FDR's former vice president, Henry Wallace—who came close to being nominated instead of Harry Truman, and was a socialist in everything but name—was out of politics. The defense industry was now permanent and exerted its influence on both domestic and foreign policy in America. The bottom line was that the Soviet Union had to be contained. Former US ambassador to Russia George Kennan warned Americans of Russian expansionism with his Long Telegram from Moscow in 1946, and his 1947 article "The Sources of Soviet Conduct." His thoughts on what he called containment became the basis of US foreign policy for the next 54 years.

British dominance in the world was based on race; French dominance was based on culture. Soviet challenge to American dominance came in the form of an economic class struggle, and struck a responsive chord in the Third World. American dominance during the Cold War was based on a national mission—containing socialism and communism—and a racial classification of people. Unlike the British, the Americans had only one consistent threat: the Soviet Union.

This allowed the US government to develop a single-minded foreign policy that united both parties. The threat from the Soviets, whether real or perceived, not only unified the American position at home, but also encouraged allies to invite the Americans to increase their military, economic, and political role. The United States was literally invited to create an empire.

National interest, concern for others, and ideology came together to drive Cold War US foreign policy. President John F. Kennedy's famous line from his inaugural speech captured this bipartisanship and focus: "We shall pay any price, bear any burden, meet any hardship, support any friend, oppose any foe to assure the survival and success of liberty." An American empire was established in four of the six major power centers in the world: the United States, Great Britain, Western Europe, and Japan.

Europe and Japan were easy for the United States to deal with compared to the Middle East. British and American leaders argued over the Middle East. The British felt that US foreign policy in the Middle East was subverted by big oil companies and the Jewish lobby. The US Central Intelligence Agency (CIA) helped orchestrate a coup that removed Iranian prime minister Mohammad Mosaddeq in 1953. Mosaddeq planned to nationalize the Iranian oil industry and the CIA feared he was steering the country toward an alliance with Russia. After the assassination, the United States then supported the installation of the pro-Western Shah of Iran, Mohammad Reza Pahlavi. The old saying about US foreign policy is that the flag follows the dollar. In other words, if US corporations are heavily invested somewhere and trouble breaks out, the US military or CIA, or both, will come to the rescue. US oil companies had a 40 percent share of the oil in Iran and were not about to risk losing that.

US interests were established and represented around the world. By the 1960s, the United States had 450 bases in 36 countries, and one million members of its military stationed abroad. Unlike previous hegemonic powers, America imposed its policy through the will of the people in the countries it interacted with, an "invitation to empire," as Norwegian historian Geir Lundestad said. The Marshall Plan was a prime example of how this worked. From 1945 through 1947, Americans were providing direct financial aid to a war-torn Europe. The brand new United Nations (UN) was providing humanitarian aid. In 1947, President Harry S. Truman appointed George Marshall to be secretary of state. In just a few months, Marshall, with the help of George Kennan, William Clayton, and others, came up with the Marshall Plan. The plan was officially known as the European Recovery Program (ERP). The Marshall Plan's mission was to rebuild the economies of Western Europe and bolster the morale of a suffering people. The lesson of World War I lingered in the minds of those who remembered Hitler's rise to power before World War II. Economic revitalization was the key to political stability and resistance to the advance of Soviet communism in Europe. Sixteen nations, including Germany, became part of the program and received nearly $13 billion in aid. The Marshall Plan funding ended in 1951.

The United States became the leader of the free world because America offered better opportunities than anyone else could or had. US policy strengthened economic multilateralism and promotion of free trade. All countries operated under a US system dominated by the dollar—the Bretton Woods system. Because of the heavy influence of American corporations, US policies and funding abroad promoted programs that would not work at home—programs that were better suited for the social democracies of Europe. This was done in order to counter any pressure from the left that could sway support toward the Soviet Union. The United States could be heavy handed, as with Iran and Guatemala, and failed when it did not have broad popular support (e.g., the failed Bay of Pigs invasion of Cuba). The US anti-imperial imperialism (discussed in the earlier chapter on the Spanish-American War) sent mixed messages to developing countries around the world. The United States' efforts to rebuild Japan and Germany worked so well that those two countries began to have negative economic effects on the US, becoming competitors and actually overtaking the United States in some areas (e.g., Japanese high-mileage cars during the gas shortage of the 1970s). The Communist victory in China in 1949 was the biggest blow to American foreign policy, and prompted Senator Joseph McCarthy's anti-Communist witch hunts of the early 1950s.

Origins of Mistrust

This would be a good point to go over the circumstances behind the ideological split between Russia and the United States. In other words, how did the Cold War start? Most historians point to the Truman Doctrine of 1947 when President Truman threw down the gauntlet over Russia's Communist influence and interference in Greece and Turkey. The Soviets already had half of Europe after World War II and seemed to be spreading their influence far and wide. Truman's announcement, as part of the new strategy of containment, would reverberate throughout the Cold War era and set a tone for harsh rhetoric used by both sides. But everything was not well in US–Soviet relations prior to the Truman Doctrine. The origins of the Cold War go deeper. As with any bad relationship, both sides believed themselves to be the aggrieved party.

The Russian Revolution of October 1917 was the true beginning of the Cold War. This was the first Communist revolution in world history. Vladimir Ilyich Ulyanov (later using the name Lenin) took the debate about Communist revolution—circulating since Karl Marx published *The Communist Manifesto*—into the streets and made it reality. The Bolsheviks (Russian Communists) took on the non-Communist Russians (Mensheviks) in a bloody civil war that last for three years. Lenin did not threaten the United States directly, but did so indirectly by calling for a worldwide Communist revolution and the burying of capitalism. This got the American government's and business leaders' attention. It also got the attention of capitalists around the world. As Winston Churchill, then secretary of war for Great Britain, said, "The foul baboonery of Bolshevism, must be strangled in its cradle." Russia was on the side of the Allies in World War I prior to the Communist revolution. With a civil war raging in Russia, they were forced to drop out of the war in 1918. This made the war that much more difficult for the United States and the other Allies. Russia had threatened to destroy capitalism and dropped out of the war, threatening the European democracies—the United States and other countries believed it was time to intervene.

In 1918 the United States, along with Great Britain, France, Japan, and others, invaded Russia during its civil war. The primary objective of this intervention was to re-establish an eastern front after the collapse of the Russian government during the 1917 Communist revolution. The Allies also feared Communist ambitions in other countries. This intervention lasted until 1922, although the United States left in 1920. The Allied incursion was not successful. The non-Communist White Russians were doomed from the start in the civil war with the Red Russians (Communists). Moreover, the intervention fed Russian Communist fears of future invasions and attacks by Western nations. The Communists used the Allied intervention as a useful propaganda tool. It could be used to justify fear of capitalist countries and the creation of the Soviet bloc of Eastern European nations, as a buffer against invasion.

The Comintern (Communist International) was founded in Moscow in March 1919, based on Lenin proclaiming the end of capitalism and predicting the eventual victory of Communist revolution around the world. The organization helped fund Communist organizations around the world, including in the United States. From the US perspective, it is one thing to call for revolution; it is quite another to actively organize and fund revolution.

In retaliation for Russia's revolutionary activities, the Bolshevik's failure to repay debts owed to America, and the seizure of American property, the United States refused to recognize Russia's right to exist as a nation starting in December 1917. This means that the United States did not exchange ambassadors or enter into any formal agreements with Russia. On November 16, 1933, President Franklin Roosevelt ended almost 16 years of American non-recognition with the Soviet Union in a series of negotiations in Washington, D.C.

The non-aggression pact between Hitler and Stalin (also known as the Nazi–Soviet Pact) divided Poland and signaled that World War II in Europe was about to begin. It also convinced the United States that Stalin and the Russians were not to be trusted.

The United States wanted to launch an attack on German-occupied France as early as 1942, but Winston Churchill convinced Roosevelt that it would be better to attack what he called the soft underbelly of Europe, through North Africa and Italy. The Russians wanted an attack on the Western Front through France, thereby establishing a strong second front and relieving pressure for the Soviets on the Eastern Front. This delay of a second front cost the Russians dearly and annoyed Stalin to no end. The Italian campaign did not result in a swift movement into Germany from the south, as Churchill had hoped. The fighting in Italy was fierce. When America launched the D-Day invasion, the Russians were able to speed up their offensive in the east against weakened German forces. Had the Allies invaded France in 1943 instead of Italy, the war in Europe may have ended one year earlier. Stalin would remember this delay and even though Russia was allied with the United States, would never forgive them for waiting.

The last grievance, from the Soviet side, was the United States' refusal to share atomic bomb secrets with its Russian allies. The British had full knowledge of the Manhattan Project, but the United States did not trust the Russians with this super-secret atomic bomb project. Stalin had his spies in the United States and eventually got the information he needed to develop a Russian bomb.

CONTAINMENT

US diplomat and historian George F. Kennan criticized US foreign policy for its excessive moralism and legalism. Kennan's important contribution to US foreign policy is containment, which was conceived at the beginning of the Cold War. He is known as the father of containment. Containment remained the United States' foreign policy strategy until September 11, 2001. He first articulated this policy in his X Article published in *Foreign Affairs* in 1947, when he said that the United States needed long-term patience and vigilance in containing Soviet expansionist tendencies. He had already warned US officials in his 1946 Long Telegram that the United States should be careful not to overreact to Soviet aggression. Kennan stressed using economic and political means, rather than military force, to deal with the threat of Soviet Communist expansion. Above all, he encouraged remaining cool, calm, and collected in dealing with the Russians. Containment, then, was the US foreign policy designed to stop the spread of communism. To implement containment, Kennan suggested four elements or tools: military, psychological, economic, and diplomatic.

FIGURE 8.2. George F. Kennan

MILITARY CONTAINMENT

The military can be used either offensively or defensively. One example of the offensive use of the military to stop the spread of communism was Operation Urgent Fury in 1983. Cubans were building a military airfield on the island nation of Grenada with the help of the Soviet

Union. President Reagan did not want to let the Russians build a bomber-capable airfield in the Caribbean. A force of 8,000, including the 82nd Airborne Division, Special Forces, and Marines, invaded Grenada. A total of 19 US military forces were killed and more than 100 wounded. An example of a defensive operation would be the occupation of Western Europe after World War II. The United States had a force of up to 250,000 stationed permanently in West Germany throughout the Cold War. The mission was to prevent a Soviet Communist incursion into Western Europe, at great expense. The United States had tanks, fighter and bomber aircraft, artillery, infantry, nuclear missiles, helicopters, and everything else it needed to deter a Soviet invasion. The problem with using the military to contain communism is that it is expensive and could potentially ratchet up the tensions between the superpowers (especially in offensive operations).

PSYCHOLOGICAL CONTAINMENT

Psychological containment is much cheaper than using the military. Printing posters, radio broadcasts, movies, leaflets, all can be very effective in getting an official government message out. This type of containment is really propaganda. The secret to propaganda is to take complex ideas and a find an easy solution to these problems by boiling them down to a simple catchphrase. At that point, you simply repeat that message over and over. The purpose of propaganda is to get people to believe something, and then take action based on that belief. Anti-Communist propaganda would convince people that communism offers absolutely no advantages. President Ronald Reagan used to refer to the Soviet Union as the evil empire. That phrase is clever and very effective propaganda. Democracies can also use propaganda, not just totalitarian regimes. In fact, the average person is constantly bombarded by propaganda from their own government, foreign governments, special interest groups, commercial advertisers, corporations, and other entities and groups. The easiest way to control people is to create either anger or fear. Propaganda does this very effectively.

ECONOMIC CONTAINMENT

Economic containment is also cheaper than military containment. By offering most-favored-nation trading status, or extending loans or credits to other countries, the United States can spread goodwill, serve humanitarian purposes, and create a relationship and bond that can pay political dividends later on. The Marshall Plan, US aid to rebuild Europe after World War II, was a good example of economic containment.

DIPLOMATIC CONTAINMENT

Diplomatic containment was simply being able to convince other nations that supporting US policy in the Cold War was the right thing to do. A successful diplomat is worth their weight

FIGURE 8.3. American Cold War propaganda

in gold. The art of diplomacy is getting someone else to have things your way. The United Nations was an example of diplomatic containment. Voting blocs developed that supported the US-led, Western view. The United States also developed organizations like the North Atlantic Treaty Organization (NATO), which was a collective security arrangement made by like-minded allies.

STRATEGIES OF CONTAINMENT

The way in which the United States uses the elements or tools of containment define the strategy. Two primary strategies developed during the Cold War: perimeter defense and strong-point defense. With perimeter defense, the United States would ensure that the Soviets could not break out of their present borders anywhere in the world. In other words, America defends the world against any Soviet Communist aggression. With strong-point defense, the United States selects certain countries or regions to defend, based on their strategic value to US national interests, and is not overly concerned with other countries or regions that do not hold such value. There are advantages and disadvantages to both strategies. With perimeter defense, the American ideal of promoting democracy and freedom is upheld. It would not matter whether a country had strategic value to the United States, Americans will defend anywhere, anytime. So, from a moral and ethical standpoint, perimeter defense is better. But, from a resource allocation standpoint, strong-point defense is better. The United States does not have unlimited power or resources. By choosing certain regions or countries to defend, the United States can preserve its precious resources and not waste them defending places that hold no strategic value. American presidents during the Cold War have flip-flopped between these two strategies.

THE KOREAN WAR, 1950–1953

The Korean War was the first war of the Cold War. It is also known as the forgotten war, because it is stuck between the great victory of World War II and the tragedy of Vietnam. Korea was liberated in 1945 after the defeat of Japan. The United States occupied the Korean Peninsula south of the 38th parallel, and the Soviet Union controlled the area north. Communist leader Kim Il-sung took power in the north, while the south became democratic. Supported by the two superpowers, North and South Korea each wanted to reunite the country under their own rule. The war started in June 1950 when the North Koreans crossed the 38th parallel and invaded South Korea.

The United Nations passed a resolution to reestablish the border between North and South Korea at the 38th parallel and called for military assistance for South Korea. The North Korean forces overwhelmed the South Koreans and pushed them back to a small area around Pusan in the southern end of the peninsula. Then, under the UN flag, General Douglas MacArthur orchestrated an amphibious landing at Inchon on September 15, 1950, and forced the North Koreans back north of the 38th parallel. The original objective had been achieved fairly quickly. Unfortunately, the UN forces then pursued a second objective of reunifying the peninsula, so they pushed in to North Korea and got very near the Chinese border by September 1950. The United States did not heed the Chinese warnings against intervening, and General MacArthur dismissed the threats as not credible. In October Chinese forces crossed the Yalu River and entered the war.

By April 1951, General MacArthur had been fired by President Truman. MacArthur's replacement, General Matthew Ridgeway, was able to push the Chinese and North Koreans north of Seoul and the 38th parallel. Armistice negotiations opened in July 1951 as the fighting continued. The war featured the first combat by jet aircraft on both sides. Negotiations finally reached a breakthrough in 1953 and an armistice went into effect on July 27. It was just a cease-fire agreement, not a formal peace treaty. Both sides agreed to the creation of a demilitarized zone (DMZ) along the front, approximately 250 miles along and 2.5 miles wide. The demilitarized zone between North and South Korea is one of the most heavily fortified borders in the world. South Korea has since developed into one of most vibrant world economies, while North Korea is poor, isolated, and the people live in a police state.

CONCLUSION

As German philosopher Friedrich Nietzsche wrote: "He who fights with monsters should look to it that he himself does not become a monster. And when you gaze long into an abyss the abyss also gazes into you." The Cold War lasted for approximately 45 years and the legacies are still with us. The Third World nations, which served as a battleground for the two superpowers, are still in economic and political turmoil, especially in Africa. The US economy has never recovered fully from the long drawn out Cold War as is evident in our deteriorating economy, substandard public schools, and crumbling infrastructure. The Soviet Union collapsed but Russia appears to be on the rise. Nuclear weapons are now in the hands of 10 nations and North and South Korea are still ever vigilant along a tense border without an official peace treaty. In order to fight communism the United States teamed up with dictators around the world who expressed anti-communist views following the old Mafia principle of "the enemy of my enemy is my friend."

The United States was the self-proclaimed arsenal of democracy during World War II. American gross national product doubled from 1941 to 1945. President Franklin D. Roosevelt put the military and corporations in charge of mobilization for war. The US government even suspended anti-trust laws. In 1940, the top 100 companies in the United States produced 30 percent of all goods. By 1945, the top 100 companies in the United States produced 70 percent of all goods. What had been a makeshift defense industry that would rise up only when needed became a permanent fixture after World War II. One cannot help but think that this is all planned out to benefit what President Dwight D. Eisenhower called the military industrial complex. Eisenhower warned us of this in his 1961 farewell address: "This conjunction of an immense military establishment and a large arms industry is new in the American experience … In the councils of government, we must guard against the acquisition of unwarranted influence, whether sought or unsought, by the military-industrial complex. The potential for the disastrous rise of misplaced power exists and will persist."

Eisenhower wanted to make his military industrial complex speech earlier in his presidency, but was unable to. He would read articles and see ads for new weapons systems and get angry and throw them in his fireplace in the oval office. He thought that defense companies should not try to seek budgets for weapons systems for commercial gain, it should be for reasons of national defense.

I worked on the B-1B bomber project for Boeing Military from 1986 to 1990. After my time in the US Army I got a job at Boeing. I was a buyer working on avionics contracts with the US Air Force when one day I was looking at old contract documentation. I found some files from the Carter era. The B-1A was axed by President Carter, but the documentation showed that Boeing kept the B-1 project going using its own money until Ronald Reagan was elected and he turned the project back on. This could be just coincidence, but I could not help but think that Boeing knew something ahead of time. Boeing is a very conservative company, so I know they had an idea that whoever would come into the presidency next would buy into the B-1 project. Maybe just coincidental, but Boeing moved their corporate headquarters to Chicago in 2001 just before 9/11. People in Seattle were outraged that Boeing would leave the city where the company was founded in 1917. Boeing is not just a commercial airplane company; the company includes McDonnell jet fighters, Douglas commercial aircraft, Hughes helicopters, Hughes Space, North American Aerospace, and many other entities. The company said they wanted to develop global growth opportunities. Boeing got many military contracts from the subsequent global War on Terror after their corporate move. Perhaps just coincidentally, Barack Obama, then a US senator from Illinois, gave the keynote speech at the Democratic National Convention in 2004. You could tell that he was being groomed for higher office. That is the way the media played it. He was then elected in 2008. Obama has his powerbase in Chicago. Is there a Boeing connection?

The US Navy's battle fleet is larger than the next 13 navies combined, 11 of which are our allies. The United States has 20 times more advanced stealth fighters than China. Yet we continue to build up our defenses. Why? It is very difficult to control the power of the nation's defense industry. There are only a few giant defense contractors, so there is not much competition to drive the price down. These companies are also quite adept at both lobbying and marketing to promote their interests. Defense companies like Boeing spread the jobs around the country, to lock in nationwide political support. It is said that a new Cold War is beginning with Russia under Vladimir Putin. That is very good news for the Military Industrial Complex.

TIMELINE

1945

February 8: At the Yalta Conference, the Allies (United States, Soviet Union, Great Britain, and France), divide Germany into four occupation zones.

April 12: President Franklin D. Roosevelt suffers a stroke and dies in Warm Springs, Georgia.

July 24: At the Potsdam Conference, President Harry S. Truman tells Stalin that the United States has a powerful super weapon.

August 2: At the Potsdam Conference, Berlin is divided into four zones occupied by the Allies.

August 6: An atomic bomb is dropped on Hiroshima.

August 8: The Soviet Union declares war on Japan and invades Manchuria.

August 9: An atomic bomb is dropped on Nagasaki.

September 2: The Japanese formally surrender unconditionally onboard the USS *Missouri*.

October 24: The United Nations is founded.

1946

January: The Chinese civil war between Communist and Nationalist forces resumes.

February 22: George F. Kennan writes his Long Telegram, describing his interpretation of the objectives and intentions of the Soviet Union.

March 5: Winston Churchill warns of an Iron Curtain descending across Europe.

July 4: The Philippines gains independence from the United States.

December 19: The First Indochina War (French-Viet Minh War) begins in Vietnam.

1947

March 12: President Harry S. Truman announces the Truman Doctrine.

April 16: Bernard Baruch calls deteriorating relations between the Soviet Union and the United States the Cold War.

May 22: The United States gives $400 million of military aid to Greece and Turkey.

June 5: Secretary of State George Marshall outlines the Marshall Plan.

August 14: India and Pakistan gain independence from the United Kingdom.

1948

February 25: The Communist Party takes control in Czechoslovakia.

April 3: Truman signs the Marshall Plan, which amounts to $13 billion in economic assistance to Europe.

May 10: Syngman Rhee becomes president of South Korea.

June 24: Stalin orders a blockade of all land routes from West Germany to East Germany; Berlin Airlift begins.

September 9: The Soviet Union declares that the Democratic People's Republic of Korea (North Korea) is the only legitimate government in Korea and instates Kim Il-sung as prime minister.

1949

April 4: The North Atlantic Treaty Organization (NATO) is founded in order to resist Soviet expansion into Europe.

May 11: The Soviet blockade of Berlin ends.

June 8: Anti-Communist hysteria continues as American celebrities are accused of being members of the Communist Party.

August 29: The Soviet Union tests its first atomic bomb.

September 15: Konrad Adenauer becomes the chancellor of the Federal Republic of Germany (West Germany).

October 1: Chairman Mao Zedong declares the creation of the People's Republic of China (Communist China).

October 7: The Soviets declare their part of Germany to be the German Democratic Republic (East Germany).

December 27: Indonesia gains it independence from the Netherlands.

1950

February 16: The Soviet Union and the People's Republic of China sign a mutual defense agreement.

March 11: Nationalist Chinese leader Chiang Kai-shek moves his capital to Taipei, Taiwan.

April 17: National Security Council Memo 68 (NSC-68) makes a militarized form of containment the official US foreign policy.

June 25: North Korea invades South Korea.

September 30: UN forces land at Inchon.

October 2: UN forces cross the 38th parallel, into North Korea.

October 22: China intervenes in the Korean War.

1951

March 29: Julius and Ethel Rosenberg are convicted of giving atomic secrets to the Soviet Union.

April 11: President Truman fires General MacArthur.

1952

April 28: Japan becomes a sovereign state again.

June 30: The Marshall Plan ends.

October 2: Great Britain tests its atomic bomb.

November 1: First thermonuclear bomb (H-bomb) is detonated by the United States.

1953

January 20: Dwight D. Eisenhower becomes president of the United States.

March 5: Joseph Stalin dies.

July 27: An armistice agreement ends the Korean War.

August 19: The CIA orchestrates a coup to oust Iranian prime minister Mohammad Mosaddeq.

September 7: Nikita Khrushchev becomes leader of the Soviet Union.

1954

January 21: The USS *Nautilus* (first nuclear submarine) is launched.

April: The Non-Aligned Movement is started by Nehru of India, Sukarno of Indonesia, Tito of Yugoslavia, Nasser of Egypt, and Nkrumah of Ghana.

May 7: The Viet Minh defeat the French at Dien Bien Phu. The French withdraw completely from Vietnam shortly thereafter.

May 9: West Germany joins NATO and begins rearmament.

May 14: The Warsaw Pact is founded in Eastern Europe.

June 2: Senator Joseph McCarthy claims Communists have infiltrated the CIA and the defense industry.

June 18: Jacobo Árbenz, head of a leftist Guatemalan government, is overthrown in a CIA-sponsored coup.

August 11: Communist China shells Taiwan in the Taiwan Strait Crisis.

1956

July 26: Nasser nationalizes the Suez Canal.

October 23: Hungarian revolt is crushed by the Soviet military.

October 29: In the Suez Crisis, France, Israel, and the United Kingdom attack Egypt and try to remove Nasser from power.

December: Communist insurgency begins in South Vietnam.

1957

May 2: Senator Joseph McCarthy dies.

October 1: The Strategic Air Command initiates a 24/7 nuclear alert.

October 4: The Soviet Sputnik satellite is launched.

November 7: The US government encourages Americans to build backyard bomb shelters.

November 15: Khrushchev claims that the Soviet Union has missile superiority over the United States.

1958

July 14: A coup in Iraq, backed by the Soviet Union, removes the pro-British monarch.

August 23: China begins to bomb Quemoy in the Second Taiwan Strait Crisis.

October 4: The National Aeronautics and Space Administration (NASA) is formed.

1959

January 1: Fidel Castro becomes the leader of Cuba, following the success of the Cuban Revolution.

July 24: Vice President Richard Nixon and Soviet premier Nikita Khrushchev have what is called the Kitchen Debate.

September: Khrushchev visits the United States for 13 days and is not allowed to go to Disneyland.

December: Viet Cong (VC), also known as the National Liberation Front, is formed in Vietnam.

1960

February 16: France tests its first atomic bomb.

May 1: American CIA pilot Francis Gary Powers is shot down in his U-2 spy plane over Russia.

June: A Sino-Soviet split occurs between China and the Soviet Union.

1961

January 20: John F. Kennedy becomes president of the United States.

April 12: Soviet cosmonaut Yuri Gagarin becomes the first human in space and first to orbit the earth.

April 17–19: The CIA-orchestrated Bay of Pigs invasion of Cuba fails.

May 25: John F. Kennedy announces that America will put a man on the moon by the end of the decade, which starts the Apollo program.

August 13: The building of the Berlin Wall begins by the Soviet Union and East Germany.

October 31: The Soviet Union detonates the most powerful H-bomb in history (50 megatons).

1962

October 16: The Cuban Missile Crisis begins.

1963

June 20: A hotline is established between Washington and Moscow.

November 2: South Vietnamese prime minister Ngo Dinh Diem is assassinated in a military coup.

November 22: President John F. Kennedy is assassinated in Dallas. Lyndon B. Johnson becomes president of the United States.

1964

August 2: The USS *Maddox* is attacked in the Tonkin Gulf.

August 7: The Tonkin Gulf Resolution authorizes use of force against North Vietnam.

October 14: Leonid Brezhnev becomes the new Soviet leader.

October 16: China tests its first atomic bomb.

1965

March 8: US Marines land in Danang, South Vietnam, beginning the ground war. President Johnson orders sustained bombing of North Vietnam.

April 28: US forces invade the Dominican Republic.

November 14: At the Battle of Ia Drang, US troops engage regular North Vietnamese forces.

1966

March 10: France withdraws from NATO.

August 26: The South African Border War begins.

1967

June 5: The Six-Day War begins, between Israel and Egypt in the Sinai Peninsula.

November 29: Robert McNamara resigns as US secretary of defense.

1968

January 30: Tet Offensive begins in South Vietnam.

March 30: President Johnson stops bombing North Vietnam and announces he is not running for reelection.

1969

January 20: Richard Nixon becomes president of the United States.

March 2: Border clashes occur between the Soviet Union and China.

March 17: The United States begins bombing Cambodia.

July 20: Apollo 11 lands on the moon.

July 25: The United States begins withdrawing troops from Vietnam through a process called Vietnamization.

September 1: Muammar al-Gaddafi takes over Libya in a coup.

1971

February 8: The South Vietnamese Army enters Laos.

September 11: Nikita Khrushchev dies.

October 25: The UN general assembly recognizes Communist China as the sole legitimate government of China.

December 3: India and Pakistan go to war over Bangladesh.

1972

February 21: President Nixon visits Communist China.

May 26: Detente policy leads to Strategic Arms Limitation Talks (SALT I) agreement between the Soviet Union and the United States.

September 1: Bobby Fischer defeats Russian Boris Spassky to become the first American chess champion.

December 18: President Nixon announces the Christmas bombing campaign in North Vietnam.

1973

January 27: The United States signs the Paris Peace Accords and ends American involvement in the Vietnam War.

September 11: The CIA backs a coup in Chile.

October 6: The Yom Kippur War begins, with Israel fighting Egypt and Syria.

1974

August 9: President Nixon resigns due to the Watergate scandal and Gerald Ford becomes president of the United States.

1975

April 18: The Communist Khmer Rouge seizes power in Cambodia.

April 30: North Vietnam takes Saigon and wins the Vietnam War.

May 12: The Mayagüez incident takes place with a US ship seized by the Khmer Rouge.

June 25: Civil wars break out in Angola and Mozambique involving American and Soviet support.

July: The Apollo–Soyuz joint US–Soviet test project begins.

November 29: Communist Pathet Lao takes over in Laos.

1976

January 8: Chinese premier Zhou Enlai dies.

September 9: Mao Zedong dies.

1977

January 20: Jimmy Carter becomes president of the United States.

1978

April 27: The president of Afghanistan is murdered in a coup led by pro-Communist rebels.

December 25: A Communist regime is installed in Afghanistan.

1979

January 7: Vietnam gets rid of the Khmer Rouge.

January 16: The Iranian Revolution removes the Shah from power.

February 17: China launches an attack on North Vietnam.

May 9: War breaks out in El Salvador between Marxist insurgents and the American-backed government.

June 18: President Jimmy Carter and Soviet leader Leonid Brezhnev sign the SALT II agreement.

July 3: President Carter authorizes funding to help groups fighting against the pro-Soviet regime in Afghanistan.

July 17: Marxist Sandinistas overthrow the pro-American dictator in Nicaragua.

November 4: Iranian students take over the US embassy and capture Americans.

December 24: The Soviet Union invades Afghanistan.

1980

March 21: The United States announces a boycott of the 1980 Summer Olympics in Moscow.

May 4: Tito, Communist leader of Yugoslavia, dies.

November: Ronald Reagan is elected president of the United States.

1981

January 20: The Iran hostage crisis ends.

November 23: The CIA begins to support anti-Sandinista Contras in Nicaragua.

December 13: The military declares martial law in Poland to crush the Solidarity trade union movement.

1982

April 2: The Falklands War begins between the United Kingdom and Argentina.

June 6: Israel invades Lebanon.

November 10: Leonid Brezhnev dies.

November 14: Yuri Andropov becomes leader of the Soviet Union.

1983

March 8: President Reagan calls the Soviet Union an evil empire.

March 23: President Reagan proposes the Strategic Defense Initiative (SDI) and opponents call it Star Wars.

September 1: Civilian Korean Air Lines Flight 007 is shot down by Soviet military aircraft.

October 25: US forces invade the Caribbean island of Grenada (Operation Urgent Fury).

1984

February 13: Konstantin Chernenko is named general secretary of the Soviet Communist Party.

July 28: The Soviet Union boycotts the 1984 Summer Olympics in Los Angeles.

October 31: Indira Gandhi is assassinated.

1985

March 11: Mikhail Gorbachev becomes leader of the Soviet Union.

November 21: Reagan and Gorbachev have a summit meeting in Geneva, Switzerland.

1986

February 25: Ferdinand Marcos is overthrown in the Philippines and Corazon Aquino is elected as the first female president of the Philippines.

April 26: The Chernobyl disaster takes place.

October 17: President Reagan approves $100 million of military aid for the Contras.

November 25: The Iran–Contra affair.

1987

January 16: Gorbachev supports economic restructuring of the Soviet Union known as perestroika. He also favors an opening of society that he calls glasnost, which is an opening of society.

June 12: President Reagan asks Gorbachev to tear down the Berlin Wall.

November 18: The Iran–Contra scandal hearings conclude.

December 8: The Intermediate-Range Nuclear Forces (INF) Treaty is signed by Reagan and Gorbachev.

1988

May 15: The Soviet Union withdraws from Afghanistan.

December 7: Gorbachev announces that the Soviet Union will not interfere with Eastern Europe.

1989

January 20: George H. W. Bush becomes president of the United States.

June 4: The Tiananmen Square Massacre takes place in Beijing.

June 4: Semi-free elections are held in Poland.

October: East German Communist leader Erich Honecker is ousted.

October 18: Free elections are allowed in Hungary.

November 9: The Berlin Wall is breached.

December 16–25: Romanians overthrow the Communist government.

December 29: Václav Havel becomes president of Czechoslovakia.

1990

January 31: The first McDonald's in Moscow opens.

March 11: Lithuania becomes independent.

May 29: Boris Yeltsin is elected president of Russia.

August 2: Iraq invades Kuwait, beginning the Gulf War.

October 3: Germany is reunified.

1991

February 28: The Gulf War ends.

July: The Warsaw Pact is dissolved.

December 25: President George H. W. Bush acknowledges the end of the Cold War.

December 25: Mikhail Gorbachev resigns as president of the USSR.

December 31: The Soviet Union ceases to exist.

CREDITS

1. Fig. 8.1. "Titan II Intercontinental Ballistic Missile," U.S. Air Force, http://commons.wikimedia.org/wiki/File:Titan_II_ICBM.jpg. Copyright in the Public Domain.
2. Table 8.1. Nuclear Weapons: Who Has What? http://www.cnn.com/interactive/2013/03/world/nuclear-weapon-states/. Sources: Federation of American Scientists, CIA World Factbook, Nuclear Threat Initiative, U.S. Census Bureau
3. Fig. 8.2. "George F. Kennan," http://commons.wikimedia.org/wiki/File:Kennan.jpeg. Copyright in the Public Domain.
4. Fig. 8.3. Catechetical Guild Educational Society, "American Cold War Propaganda," http://commons.wikimedia.org/wiki/File:Is_this_tomorrow.jpg. Copyright in the Public Domain.

INTOLERANCE

BY DR. BRUCE OLAV SOLHEIM WITH ART BY GARY DUMM

AFTER WORLD WAR II, THE U.S. ARMY HOUSED ITS TROOPS IN FORMER NAZI MILITARY BUILDINGS IN WEST GERMANY.

THIS IS THE UNITED STATES ARMY EUROPE (USAEUR) CREST. IT DEPICTS THE SWORD OF FREEDOM. WE LIBERATED MILLIONS OF PEOPLE AFTER WORLD WAR II.

I LIVED IN FORMER NAZI BARRACKS, IN 1979. IT WAS AN INTEGRATED FOUR-MAN ROOM. TWO WHITES, TWO BLACKS.

OUR OTHER WHITE ROOM MATE WAS IN THE KU KLUX KLAN.

I HAD NEVER MET A KLANSMAN BEFORE. HE DID NOT APPROVE OF MY FRIENDSHIP WITH OUR BLACK ROOM MATES.

I GREW UP IN A TOLERANT AND LOVING HOME. MY MOM AND DAD DID NOT DISCRIMINATE OR HOLD ANY PREJUDICES IN THEIR HEARTS.

LIVING UNDER NAZI RULE DURING THE WAR SHOWED THEM HOW UGLY INTOLERANCE WAS.

CHAPTER NINE

THE MODERN CIVIL RIGHTS ERA

OBJECTIVES

1. Understand the connection between World War II and the modern civil rights movement.
2. Identify some of the major civil rights leaders.
3. Understand the legacies of Dr. Martin Luther King, Jr. and Malcolm X.
4. Determine the impact of various civil rights movements.

PERSONAL HISTORY

In my high school in rural King County, north of Seattle, Washington, we had about 700 students. Of those, only 3 or 4 students were African American, maybe 6 were Asian, there was a Pacific Islander or 2, and a few Mexican Americans—not exactly diverse. Our mascot was a Viking and our principal was Norwegian. When I joined the Army on Halloween 1978, I had no idea that I was about to get a lesson in ethnic and racial diversity. I was lucky that I grew up with parents who were open and accepting of all people. I never heard them speak ill of any ethnic, racial, or religious group. My mom had a copy of *The Feminine Mystique* by Betty Friedan on our bookshelf. I really did not understand the significance of that until later in my life. My mom was 40 years old when I was born and arrived at a pro-feminist view late in life. I remember mom arguing with dad over a night class she wanted to take. Both of them had 6th-grade educations, but were very smart. None of her other friends were taking night classes; she was a maverick of sorts. She also liked to make her own clothes and loved the bright colors that were very popular in the 1960s and 1970s. My father did not like the feminist views my mother had, but he never won any arguments as far as I could tell. There were no marriage counselors for that generation—they just kept going, no matter what. Divorce was not an option.

In 1970, when Native Americans were protesting over what was going to be done with Ft. Lawton (an old US Army fort in Seattle), my mom took me to the protests. Developers wanted to build luxury homes, hotels, and resorts, because the land was highly prized and had a beachfront on the Puget Sound. I remember she wore a headband not unlike the ones the Native American protesters were wearing. Up to that point the only Native Americans I had seen were the ones in John Wayne movies, Tonto, and winos on skid row in Seattle. My mom was definitely tuned into the social changes that were going on in the 1960s. When Dr. Martin Luther King, Jr. was assassinated, my parents grieved. My best friend from down the street told me his parents were glad King was shot. My parents also supported César Chávez and the United Farm Workers when they started the grape boycott. I was not allowed to eat grapes and was not happy about that.

Now I appreciate everything they taught me. Now, I have taught my children tolerance and love just as my parents did for me.

WORLD WAR II

It is probably safe to say that had it not been for World War II, the modern civil rights era might have been delayed. Basically, the Second World War opened the door for sweeping changes in civil rights for women and ethnic minorities in America. The Great Depression had hit minorities especially hard, although some gains were made as a result of FDR's New Deal. When World War II began, most African Americans still lived in a segregated South under harsh and unfair Jim Crow laws. At the beginning of the war, only 2 percent of eligible African Americans in the South were registered to vote. During the war, over a million black soldiers served in uniform. A shortage of workers in defense plants in the North and the West led to a migration of African Americans from the South. High-paying union jobs were available to minorities that had not been available before. Women took these jobs as well. During the war, more than half of the defense plant workers were women. These opportunities gave women and many ethnic minorities a chance to make a decent wage doing important work, economic independence, and upward economic class mobility. When the war was over and women and minorities were asked to go back to the way things were before, the resistance was immediate. Pressing for rights in the South opened a backlash from segregationists like Governor George Wallace of Alabama and Senator Strom Thurmond of South Carolina, among many others.

Another factor in stimulating the beginning of the modern civil rights movement was the rhetoric behind America's war against Hitler's Germany and Imperial Japan. The United States was a democratic nation fighting to free millions of people from the tyranny of a racist and fascist dictator in Germany and an undemocratic military-led regime in Japan. American propaganda pointed out how diverse the United States was and emphasized citizen access to civil rights, regardless of color or creed. After the war, minority groups in America did not forget what was said in wartime propaganda and used that effectively in justifying and bolstering the modern civil rights movement.

Many ethnic minorities served honorably in World War II, despite the military being segregated. Navajo code talkers were vital in the Pacific, the Japanese American 442nd Infantry was one of the most highly decorated units in Europe, and African Americans served proudly and proved the racists wrong when the Tuskegee Airmen had the best record for bomber escort during the war. As a result, there was greater (although not universal) sympathy from white Americans for the civil rights movement. Demographics had changed as a result of wartime jobs and politicians had to recognize more ethnically diverse districts.

Although Congress did not respond to pressure from ethnic minorities and women to address the issue of civil rights, President Truman was upset about the way African Americans were being treated in particular. On December 5, 1946, Truman established the president's Committee on Civil Rights. The committee investigated the status of civil rights in America and was asked to propose solutions to protect the civil rights of all Americans. In 1947 Truman became the first president to address the National Association for the Advancement of Colored People (NAACP).

In December 1947, the president's Committee on Civil Rights issued a report. Among the recommendations were strengthening existing civil rights laws, making the Civil Rights Commission a permanent body, forming a Joint Congressional Committee on Civil Rights, establishing a Civil Rights Division in the Department of Justice, developing federal protection from lynching, creating a Fair Employment Practices Commission, and abolishing unfair voting laws (i.e., poll taxes). Truman sent a special message to Congress on civil rights in February 1948 and demanded that the commission's recommendations be implemented.

DESEGREGATION OF MAJOR LEAGUE BASEBALL

The uniform number 42 has been retired by Major League Baseball. That number belonged to Jackie Robinson. Jack Roosevelt Robinson was born in Cairo, Georgia, in 1919. His early life

FIGURE 9.1. Jackie Robinson

was not easy. His family members were all sharecroppers and Jackie was raised by his single mother in a town filled with prejudice. He excelled in sports and ended up at the University of California, Los Angeles (UCLA), where he was a four-sport athlete: baseball, football, basketball, and track. In 1941 he enlisted in the US Army and became a second lieutenant before legal troubles emerged due to racial discrimination. Honorably discharged, he then played one season of baseball in the Negro Leagues in 1945.

In 1947, Brooklyn Dodgers president Branch Rickey signed Jackie with the plan to break the color barrier in the major leagues. The last African American to play professional baseball was in 1889. The first Latin American major league player was Luis Castro. Born in Colombia, he played 42 games for the Philadelphia Athletics in 1902. The segregation policy in Major League Baseball reflected segregation in the rest of American society in the aftermath of Reconstruction. Jackie was faced with tremendous challenges—physical, mental, and social—when he joined the Dodgers. Other players deliberately tried to hurt him, many of his own teammates ignored him, and crowds heckled him. Branch Rickey asked Jackie not to react to any of the mistreatment for one year, which he was able to do with great moral and physical courage. By meeting this challenge, Jackie opened the door for other African American players. As a result of his tremendous success, Jackie was inducted into the Baseball Hall of Fame in 1962. Once every baseball season, in a tradition started by future Hall of Famer Ken Griffey, Jr., all major league players wear Jackie Robinson's number 42 in tribute.

Born in 1934 in Puerto Rico, Roberto Clemente was probably the finest major league baseball outfielder who ever lived. He debuted with the Pittsburgh Pirates in 1955, right in the middle of the modern civil rights era. Clemente experienced frustration because of racial tension with the fans, the media, other players, and even some of his teammates. The Topps Company, which dominated the baseball card industry, refused to allow Clemente to use his real name on his baseball cards. They insisted on him being called Bob. They claimed that the name Roberto sounded too ethnic. It was not until 1971 that his card displayed his real name. Clemente said that he had been taught never to discriminate against anyone based on ethnicity. Clemente was not only a great outfielder; he was also a tremendous hitter. He was able to get 3,000 hits in his career and is a member of the Baseball Hall of Fame. Unfortunately he died in 1972 in a plane crash trying to deliver food and medical supplies to people in Nicaragua who had suffered through an earthquake. In 1973, Major League Baseball established the Roberto Clemente Award for the major league player who does most to help others through humanitarian and charitable causes.

DESEGREGATION OF THE MILITARY (1948)

In an often overlooked, but critical, step in the modern civil rights era, President Truman banned segregation in the US military by issuing Executive Order 9981 on July 26, 1948. Senior military officials complained, but the Korean War that began in 1950 soon proved that integrated combat units were effective and necessary, in spite of some generals warning that integration would lead to a loss of combat effectiveness. At the end of the Korean War, President Eisenhower used the integrated US military as an example of American freedom. The Soviet Union had started to use American segregation and racial problems in its Communist propaganda, which claimed that American society was racist. This desegregation of the military came six years before the Supreme Court's *Brown v. Board of Education* ruling that desegregated the entire country. It is important to look at some key individuals in the struggle for civil rights in America, keeping in mind that good people have to struggle and work very hard for justice.

Brown v. Board of Education (1954)

In 1954 the US Supreme Court overturned the *Plessy v. Ferguson* ruling of 1896. *Plessy v. Ferguson* gave an official constitutional blessing to segregation. The Supreme Court concluded in the 1954 decision that "separate educational facilities are inherently unequal." The

FIGURE 9.2. Supreme Court Justice Thurgood Marshall

case was named after Oliver Brown of Topeka, Kansas, an African American man whose daughter Linda was forced to go to an all-black school many miles away even though there was an all-white school in their own neighborhood. One of the lead attorneys was Thurgood Marshall, who later became the nation's first African American Supreme Court Justice. The backlash to the *Brown v. Board of Education* decision was immediate, as many southern whites refused to let African Americans into their public schools. When they were forced to comply with the decision, these segregationists pulled their children out of the public school system. *Brown v. Board of Education* set the stage for the legal and social change to come. One of the first major tests of the impact of *Brown v. Board of Education* came in 1955 in Montgomery, Alabama.

THE MONTGOMERY BUS BOYCOTT (1955–1956)

Civil rights activist Rosa Parks was born in 1913, in Tuskegee, Alabama. Her decision to refuse to give up her seat to a white bus passenger led to a city-wide boycott, national media attention, and an opportunity for Dr. Martin Luther King, Jr. to rise to prominence on the national stage. Rosa became a catalyst for the modern civil rights movement.

Rosa was raised by former slaves in rural Alabama and went to segregated schools. She joined the NAACP in 1943 and was very active. In 1955 Rosa was living in Montgomery, Alabama, where the Montgomery City Code required that all public transportation be segregated. On December 1, 1955, Rosa Parks took a seat in the front of a segregated public bus. Eventually, the bus filled up and the driver noticed that several white passengers were standing. He asked four black passengers to give up their seats. Three gave up their seats, but Rosa refused and remained seated. She later said that she was tired of giving in. The police arrested Rosa and later she was released on bail. The NAACP began to organize a boycott of Montgomery's city buses. They formed the Montgomery Improvement Association and elected Dr. Martin Luther King, Jr., minister of the Dexter Avenue Baptist Church in Montgomery, to lead the boycott.

In response to the events in Montgomery, and due to a lawsuit brought to the US District Court, the court declared racial segregation laws unconstitutional. The City of Montgomery appealed, but in November 1956, the US Supreme Court upheld the lower court's ruling. This ruling, coupled with the fact that downtown businesses were suffering financial losses and the bus company was going bankrupt, meant the City of Montgomery had to relent and comply with the court order. The combination of legal action, activism by the African American community, and leadership by Dr. King, made the Montgomery Bus Boycott one of the most successful mass movements against racial segregation in history. In 1996, President Bill Clinton awarded Rosa Parks the Presidential Medal of Freedom, and the following year, she was awarded the Congressional Gold Medal. She died in 2005 at the age of 92.

DR. MARTIN LUTHER KING, JR.

Martin Luther King, Jr. was born on January 15, 1929, in Atlanta, Georgia. In 1948, King earned a sociology degree from Morehouse College, and then attended the Crozer Theological Seminary in Chester, Pennsylvania. During his last year in seminary, King met theologian Reinhold Niebuhr, who became his mentor. King then enrolled at Boston University, eventually earning his Ph.D. degree. In 1954, King became pastor of the Dexter Avenue Baptist Church of Montgomery, Alabama. The media coverage of the boycott made King a national civil rights leader. In January 1957, King, Ralph Abernathy, and 60 other ministers and civil rights activists founded the Southern Christian Leadership Conference (SCLC) to utilize the moral authority and organizing power of black churches. King gained a national platform. In 1959 King visited Mohandas K. Gandhi's birthplace in India. The trip had a profound influence on King, who then renewed and increased his commitment to the American civil rights struggle.

By August of 1960, the sit-ins King had organized were successful in ending segregation at lunch counters in 27 southern cities. King then returned to Atlanta to become co-pastor with his father at Ebenezer Baptist Church. In the spring of 1963, King organized a demonstration in downtown Birmingham, Alabama. City police turned dogs and fire hoses on demonstrators. King was arrested and put in jail along with his supporters and the event drew nationwide attention. In August 1963, King's March on Washington drew more than 200,000 people to the Lincoln Memorial, where he made his famous "I Have a Dream" speech. King's speech led to the passage of the Civil Rights Act of 1964, authorizing the federal government to enforce

FIGURE 9.3. Martin Luther King, Jr.

desegregation of public accommodations and outlawing discrimination in publicly owned facilities. King earned the Nobel Peace Prize in 1964 and was gaining international exposure.

From late 1965 through 1967, King expanded his civil rights movement into larger American cities, including Chicago and Los Angeles. Young black-power leaders in the North and the West thought his methods were too weak and too late. King then refocused and expanded his civil rights efforts to include ending the Vietnam War. His message shifted from equality to an attack on the capitalist economic system and national security structure that he felt promoted inequality. His Poor People's Campaign, because of his international standing, served as a significant threat to the power structure in the United States. King was becoming increasingly radical, and he was warned by other civil rights leaders to moderate his views. In the spring of 1968 he came to Memphis to help sanitation workers who were on strike. Then, on April 4, 1968, while standing on a balcony outside his room at the Lorraine Motel, King was shot. The shooter, James Earl Ray, was later caught. King's assassination caused riots and demonstrations in more than 100 cities across the United States. In 1969 Ray pleaded guilty to killing King, but later he recanted his confession. Ray told many people that he was just part of a conspiracy, but no investigation was ever conducted. Ray died in prison on April 23, 1998. Dr. Martin Luther King's complete vision has not been fulfilled and his legacy has been homogenized to the point that his calls for economic and social justice through democratic socialism are not taught in public schools. It is not just coincidence that King was killed just one year after he began to broaden his appeal, radicalize his message, turn against the war, and attack the power structure of American society.

MALCOLM X

Malcolm Little was born on May 19, 1925, in Omaha, Nebraska. Malcolm's father, Earl Little, was a preacher and supporter of black nationalist leader Marcus Garvey. Malcolm's family was harassed because of his father's black nationalist views and as a result the family moved to Michigan. In 1931, Malcolm's father was murdered by white supremacists, although the local police called it suicide. Malcolm's mother did not recover from her husband's death and was eventually committed to a mental hospital. Malcolm was the only black child in his class and when he told his teacher he wanted to be a lawyer, the teacher said that was not an appropriate ambition for a Negro. Losing hope, Malcolm later moved to Boston, where he began a career of crime. In 1946 he was arrested and sentenced to ten years in jail. Malcolm spent his time in prison reading and learning, trying to make up for dropping out of high school. Malcolm joined the Nation of Islam while in prison, and when he was released in 1952 he changed his name to Malcolm X, the X being a tribute to a lost African name.

Malcolm X moved to Detroit, Michigan, where he worked with the leader of the Nation of Islam, Elijah Muhammad. Malcolm later went on to start Nation of Islam temples in many cities in the eastern United States. He was a passionate, very articulate, and charismatic speaker

FIGURE 9.4. Malcolm X

who tended to alienate and frighten most white people, and even some black people, with his rhetoric. By the early 1960s, Malcolm X had emerged as a leading voice of a radical wing of the civil rights movement, presenting an alternative to Dr. Martin Luther King, Jr.

In 1963, Malcolm X found out that Elijah Muhammad had fathered children outside of his marriage. His open disapproval of Muhammad, coupled with Malcolm's increasing popularity and his off the cuff remarks after the JFK assassination, caused the Nation of Islam to remove him in 1964. That same year, Malcolm X travelled to Africa and the Middle East, and converted to what he called true Islam. He came to see the American civil rights movement as part of a global anti-colonial struggle, and increasingly embraced socialism and pan-Africanism. He went on a pilgrimage to Mecca and worshipped with fellow Muslims who had blue eyes and blonde hair. This had a profound impact on Malcolm, as he came to see his cause as being much broader than he had first imagined. At that point he changed his name to El-Hajj Malik El-Shabazz.

After his epiphany during his time in Mecca, Malcolm was set to turn his ideological trans-formation into a new, more moderate direction that would have coincided with Martin Luther King, Jr.'s turn toward socialism. What could have been a great and powerful partnership never came to be because Malcolm was assassinated by members of the Nation of Islam on February 21, 1965, at the Audubon Ballroom in New York. He was only 39 years old. Malcolm was being watched by the FBI and the CIA. It is not surprising that Malcolm X was killed when his views became more moderate, making him a greater threat to the power structure in America.

CÉSAR CHÁVEZ

César Chávez born near Yuma, Arizona, on March 31, 1927. When he was young, Chavez and his family worked in the fields as migrant farm workers. Cesar was a community and labor organizer in the 1950s, and he went on to found the National Farm Workers Association in 1962 and the United Farm Workers (UFW) in 1972. The UFW had its first strike against grape growers in California in 1965. In early 1968, Chavez called for a national boycott of California table grape growers. As a result of this pressure, several growers signed contracts with the union. César Chávez used nonviolent means to bring attention to the terrible working and living conditions for farm workers. He led marches, called for boycotts, and went on several hunger strikes. Chávez also brought attention to the dangers of pesticides. His dedication and sacrifice led to support from Robert F. Kennedy and Jesse Jackson. César is one of the greatest civil rights and labor leaders in US history and he influenced the rise of Chicano activism in the 1960s and 1970s and the Latino civil rights movement as well. Like all true civil rights leaders, César put his life on the line. It is believed that César's hunger strikes contributed to his early death at age 66 on April 23, 1993.

FIGURE 9.5. César Chávez

BETTY FRIEDAN

Betty Friedan was born as Bettye Naomi Goldstein on February 4, 1921, in Peoria, Illinois. Friedan graduated from Smith College in 1942 with a degree in psychology. She then moved to New York City to work as a reporter. In 1947 she married Carl Friedan. They had three children. Feeling restless and unfulfilled as a homemaker, she began to wonder if other women felt the same way she did. Friedan surveyed other graduates of Smith College and that research became the basis of her book *The Feminine Mystique*, published in 1963. In that book, Friedan encourages women to seek new opportunities for themselves and not to be limited by choices imposed upon them by society. The book was a sensation and debunked the myth of the happy homemaker. Her book started what is called the second-wave feminism in the United States. The first wave of feminism began with the first women's rights convention in Seneca Falls, New York, in 1846. Friedan went on to co-found the National Organization for Women (NOW) in 1966. Its goal was to bring women "into the mainstream of American society now [in] fully equal partnership with men." She also fought for abortion rights by establishing the National Association for the Repeal of Abortion Laws in 1969, which eventually led to the *Roe v. Wade* decision in 1973 supporting a woman's right to choose. Betty Friedan died on February 4, 2006.

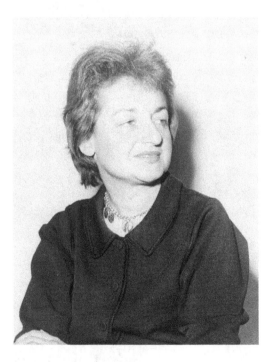

FIGURE 9.6. Betty Friedan

THE AMERICAN INDIAN MOVEMENT

The American Indian Movement (AIM) was founded in 1968 in Minneapolis, Minnesota, by Dennis Banks, George Mitchell, Herb Powless, Clyde Bellecourt, Harold Goodsky, Eddie Benton-Banai, and a number of others in the Minneapolis Native American community. Russell Means came along later, during the 1970s protests. AIM is a Native American advocacy group that was formed to address American Indian sovereignty, treaty issues, spirituality, and leadership. AIM has worked to change America's perception of Native Americans. Martin Luther King, Jr. reached out to AIM during the planning stage of his Poor People's Campaign, a few weeks before his 1968 assassination in Memphis. Around the same time, Robert F. Kennedy

FIGURE 9.7. American Indian Movement (AIM) poster

met with Black Panther representatives in California, and AIM representatives on reservations in Montana, New York, and elsewhere before his assassination on June 6, 1968, in Los Angeles.

From November 1969 to June 1971, AIM participated in the occupation of Alcatraz, an abandoned federal penitentiary in San Francisco Bay, in order to highlight the issues facing Native Americans. On February 27, 1973, tribal elders decided to make a stand and occupied a building on the Pine Ridge Indian Reservation in South Dakota, which led to a siege by the US government. The siege lasted 71 days and drew international attention to the treatment of indigenous people in the United States. The US government responded to the occupation with armored personnel carriers; F-4 Phantom jets; US Marshals; FBI, state, and local law enforcement; and vigilante groups. Two activist occupiers were killed by sniper fire. In May 1973, AIM ended its occupation. The occupation of Wounded Knee was the beginning of what Oglala people refer to as the Reign of Terror, which lasted from 1973 to 1976. Over 60 Native Americans were killed at Pine Ridge during that time and their murders were not investigated by the FBI. The turmoil ended on June 26, 1975, in a shootout with the FBI in which two FBI agents were killed. Leonard Peltier was later convicted for those murders and is still imprisoned, although Amnesty International believes the case against him is weak and circumstantial.

THE BEAT GENERATION

Before there were hippies, there were beatniks. Rejecting the culturally conservative mood of the 1950s, the literary group known as the Beats, the Beat Generation, or the Beat Movement provided literature of raw intensity that tested the limits of creative freedom. The Beat Movement was at its height from the mid-1950s until the early 1960s. Its most celebrated members were John Clellon Holmes, Jack Kerouac, Allen Ginsberg, Lawrence Ferlinghetti, Philip Whalen, Gary Snyder, and Gregory Corso. William S. Burroughs was also associated with the group,

FIGURE 9.8. Jack Kerouac

which was centered in San Francisco and in Greenwich Village in New York City. Journalist Hunter S. Thompson was also part of the Beat Generation. Many beatniks were jazz enthusiasts and a significant number were homosexual or bisexual. Promoting individuality, they attacked materialism, militarism, consumerism, and conformity. They also experimented with drugs and Eastern religions. The Beat Generation infused American writing with new vital energy, and the influence of the Beat writers has been significant, especially when coupled with the civil rights movement and the advent of rock and roll music and socially conscious folk music.

KING OF ROCK AND ROLL?

Although not traditionally covered in a chapter on the civil rights movement, rock and roll played a vital role. The roots of rock and roll music come from African American blues and jazz music, in addition to western, country, and folk music. Elvis Presley is considered the King of Rock and Roll, but the music came before him. Subject to some conjecture, Fats Domino may have recorded the first rock and roll record in the 1940s. Muddy Waters, Robert Johnson, and Howlin' Wolf all contributed to the rise of rock and roll through the blues. Many of the early African American artists were taken advantage of by record companies and lost control of their copyrights. Rock and roll's breakthrough came from white musicians like Bill Haley, Elvis Presley, Carl Perkins, and Jerry Lee Lewis, who re-recorded earlier African American rhythm and blues hits. Later, younger African American artists, like Chuck Berry, Little Richard, and Bo Diddley, emerged into an established rock and roll market, and they

FIGURE 9.9. Fats Domino

were more accepted than earlier artists. Rock and Roll was firmly established by 1954 with big hit songs by Bill Haley, Elvis Presley, and Little Richard. The rebellious spirit of rock and roll is more style than substance. The music of early Bob Dylan, Pete Seeger, and others had social commentary and an element of protest, but, at the end of the day, there is no more pro-capitalist industry than the music industry.

THE FREE SPEECH MOVEMENT

The Free Speech Movement at the University of California, Berkeley, began with a sit-in by 1,000 students in Sproul Hall on December 2, 1964. The next day, 800 of those students were arrested. The informal leaders were students Mario Savio, Michael Rossman, Brian Turner, Bettina Aptheker, Steve Weissman, Art Goldberg, and Jackie Goldberg, among others. The students demanded freedom of speech, the pursuit of academic freedom, and the right to pursue political activities on campus. To that point, the administration had essentially parental control over the students on campus. The Free Speech Movement leaders believed that the university should be run by the students and the faculty. In Savio's phrase, the job of the administration should be merely "to see that the sidewalks get swept." The Free Speech Movement spread to other campuses around the United States, liberating young students to speak their minds without fear. Not surprisingly, college campuses became hotbeds for war protesting over the American war in Vietnam. These campus free speech rights are still in effect today, but they are constantly challenged by over-zealous college administrators and protesters alike. Just recently several community colleges and universities around the United States were legally challenged by free speech organizations who believed that these campuses were being regressive in terms of free speech on campus. Most of these cases resulted in out of court settlements and re-establishment of free speech rights.

THE GAY LIBERATION MOVEMENT

The Stonewall riots were a series of spontaneous demonstrations by members of the gay community in response to a police raid on June 28, 1969, at the Stonewall Inn, in the Greenwich Village neighborhood of New York City. These demonstrations are considered to be the single most important event leading to the gay liberation movement and the modern fight for gay and lesbian rights in the United States. Challenges to old laws dealing with sexuality have been ongoing ever since. Same-sex marriage was upheld by the Supreme Court as legal nationwide in 2015. In 1994, President Bill Clinton instituted the Don't Ask Don't Tell (DADT) policy for the military. Gays and lesbians could serve as long as they stayed in the closet. The US Department of Defense overturned its Don't Ask Don't Tell policy in 2011. Gays and lesbians can now serve openly in the military. The

FIGURE 9.10. The Stonewall Inn

military, which is usually thought of as old fashioned and behind the times, tends to be ahead of the rest of American society. This was not unlike the desegregation of the military in 1948, which came six years before the *Brown v. Board of Education* decision.

How Far Have We Come?

It would be easy to assume that since we have had a president who is part African American and part white, that the United States has overcome its problems with racism. It is also easy to assume that because gays and lesbians can serve in the military, and can get married, that we have overcome homophobia. It can also be assumed that, since women hold more and more positions of power in both the public and the private sectors, our difficulties with sexism are over. In spite of these advances, it is sad that these problems persist in America. Here are some frightening statistics.

These statistics show that we still have a way to go before we can say that we have equal opportunity in America. One look at the makeup of Congress also points out this fact. Women, although they are the majority of the US population, hold only 19.4 percent of the seats in Congress. The current Congress is 80 percent white, 8.6 percent African American, 3.2 percent Hispanic, and 2.1 percent Asian. The general population of the United States is 63 percent white, 12.4 percent African American, 17 percent Hispanic, and 4.4 percent Asian. Ethnic minorities continue to be underrepresented in Congress.

The Pine Ridge Indian Reservation had the lowest per capita income in the entire United States in 2010. Much of the trouble comes from high rates of alcohol or drug dependency, dysfunctional families, and educational failures. Unemployment on Pine Ridge is estimated at around 70 percent. Most of those who work have jobs with the government or for the Oglala

AMERICANS LIVING BELOW THE POVERTY LINE, 2010

Native Americans	27.0 percent
Hispanics	26.6 percent
African Americans	25.8 percent
Asians	12.1 percent
Whites (non-Hispanic)	9.9 percent

FIGURE 9.11. Poverty in America

Sioux tribe itself. Half the population over age 40 on Pine Ridge has diabetes, and tuberculosis runs at eight times the national rate. Around 66 percent of adults are alcoholics; 25 percent of the children are born with fetal alcohol syndrome. The life expectancy is somewhere around 48, which is about the same as for people living in sub-Saharan Africa. Fewer than 10 percent of children graduate from high school.

CONCLUSION

It can take many years of part-time teaching to land a full-time position in college teaching. For six years, while teaching part-time for less than half the pay of a full-time professor, I sent applications out for full-time positions everywhere in the United States and some overseas. Some people told me that the trouble I had getting a full-time teaching job was because I was white and male and only minorities and women were being hired. I chose not to believe that. Women and minorities continue to be underrepresented in academe and racism is persistent in America. But, I also think that there is a vital economic component as well. Dr. Martin Luther King, Jr. made this clear when he started his poor people's campaign. I think that unfairness comes from economic class bias as well as racial, gender, and sexual orientation bias. Harvard, Princeton, Columbia, and Yale graduates get job offers immediately, at least in history. I was told, unofficially of course, that universities want to hire faculty from more prestigious schools because it attracts more donors and research funding. I have found that there is no worse snobbery than intellectual snobbery. When I have delivered papers at academic conferences, they introduce the panel members. One time, I was on a panel and this one historian was introduced as Dr. Smith, a Harvard graduate. When it came to my introduction, they said: "And here is Bruce Solheim." Mid-level schools like Bowling Green State University, where I graduated, generate little interest among potential hiring committees at colleges and universities. Getting into these highly ranked institutions should be based strictly on merit, but we all know that is simply not true. The rich make sure their children get into the best schools and get the top job opportunities. It has come to the point now where the poor working class can ill afford a college education for their children, much less an education at the elite universities. Private prep schools ensure that the children of the rich are better prepared than most students coming from the public school system. It is not impossible for a working-class student to get into Harvard, but it is beyond difficult. Rather than have a national dialog and address real issues of economic class inequality, persistent racism, sexism, and homophobia, those in power trick poor working-class people, minorities, and women into fighting over the scraps.

TIMELINE

1896

May 18: The *Plessy v. Ferguson* decision upholds the constitutionality of segregation.

1920s

The Harlem Renaissance serves as a bridge between the Reconstruction era and the modern civil rights era.

1936

President Franklin D. Roosevelt gets 71 percent of the African American vote signaling a shift of voting allegiance from the Republican to the Democratic Party.

1941

June 25: President Roosevelt issues an executive order banning discrimination against minorities in defense contracts.

1942

February 19: Japanese Americans moved to internment camps.

August 4: The Bracero Program permits Mexican nationals to work in the United States at wages lower than domestic workers.

1947

April 15: Jackie Robinson plays for the Brooklyn Dodgers.

1948

July 26: The US military is desegregated.

1952

The Tuskegee Institute reports that, for the first time in the 71 years it has been keeping records, there were no lynchings of African Americans during the year.

1954

May 17: The *Brown v. Board of Education* decision declares segregation unconstitutional.

1955

August 28: 14-year-old Emmett Till is beaten, shot, and lynched by whites in Mississippi.

December 1: Rosa Parks is arrested.

1956

December 21: After a peaceful boycott led by Dr. Martin Luther King, Jr., the Montgomery, Alabama, bus system is desegregated.

1957

January 10: The Southern Christian Leadership Conference (SCLC) is established.

September 24: Federal troops mobilize to protect the nine African American students at a Little Rock, Arkansas, high school.

1959

January 3: Alaska is admitted as a state.

August 21: Hawaii is admitted as a state. Hiram Fong and Daniel Inouye are the first Asian Americans elected to the US Congress.

1960

February 1: Lunch counter sit-ins begin in North Carolina.

April 17: The Student Non-Violent Coordinating Committee is founded.

1961

May 1: The Freedom Riders start testing segregation laws.

1962

March: The National Farm Workers Association (later the United Farm Workers Union, or UFW) is founded by César Chávez.

October 1: James Meredith becomes the first African American student admitted to the University of Mississippi.

1963

April 16: Dr. Martin Luther King, Jr. writes his "Letter from a Birmingham Jail."

May: Alabama commissioner of public safety Eugene "Bull" Connor orders the use of police dogs and fire hoses on black protesters.

June 11: Governor George Wallace stands in the schoolhouse door at the University of Alabama to try to stop black students from entering.

June 12: Medgar Evers, NAACP field secretary in Jackson, Mississippi, is murdered.

August 28: Dr. Martin Luther King, Jr. delivers his "I Have a Dream" speech.

September 15: Four young black girls are killed in a Birmingham, Alabama, church bombing.

1964

Summer: The Freedom Project begins in Mississippi.

July 1: The Civil Rights Act of 1964 is passed.

August 4: The bodies of three civil rights workers, Michael Schwerner, Andrew Goodman, and James Chaney, are found in Mississippi. The KKK is blamed.

December 1: The Bracero Program is terminated.

1965

February 21: Malcolm X is assassinated in New York.

March 7: Dr. Martin Luther King, Jr. leads a march from Selma to Montgomery, Alabama.

August 10: A Voting Rights Act is approved.

August 11–17: The Watts Riots take place.

September 24: President Johnson enforces affirmative action.

1966

June 30: The National Organization for Women is founded by Betty Friedan.

October 15: The Black Panthers are founded by Bobby Seale and Huey Newton in Oakland, California.

October 29: Civil rights leader Stokely Carmichael first uses the phrase "black power" during a voter registration drive in Mississippi.

1967

April 28: Muhammad Ali, formerly known Cassius Clay, is stripped of his heavyweight boxing title for resisting the military draft.

August 30: Thurgood Marshall becomes the first African American Supreme Court justice.

July: Race riots take place in Detroit and New York.

1968

April 4: Dr. Martin Luther King, Jr. is assassinated in Memphis, Tennessee.

April through May: Race riots throughout the United States.

April 11: President Johnson signs the Civil Rights Act of 1968.

May 27: The Supreme Court rules that "actual desegregation" of schools in the South is required.

June 6: Senator Robert F. Kennedy is assassinated in Los Angeles.

July: The American Indian Movement (AIM) is founded in Minneapolis, Minnesota.

November 5: Representative Shirley Chisholm (Democrat from New York) is the first African American woman elected to Congress.

1969

June 27: A police raid on the Stonewall Inn, a Greenwich Village bar, and subsequent riots is the symbolic beginning of the gay rights movement.

1973

January 22: The Supreme Court, in *Roe v. Wade*, guarantees the right to legal abortion.

February 27: More than 200 Oglala Lakota and followers of the American Indian Movement (AIM) seize and occupy the town of Wounded Knee, South Dakota, on the Pine Ridge Indian Reservation.

July 18: Congress passes Section 504 of the Vocation Rehabilitation Act, barring discrimination against disabled people with the use of federal funds.

December 15: The American Psychiatric Association votes to remove the classification of homosexuality as a mental illness from their manuals.

1974

January 21: The Supreme Court rules that public schools must teach English to students who do not speak English.

1975

The American Medical Association calls for the repeal of all state laws barring homosexual acts between consenting adults.

1977

November 18: The first National Women's Conference, held in Houston, Texas, calls for empowerment of women and equal opportunity.

1978

June 28: The Supreme Court upholds affirmative action, but rejects fixed racial quotas.

1979

October 14: The first Gay and Lesbian Civil Rights March on Washington draws more than 100,000 people.

1982

June 30: The Equal Rights Amendment fails to be ratified.

November: Wisconsin becomes the first state to adopt a civil rights law prohibiting discrimination against gay people.

1984

The Supreme Court rules that states do have the right to outlaw homosexual acts between consenting adults.

1990

July 26: President George H. W. Bush signs the Americans with Disabilities Act, banning job discrimination against people with disabilities and requiring buildings, businesses, and public transportation to be accessible.

1993

July 19: President Bill Clinton announces a "Don't ask, don't tell, don't pursue" policy regarding homosexuals in the military.

2003

June 26: The Supreme Court struck down sodomy laws in Texas and 13 other states.

2008

November 4: Barack Obama is elected president of the United States. He is the first person of African American descent to occupy the White House.

2011

September 20: US Department of Defense drops "Don't Ask, Don't Tell."

2015

June 26: The Supreme Court decides that same-sex marriage is legal nationwide.

CREDITS

1. Fig. 9.1. Bob Sandberg, "Jackie Robinson," LOOK Magazine, vol. 19, no. 4, p. 78. Copyright in the Public Domain.
2. Fig. 9.2. "Supreme Court Justice Thurgood Marshall," http://commons.wikimedia.org/wiki/File:Thurgood-marshall-2.jpg. Copyright in the Public Domain.
3. Fig. 9.3. "Yoichi R. Okamoto, "Martin Luther King, Jr.," White House Press Office, http://commons.wikimedia.org/wiki/File:Martin_Luther_King,_Jr._and_Lyndon_Johnson.jpg. Copyright in the Public Domain.
4. Fig. 9.4. "Marion S. Trikosko, "Malcolm X," U.S. News & World Report Magazine, http://commons.wikimedia.org/wiki/File:Malcolm-x.jpg. Copyright in the Public Domain.
5. Fig. 9.5. Copyright © Joel Levine (CC by 3.0) at http://commons.wikimedia.org/wiki/File:Cesar_chavez_crop2.jpg.

6. Fig. 9.6. Fred Palumbo, "Betty Friedan," New York World-Telegram, http://commons.wikimedia.org/wiki/File:Betty_Friedan_1960.jpg. Copyright in the Public Domain.

7. Fig. 9.7. "American Indian Movement (AIM) poster," Weather Underground, http://commons.wikimedia.org/wiki/File:Pine_Ridge_-_Osawatomie_2.JPG. Copyright in the Public Domain.

8. Fig. 9.8. Copyright © Tom Palumbo (CC BY-SA 2.0) at http://commons.wikimedia.org/wiki/File:Kerouac_by_Palumbo.jpg.

9. Fig. 9.9. Copyright © Heinrich Klaffs (CC BY-SA 2.0) at http://commons.wikimedia.org/wiki/File:Fats_Domino_Hamburg_1973_1605730021.jpg.

10. Fig. 9.10. Copyright © InSapphoWeTrust (CC BY-SA 2.0) at https://www.flickr.com/photos/skinnylawyer/7247504688/.

BROTHERS IN ARMS

BY DR. BRUCE OLAV SOLHEIM WITH ART BY GARY DUMM

VIETNAM – LATE 1960S...

THE WAR IN VIETNAM WAS DIFFERENT FROM ANY OTHER AMERICAN WAR. THERE WERE NO VICTORY PARADES; TRAUMATIZED COMBAT VETERANS CAME HOME ONE BY ONE AND WERE OFTEN MET WITH HOSTILITY OR IGNORED BY THE GENERAL PUBLIC.

ALF SOLHEIM

MY BROTHER SERVED TWO TOURS IN VIETNAM AND IS A DISABLED VET WITH PTSD AND AGENT ORANGE RELATED LEUKEMIA...

DAVID A. WILLSON

MY FRIEND DAVID SERVED AS A CLERK TYPIST OR REMF IN SAIGON. HE IS A NOVELIST AND A FINE POET. DAVID HAS BEEN FIGHTING AGENT ORANGE RELATED MULTIPLE MYELOMA FOR SEVERAL YEARS.

JOHN RONCEVICH

JOHN FOUGHT IN WWII, KOREA, AND VIETNAM. HIS FLASHBACKS, NIGHTMARES, AND PTSD CAME FROM HIS SERVICE IN VIETNAM.

WHILE VISITING THE VET CENTER PTSD THERAPY GROUP IN EAST LOS ANGELES, I NOTICED SOME OF THE VETS SLEEPING. I WAS TOLD THAT THE GROUP IS THE ONLY PLACE MANY OF THE VETS FEEL SAFE ENOUGH TO SLEEP SOUNDLY WITHOUT FEAR AND NIGHTMARES. IN THE GROUP, THEY ARE SURROUNDED AND PROTECTED BY THEIR BROTHERS.

CHAPTER TEN

THE AMERICAN WAR IN VIETNAM

OBJECTIVES

1. Discover the reasons why the United States fought in Vietnam.
2. Comprehend how the United States failed to achieve its objectives in the Vietnam War.
3. Understand the impact of the Vietnam War at home.
4. Examine the legacies of the Vietnam War.

PERSONAL HISTORY

I have taught a Vietnam War history course since 1994 and have always assigned interview assignments to the students. They are asked to interview a Vietnam War–era person. Many of them interview their fathers. One young student came up to me one day, very upset, and I asked him what was wrong. He said that he had asked his father what it was like in Vietnam during the war. His father then made a fist and swung it at his son as hard as he could, stopping just short of the frightened student's face.

"Like that," he said, "only all the fucking time." Of all of the stories I have heard from students and veterans, this one continues to impact me the most. My friend, University of Southern California professor Viet Nguyen, said,

"All wars are fought twice, the first time on the battlefield, the second time in memory." This was never truer than with the American war in Vietnam.

My father's merchant ship arrived in Saigon, Vietnam, in 1939, just before the Japanese invasion of Southeast Asia. Little did he know that 30 years later his son (my brother) would arrive in Saigon—not by ship, but by airplane. My first memory of anything outside of my own immediate family was the assassination of President John F. Kennedy. My father came home from work early, something that he never did. My brother collected newspaper clippings. My parents were very upset, as they were big Kennedy supporters. We only had one presidential portrait hanging in our home—John F. Kennedy. Events seemed to be spiraling out of control in Southeast Asia after Kennedy's assassination, and my parents never believed that Oswald acted alone. My brother volunteered for the US Air Force in 1967 in order to avoid being drafted. Draftees had no choice as to branch or job—most ended up in the Army or Marine Corps and were combat infantry. My brother chose radio school and ended up in South Carolina, and then later in the Philippines. He worked in air conditioned buildings and had a nice clean uniform every day. It was not long until he began receiving letters from his buddies who had not been so lucky and had been drafted and sent to Vietnam. My brother began to feel guilty. Against my mother's wishes he volunteered to go to Vietnam, telling her that he would get more pay.

My brother was assigned in Saigon and once again had a nice job and a decent office to work in. He did write about the occasional VC attack, but had settled into a routine in the midst of the war. This did not last long, as he was then assigned in Quang Tri and Phu Bai in the northern part of South Vietnam. He worked as a mobile radio operator attached to US Marine and Army units. He had found a war. One night while his base was being attacked, he felt he was not going to make it. He remembered calling out for our mother. Half a world away in Seattle, my mother woke up in the middle of the night and told me and my father that she heard my brother's voice and that he was frightened. We figured out later that she heard his voice at precisely the same time my brother called out to her. Every night on the news we watched the body count and film footage from the war. We also saw the war protesters. My dad had no use for the protesters. In fact, he used to take us to the University District in Seattle to see "the freak show," as he called it. We would drive up and down University Avenue and he would point out all of the "spoiled rich kids" who were on drugs and "not serving their country" like my brother. Later in the war, my parents had modified their thoughts about the protesters when the protests moved from the college campuses to neighborhoods and cities, and war veterans joined their ranks. Even my brother began to change. We noticed he signed his letters home with peace symbols and began to question why we were in Vietnam. When my brother returned after two tours of duty in Vietnam and four years in the Air Force, he had changed, almost as if he was another person. The day he came home from Vietnam he locked himself in his room and would not come out for a long time.

Seven years after my brother returned from Vietnam, I joined the army. All of my sergeants had served in Vietnam. Later, when I went to flight school to learn to fly helicopters, my instructor pilots were Vietnam veterans. In 1994, after earning my doctorate in history, I started teaching a Vietnam War history course at Green River Community College in Auburn, Washington. The classroom was the same one that had been used by a previous professor who had died. The classroom had an unusual feel to it. The first day of my class I thought I would start the class off with some video comedy. I chose clips from Eddie Murphy's movie *Trading Places* and Rodney

Dangerfield's *Back to School*. I noticed that one man who sat in the back of the class was not laughing at the humorous scenes, unlike the other students. In fact, he looked very agitated. I had finished my first-day routine, discussed my teaching philosophy, and released the class, when he came up to see me. Some other students lingered as he began to speak.

"That film clip showed something that I just cannot tolerate," he said.

"What was that?" I asked hesitantly.

"I cannot stand imposters … people who say that they were soldiers when they were not. That makes me god-damned mad!" I could see that he was in his late forties and that he was in a great deal of pain, perhaps both mentally and physically. He implied that I was lying when I had said I was a veteran. I told him I had indeed been in the army and would not lie about that. As luck would have it, I had my DD Form 214 (army discharge certificate) with me that day. It was a coincidence because I was making a copy of it to send in with a job application.

"I've put lots of imposters in the hospital," he said, "and I'm not afraid of the law." He was getting more angry and agitated, and began inching closer to my face. His eyes were bulging and his fists began to squeeze harder. Without any further hesitation, I produced the document and gave it to him. He examined it closely, very closely. My adrenaline was pumping as I thought about how I would protect my few remaining students and myself. Then his shoulders heaved downward as if his anger had been released through a relief valve. He looked at me with sorrowful eyes and said:

"I'm sorry, you have to understand, my twin brother died in Vietnam, this is serious shit to me." He never came back to the classroom. The walls of that classroom witnessed many years of teaching the Vietnam War, during and after. There was a familiar sound in the room that I noticed the first day I was there—it sounded like a Huey helicopter. After a few days, I tracked the sound to its source. The sound came from the back of the room by the clock. The clock hands did not move with a ticking sound; rather, they moved with a whop, whop, whop sound, like a Huey helicopter.

Vietnamese History

According to the ancient military treatise by Sun Tzu, the first rule of war is to know your enemy. So what did Americans know of the Vietnamese when they started financing the French colonialists in their war against the Vietnamese Communists (Viet Minh) led by Ho Chi Minh in the early 1950s? Most Americans did not know that the Vietnamese had been struggling for their independence since 100 BC. There are three basic things everyone should know about Vietnamese history:

1. The Vietnamese are an ancient people.
2. Vietnamese people have a history of successful struggle against foreign invaders.
3. The traditional enemy of Vietnam is China.

The Viet people originated in the Red River valley of North Vietnam in the first millennium BC. Just because people live in thatched-roof huts with dirt floors does not mean that they are ignorant. The Vietnamese people were perfectly adapted to their environment. After nearly 3,000 years, a people can learn a lot. American policy makers never really understood or appreciated the ancient wisdom of the Vietnamese people.

Vietnam was invaded by China in 100 BC. Generations of Vietnamese then struggled and fought the Chinese until AD 900, when they were finally expelled. In the 1850s the French arrived to colonize Indochina, which included Vietnam, Laos, and Cambodia. Nearly 100 years later, the French were defeated in 1954 by the forces of Ho Chi Minh's Viet Minh army and they left for good. For five years during World War II, the Japanese controlled Vietnam. They were defeated and left in 1945. The United States picked up where France left off in 1954 by attempting to build an independent South Vietnamese state. US troops were sent in to Vietnam in 1965 and the last US troops left in January 1973. The Vietnamese people never lose because they never give up. Because China borders Vietnam, and was the only country to keep its grip on Vietnam for a significant period of time, Vietnamese people have a great respect for the country they call the Great Dragon. Had American policy planners understood these three basic things about Vietnamese history, they may have come up with a different strategy for implementing US security interests in Southeast Asia.

THE AMERICAN WAR IN VIETNAM

When Ho Chi Minh, a Vietnamese nationalist leader since World War I, declared independence for Vietnam in 1946 after the Japanese were defeated, he expected the United States to support the Vietnamese people's right to self-determination. The United States instead decided to side with the French, who wanted to reestablish their colony in Vietnam. War broke out between the French and the Viet Minh in 1946. By 1953 the United States was paying for 80 percent of the French war effort as part of our Cold War strategy. Eventually the French were defeated at Dien Bien Phu in 1954. At the subsequent peace negotiations in Geneva, the Viet Minh and France agreed (in the Geneva Accords) to temporarily divide Vietnam in half at the 17th parallel. Unifying elections were to take place in 1956.

Meanwhile, a Catholic named Ngo Dinh Diem was named president of South Vietnam under the French and accepted by the Americans as a legitimate alternative to Communist Ho Chi Minh. When Diem decided to not hold elections in 1956, because he knew he would lose to Ho Chi Minh, the United States backed his decision and began a nation-building effort in South Vietnam, providing millions of dollars of funding to the South Vietnamese Army (ARVN) and government. At this point, Ho Chi Minh knew that reunification of Vietnam would have to be by force. Throughout the 1950s, President Dwight D. Eisenhower kept the number of military advisers to a minimum. John F. Kennedy would dramatically increase the number of advisers in the early 1960s. Before Eisenhower left office, he gave his farewell address. In that famous address Eisenhower referred to something he called the

FIGURE 10.1. Nguyen Ai Quoc (Ho Chi Minh)

military–industrial complex. Eisenhower warned us that the permanent arms industry that had been established after World War II could lead to misplaced power and undue influence by the military–industrial complex (a combination of defense industry, military, and government power). If this was to happen, our liberties and way of life would be endangered. Given the fact that Eisenhower was a conservative, pro-business Republican who served as supreme allied commander in Europe during World War II, his warning should have been taken very seriously.

The North Vietnamese began infiltrating and invading South Vietnam with men and material. Not long after, the South Vietnamese who resisted Ngo Dinh Diem formed the National Liberation Front, also known as the Viet Cong (VC), in 1960. The VC were guerrilla fighters bent on toppling the South Vietnamese government backed by the United States. America provided money, supplies, weapons, and training for the South Vietnamese government, with the intent of creating a strong and independent South Vietnamese state that could repel the North Vietnamese Communists. The problem was that the more aid the United States gave to South Vietnam, the less independent they became. Without a strong sense of national cohesion, South Vietnam could not survive. By the fall of 1963 the Diem government was starting to lose its grip

FIGURE 10.2. Dwight D. Eisenhower, John Foster Dulles, and Ngo Dinh Diem

on power and was forced to crack down on the protesting Buddhists. Since Diem was a Catholic, the attack against the Buddhists (Vietnam is about 95 percent Buddhist) backfired on him. As a result the South Vietnamese military began to plan a coup, with US government backing. It should be noted that President Kennedy did not know that Diem and his brother Nhu would be killed in the operation. With Diem and his brother gone, all of the succeeding South Vietnamese leaders threw off any restraint regarding use of American forces. Only one obstacle remained in the way of a major war in Vietnam.

JOHN F. KENNEDY

President John F. Kennedy (JFK), the 35th president of the United States, was the first Catholic ever elected to that office. He was the son of Joseph Kennedy, who served as ambassador to England before World War II. Young Jack Kennedy was a naval war hero in World War II. His boat, the PT 109, was rammed by a Japanese destroyer and he helped rescue 11 members of his crew. Although JFK took responsibility for the failed Bay of Pigs invasion of Cuba in 1961, he did lead America through one of the most significant crises in US history: the Cuban Missile Crisis in October 1962. His handling of the Cuban Missile Crisis is still taught as a model for crisis management. This incident was the closest the world has come to all out nuclear war. Kennedy's assassination in November 1963 was of great significance, especially as it relates to the Vietnam War.

FIGURE 10.3. President John F. Kennedy

THE DUAL ASSASSINATIONS

NGO DINH DIEM

President Ngo Dinh Diem was not a very popular or effective president, but he did resist all attempts to bring US troops into combat in South Vietnam. He wanted US dollars, equipment, training, and military advisers, but no US troops. As he became less democratic in order to crack down on dissent, especially by Buddhists, the US government had to disapprove of Diem and his actions. President Kennedy sent a signal to Diem in an interview with newsman Walter Cronkite in which he hinted that perhaps a change in personnel would be in order. Kennedy did not want Diem to be killed, but the CIA did give a green light to the coup. Diem and his brother Nhu were killed by ARVN generals on November 2, 1963. General Duong Van Minh (Big Minh) assumed the leadership of South Vietnam after Diem's assassination. Former US ambassador Frederick Nolting felt that it was wrong not to tell Diem that the United States favored the coup, especially after being allies for nine years. The key point to take away is that the only resistance to allowing US troops to fight in South Vietnam was removed with Diem's assassination.

JFK ASSASSINATION

Only 20 days after Diem was assassinated, President Kennedy was assassinated in Dallas, Texas. JFK assassination conspiracy theories abound. There are more books in the Library of Congress about the JFK assassination than there are about Elvis. Nearly 80 percent of the American people believe that there was some sort of conspiracy involved with the assassination of JFK. Yet, even after a release of documents and a congressional investigation in the late 1970s, no definitive proof exists. Conspiracy theorists point to the fact that all principals and witnesses are dead and that the government has had many decades to clean up any smoking gun in the files. What we do know is that shortly after Kennedy's assassination, President Lyndon B. Johnson dramatically expanded the war in Vietnam. What would Kennedy have done in Vietnam? Kennedy told some of his inner circle that he would pull out the military advisers after the elections of 1964. To others he said that the United States must hold the line in Vietnam, but he did not elaborate on just how he would do that.

His supporters argue that JFK held the dual objectives in Vietnam of stopping communism and relying on indigenous military support to do so. His detractors contend that those objectives were incompatible, since the administration had misread the nationalist political current in Vietnam and chose to support an unpopular and weak government that would eventually fall, leading to heavy US military involvement in order to achieve the first objective. Kennedy's ad hoc style of leadership makes predicting his eventual course in Vietnam uncertain. Some say he would have found a way out, others say he would have done much the same as Lyndon Johnson did. Evidence seems to indicate that Kennedy was holding two different ideas at once, but did indeed plan the withdrawal of advisers from Vietnam. According to Secretary of Defense Robert McNamara, in the November 2, 1963, National Security Council meeting, Kennedy's action had three elements: (1) complete withdrawal from Vietnam by December 31, 1965; (2) withdrawal of the first 1,000 troops by the end of 1963; and (3) a public announcement to set these decisions in concrete. In other words, had Kennedy not been assassinated, there would not have been a Vietnam War.

Lyndon B. Johnson (LBJ) fell into the trap that Kennedy and even Johnson himself had recognized. Johnson decided to allow covert action (OPLAN 34A) authorizing commando raids on the North Vietnamese coastline. A Norwegian intelligence officer named Alf Martens Meyer recruited three Norwegian sailors to participate in these raids. The Norwegians ran SWIFT boats from Da Nang, with South Vietnamese commandos onboard. These coastal raids precipitated the Tonkin Gulf incident, and subsequently the Tonkin Gulf resolution that authorized the Vietnam War. Recent tapes released from the Johnson Library indicate that LBJ was aware of the trap that Vietnam presented very early in the war. The question remains, why did he then proceed with the war? What is clear, however, is that the Kennedy administration left its successors with a heavy burden. JFK had apparently ruled out a diplomatic solution in Vietnam, but he did not have a clear vision for a military solution, either. Kennedy's government had played a role in Diem's overthrow, and that act deepened America's involvement in Southeast Asia. Kennedy's assassination in Dallas only three weeks after Diem's signaled a turning point for the United States in Vietnam.

Everyone agrees that on November 22, 1963, President John F. Kennedy was assassinated, and that the head shot was the fatal wound. Beyond that, there is not much agreement. President Kennedy, Texas governor John Connally, and a bystander named James Tague were all hit by bullets that day. Kennedy was killed by a fatal shot to the head from a high-powered

FIGURE 10.4. Lee Harvey Oswald being shot by Jack Ruby

rifle, while Connally was critically injured and James Tague hit by a fragment on his cheek. Lee Harvey Oswald was named the lone assassin by a presidential commission headed by Supreme Court Chief Justice Earl Warren. The Warren Commission report said that Oswald fired three shots from the sixth floor of the Texas School Book Depository. Oswald was assassinated by a Mafia-connected nightclub owner named Jack Ruby in the basement of the Dallas Police Station on November 24, 1963. There was no trial.

JFK was shot in his open-top limousine while travelling through Dealey Plaza in Dallas, Texas, at 12:30 p.m. on November 22, 1963. The fatal shot occurred on Elm Street just after the car took a sharp turn from Houston Street, heading toward the triple underpass. The Warren Commission findings say that three shots were fired by Oswald from a World War II Italian Carcano bolt action rifle on the sixth floor of the Texas School Book Depository. They claim that the first shot missed the motorcade entirely, and the second shot hit Kennedy and Connally. The third shot hit Kennedy in the head and killed him.

The question as to why JFK was killed remains contested. The official US government version, as revealed by the Warren Commission, says that Oswald, the lone assassin, was a Communist and wanted Kennedy dead because of his treatment of Cuba. Conspiracy theorists have pointed to many other potential players in the assassination: the Mafia, CIA, FBI, Fidel Castro, anti-Castro Cubans, and Russians. The most significant result of Kennedy's assassination was the Vietnam War. Was JFK killed because he did not want a major war in Vietnam? Did the Mafia want to kill Kennedy because he and his brother Robert were going after organized crime, and JFK had slept with the Chicago mob boss's girlfriend? Was it retaliation for his firing of CIA director Allen Dulles and deputy CIA director General Charles Cabell after the failed Bay of Pigs invasion? Had the Kennedys stepped on J. Edgar Hoover's toes too many times? Did Castro want JFK killed as revenge for the many plots to kill him? Did the anti-Castro Cubans want Kennedy to be killed for his failure to bail them out in the Bay of Pigs? Or did the Russians want to get rid of Kennedy for embarrassing them in the Cuban Missile Crisis? No one knows for sure, but what is clear is that many people had motives.

There are many facets to the case. One interesting one is Lee Harvey Oswald. Oswald was born in New Orleans, Louisiana, in 1939 and joined the US Marine Corps in 1956. In 1959 he defected to the Soviet Union and later married a Russian girl whose father was in the KGB (the Russian version of the CIA). In 1961 Oswald returned to the United States with his Russian bride, and they were never questioned or prosecuted. This fact alone seems to indicate that Oswald was a CIA operative. And why did Jack Ruby kill Oswald? The Warren Commission says that Ruby wanted to spare Mrs. Kennedy from a long trial. Ruby never spoke officially and died in a prison hospital. People who knew Ruby, like former night club singer Beverly Oliver, say that he had no love for Kennedy and was not altruistic in the least. Oliver also said that Jack Ruby introduced her to Lee Harvey Oswald at the Carousel Club in Dallas.

"This is my friend Lee from the CIA," he told her.

Another interesting facet of the case is the Zapruder film. The 8-millimeter home movie, shot by Abraham Zapruder, shows the president being shot twice, including the fatal head shot. It also establishes the timing of the shooting sequence to 5.6 seconds. The Zapruder film seems to show Kennedy being shot from the front, because his head moves back and to the left. The key to the Warren Commission findings is in the second shot, the one that hit Kennedy (but did not kill him) and struck Governor Connally. This is known as the magic bullet. The magic bullet supposedly struck JFK and Connally, and came out in pristine condition. Most ballistics experts agree, and common sense would dictate, that a bullet passing through two people would not come out in pristine condition as the Warren Commission claimed. Although circumstantial, it is interesting to note that the mayor of Dallas during the time of the assassination was Earle Cabell, the brother of deputy CIA director Charles Cabell, whom Kennedy had fired. Also, Gerald Ford served on the Warren Commission and then later became the only US president not elected by the American people, in 1974 after Nixon's resignation. This author has his own theory: the chaotic conspiracy theory. If enough people want you dead, you will end up dead. Also, people who want you dead can work toward a common goal even if they are unaware of each other and not coordinating their plans. It is this author's contention that several assassins were in Dallas that day. Because the assassins were operating independently, each plot was separate and compartmentalized with no long chain of command and organization. Probably the most damaging evidence against the Warren Commission findings are the stories from Dr. Charles Crenshaw, Dr. Robert N. McClelland, and other Parkland doctors who said that Kennedy was hit from the front. Dr. Crenshaw treated JFK in the trauma room at Parkland Hospital and says the official autopsy is a fraud.

Escalation of the War

For Americans to go to war, there usually has to be an emotional trigger event. For the Vietnam War it was the Gulf of Tonkin incident. On August 2, 1964, the USS *Maddox* was attacked by North Vietnamese patrol boats while providing signal intelligence and support for South Vietnamese coastal raiders off the coast of North Vietnam. On August 4 another attack was reported. In response to the actual attack of August 2, and the suspected attack of August 4, President Lyndon B. Johnson ordered Seventh Fleet carrier forces to launch retaliatory strikes against North Vietnam. On August 7, 1964, Congress overwhelmingly passed the Tonkin Gulf Resolution (with only two dissenting votes), which enabled Johnson to employ military force as he saw fit against the North Vietnamese Communists. CIA deputy director for intelligence Ray S. Cline verified that the second attack never took place, but he found it not unusual that reports are inaccurate given the circumstances, where quick decisions had to be made in a crisis.

In 1977, former under secretary of state George Ball claimed in an interview that the patrols by US destroyers were primarily for provocation, to give the United States an excuse to intervene militarily. The bottom line is that the authorization for the Vietnam War was based on an incident that did not occur. This is not without precedent. The Spanish-American War was also launched based on a misconception—Spain was blamed for an explosion that blew up the USS *Maine*, when in fact it was caused by a mechanical failure. Johnson began the air war against North Vietnam using airbases in South Vietnam and aircraft carriers stationed in the South China Sea.

FIGURE 10.5. Lyndon B. Johnson

In March 1965, Johnson ordered a sustained bombing campaign, Rolling Thunder, to break the will of the Communists. US Air Force units stationed in South Vietnam flew the first raids. The problem was that base security provided by the South Vietnamese was not working, and American aircraft were being destroyed on the ground by the VC. The Air Force requested two units of Marines to protect their bases. The buildup of US military ground units was beginning. The defensive posture did not last long as US forces began offensive operations around the airbases and extended their reach. This strategy of searching for the VC and the North Vietnamese Army (NVA) and engaging them became known as "search and destroy." The US military was fighting both a conventional and a guerrilla war. The North Vietnamese and the Viet Cong were supported by both the Soviet Union and Communist China.

THE TET OFFENSIVE

The United States slowly escalated the war, with planners making sure that each month did not seem that much different from the last. By 1968 there were more than 500,000 US troops in South Vietnam. The American public was told that the war was being won because more Communists were being killed than Americans or South Vietnamese troops. The necessity of the war was supported by the Domino Theory. This overly simplistic theory held that South Vietnam, if allowed to fall, would set off a chain reaction of dominoes falling until reaching the final domino, the United States. In January and February 1968, the NVA and VC changed their strategy by trying to win the war in a single blow—the Tet Offensive

The Communists hoped that the ARVN would fall apart, causing panic with the civilian population who would then overthrow the government. The Communists did not achieve

FIGURE 10.6. Wounded US soldier during the Tet Offensive

either of these goals. The result of this failure was that they lost a large part of their forces. Tens of thousands of the best VC guerrillas had gone into the cities, and when the population did not rise up to support them, and the ARVN did not collapse, a large proportion of these fighters were killed. This weakened the VC organization in the countryside very drastically, and it never completely recovered. The Communist apparatus in the South became much more dependent on North Vietnamese support than it had been previously. The Vietnam War became more of a conventional war and less of a guerrilla war after the Tet Offensive.

The Tet Offensive was militarily a defeat for the Communists, and it had weakened them very substantially. However, it was a political victory. There were several reasons for this:

1. The Communist forces were stronger than the US government had admitted, causing a credibility gap.
2. Americans witnessed the brutality of the war, which dramatically impacted public opinion.
3. Many Americans were killed in the Tet battles.

A Gallup poll taken in November 1967 showed that only 8 percent of Americans thought the United States was losing the war. In February 1968, after Tet, 23 percent of Americans thought the United States was losing. Some, such as Military Assistance Command Vietnam Commander General William Westmoreland, blamed the media. The fact is, although the media was more critical of US action in Vietnam by 1968, it did not devise the faulty ground and air war strategies. The US government alone is to blame for ill-conceived strategies in Vietnam.

THE HOME FRONT

War protesters never achieved any level of sympathy with the American public, except for some of the veteran protesters. War protesting started on college campuses, but after 1968 began to spread into the cities and suburban areas, and college-age protesters were joined by older Americans. The American public was basically forced to choose between being a hawk or a dove. A hawk was someone who favored the war, and a dove was someone against the war. This divided families, communities, and the nation. The main purpose the war protests had was to remind everyone that a war was going on and forcing the issue into people's living rooms every night. Johnson was disappointed that the Vietnam War and the protesting were taking the spotlight off of his Great Society program.

LBJ was fighting two wars at once: the war in Vietnam and the War on Poverty. His Great Society program sought to wipe out poverty in America. His two-front war efforts bankrupted the nation. The country had not been so divided since the Civil War. Many US veterans were coming back from Vietnam with changed perspectives. Many decorated veterans flung away

FIGURE 10.7. Hugh Thompson

their medals on the steps of the Capitol in protest of the war. The Vietnam War was winding down, casualties were decreasing, but those veterans who opposed the war were also reminding America of the losses and how the war had hit home. By the time he announced his decision not to run for reelection in March, Johnson's approval rating was 35 percent. The Vietnam War had destroyed Johnson's presidency, the War on Poverty was falling apart, and the very social structure of the country was off balance by the end of 1968. Public support for the war had gone from a high of 59 percent in 1966 to 35 percent in August 1968.

President Johnson's Great Society domestic programs, built with bipartisan support, were threatened by an ever-widening war in Vietnam. In 1964 and early 1965, Johnson's commitment to South Vietnam was taken at face value by most Americans. Early antiwar groups and opponents of the war were small and little noticed. They included civil rights activists, members of the old left, women's organizations, pacifists, students, and clergymen. The draft seemed inherently unfair. College students could avoid military service if they remained in school. Prior to 1968, it was clear that African Americans were doing more than their share of the fighting. Statistics show that at the beginning of the war, blacks constituted 20 percent of the combat deaths even though they only constituted 12 percent of the total US population. With college deferments readily available, anyone who could afford to go to school could avoid the draft. As a result, much of the fighting force in Vietnam was working class or poor. Estimates are that of the enlisted men in Vietnam, 25 percent were poor and 55 percent were working class. To add to the sense of disenfranchisement, 18-year-old combat soldiers were not allowed to vote until 1971, when the Twenty-Sixth Amendment lowered the voting age.

As the war dragged on into 1967, criticism grew. The war was already turning the economy sour by 1967, as Johnson was forced to raise taxes to pay for the war in Vietnam and his War on Poverty.

Martin Luther King's assassination on April 4, 1968, rocked the nation and sparked riots in more than a hundred cities. Black power militancy increased. Unlike most political leaders, Robert F. Kennedy had sympathized with King's opposition to the war. Almost assured of a Democratic nomination, and likely the presidency, Robert F. Kennedy was shot dead on June 6, 1968, in Los Angeles. His assassin was Sirhan Sirhan, who to this day claims to have no memory of the event. Suspicion was raised once more, especially since RFK's killing had taken place only two months after King's. The country seemed to be on the brink of self-destruction after having four major assassinations in the span of only five years (John F. Kennedy in 1963, Malcolm X in 1965, and Martin Luther King, Jr. and Robert Kennedy in 1968).

If things were not bad enough, *Life* magazine published pictures of Vietnamese peasants massacred in 1968 by US soldiers in a village called My Lai. The trial of Lieutenant William Calley and others implicated in the My Lai massacre dominated the news for months. Only Calley was convicted, amid controversy and a terrible national reckoning of the nature of the war in Vietnam. The American public wavered between labeling Calley a murderer and seeing him as a victim. The court martial was carefully run by the military. The army deliberately chose very tall guards for Calley, to make him seem even smaller and less significant (he was just over five feet tall). There were heroes at My Lai. Warrant Officer Hugh Thompson was one of them. He and his crew were able to rescue many Vietnamese villagers, including children by flying them out of harm's way. It was not until 1998 that Thompson and his fellow crew members (Larry Colburn and Glenn Andreotta) were recognized for their bravery and humanity and awarded the Soldier's Medal. The continuing war was becoming more and more of a liability to the president. Nixon responded by reducing draft calls and instituting a lottery system.

NIXON'S PEACE WITH HONOR

When Richard Nixon was elected, he implemented his Peace with Honor Plan:
1. begin Vietnamization,
2. increase the bombing,
3. establish negotiations, and
4. expand the war geographically into Laos and Cambodia.

The process of Vietnamization meant that the United States would start bringing troops home and handing the war over to the South Vietnamese. The French had tried doing the same in the early 1950s. Nixon also increased bombing in an attempt to get North Vietnam to the negotiating table. It worked, but at the cost of more protesting and international disapproval, as more than 1,200 civilians per month were being killed in the US bombing of North

Vietnam. After the news leaked that Nixon had ordered troops into Cambodia to stop North Vietnamese infiltration and resupply, the Kent State University ROTC (Reserve Officers' Training Corps) hall was burned down by an arsonist. On May 4, 1970, student protesters confronted Ohio National Guardsmen. Some guardsmen fired into the crowd. Four students were killed. On May 14, 1970, two African American students were killed by Jackson police and many more were wounded. As a result, student protests erupted on hundreds of campuses, forcing many to shut down. Nixon's handling of student protests was heavy-handed and led to further polarization. He could have reached out to the more moderate antiwar groups to bridge differences, but he chose not to.

Operation Lam Son 719 was an example of Nixon's Vietnamization plan. In February and March of 1971, the ARVN invaded Laos with US logistical and air support. The objective was to take the city of Tchepone and hold it briefly, then retreat, thereby testing the effectiveness of Vietnamization. In the process the ARVN was supposed to disrupt enemy supply lines along the Ho Chi Minh trail (the series of trails and dirt roads leading from North Vietnam, through Laos and Cambodia, and into South Vietnam). The hastily planned operation was a mess from the beginning. The United States would not share intelligence information and the South Vietnamese generals were too busy fighting with each other to engage the enemy. Massive US airpower saved many of the ARVN troops, but the operation proved that the ARVN could not fight alone.

THE END OF THE WAR AND RICHARD NIXON

In February 1972, Nixon shocked the world when he visited Communist China. Nixon offered the Chinese trade recognition as China's isolation was coming to an end. Nixon played his China card in hopes of driving a negotiating wedge between Russia and China, and using China's influence to negotiate a favorable settlement in Vietnam. In spite of these efforts, on March 31, 1972, the North Vietnamese launched a new offensive, crossing over the 17th parallel into South Vietnam. Using large units and tanks, they quickly captured Quang Tri Province. Not wanting to engage US troops, but wanting to respond, Nixon ordered the mining of Haiphong Harbor and increased the bombing. Nearly a thousand American aircraft struck both North and South Vietnam. The North Vietnamese offensive was halted, temporarily.

In July 1972, during the waning days of US military involvement in Vietnam, actress Jane Fonda incurred the wrath of Vietnam veterans and their families when she arrived in Hanoi, North Vietnam, and began a two-week tour of the country. Fonda visited North Vietnamese villages, hospitals, schools, and factories damaged in the war. Her comments about what she observed at those sites, along with her criticism of US military policy, was broadcast as propaganda to US servicemen via Radio Hanoi. Fonda met with international visitors and reporters who were also in North Vietnam, and spent about an hour talking to seven American POWs and posed for photographs at an antiaircraft gun emplacement set up in a rural area just

FIGURE 10.8. Richard M. Nixon

outside Hanoi. Although her motive was to do what she could to end the war, her actions and methods were perceived as traitorous and led to her gaining the nickname: Hanoi Jane. She has since apologized and admitted that she had been naive, but the rumors and hatred persist.

Nixon and Henry Kissinger (Nixon's National Security Adviser) had forged an agreement with the Communists that allowed them to keep NVA troops in South Vietnam in exchange for the return of American prisoners of war. Nixon was unable to convince the South Vietnamese to sign, so the North Vietnamese made the agreement public in October 1972, which basically forced the South Vietnamese to go along with the agreement because it was clear the United States would go ahead with or without them. On January 11, 1973, Kissinger notified Nixon that the agreement was ready. The terms were almost the same as those presented in October when South Vietnam refused to sign. Le Duc Tho, the chief North Vietnamese negotiator, was prepared to sign. The agreement established that South Vietnam was one country with two governments. There were to be moves toward reconciliation, prisoners of war would be released, American troops would leave, and NVA forces could remain in the South. Lyndon Johnson, the president who had sent US combat troops to Vietnam eight years earlier, died the day before the agreement was signed. Sadly, over 58,000 American troops had died in Vietnam to achieve this less-than-adequate agreement. On January 27, 1973, all parties signed the peace agreement. Hanoi celebrated with fireworks, but Vietnam was still divided.

A key vote on June 19, 1973, sealed the fate of South Vietnam. On that day, Congress passed the Case Church Amendment that forbade any further US military involvement in Southeast Asia. North Vietnam was now free to invade South Vietnam without fear of US bombing retaliation. Later, in November 1973, Congress passed the War Powers Resolution that required the president to obtain the support of Congress within 90 days of sending American troops abroad. After Nixon resigned, Congress dramatically cut aid to South Vietnam. The ARVN were underfunded, demoralized, and lacking in leadership and support.

The Communists welcomed the January 1973 agreement as recognition of their legitimacy. They did not see themselves as aggressors. They saw the Americans as the aggressors. In 1973, both sides knew the struggle was not over. Two huge armies, one equipped by America, the other by the Soviet Union, were prepared for the final battle for control of a devastated country. Whether they were hawks or doves, by 1973 most Americans believed that the cost of the war, especially in terms of lives, had been too much. They came to the realization that no more Americans should die for Vietnam. After the agreement was signed, the American POWs began to come home from Hanoi. As the POW homecoming was shown on American television and the last American troops left, it was nearly forgotten that America still held a commitment to the South Vietnamese government.

WATERGATE

The so-called third-rate burglary at the Democratic National Headquarters in June 1972 did not affect the reelection of Richard Nixon, because his administration did everything they could to cover it up. Nixon had been obsessed with leaks since the release of the *Pentagon Papers* in 1971. Although none of the leaked documents related to the Nixon administration, they did reveal a pattern of deception around the true purpose of the war in Vietnam. The public trust had been betrayed, and Nixon would pay the price. His paranoia led to his order to bug the Democratic National Headquarters at the Watergate office complex, and to photograph or perhaps steal documents, despite the fact that George McGovern, the Democratic challenger, had no chance of winning. This, of course, leads one to believe that it was not just a third-rate burglary as the Nixon administration called Watergate. Recent

FIGURE 10.9. South Vietnamese refugees

research has shown that the real target of the Watergate burglars (who were all CIA affiliated) was embarrassing documents related to Nixon's involvement with the Mafia in trying to kill Fidel Castro in Cuba. Nixon had the election in the bag, so it had to be something more than just bugging the office. The Watergate story broke in June 1972 and the Nixon administration denied any link. The investigation began and indictments were handed down. In spite of this, Nixon was reelected in November 1972. In March 1973 the Senate began investigating the Watergate scandal. On May 18, 1973, the Senate Watergate Committee began its nationally televised hearings. The Watergate hearings revealed a link to the Vietnam War and Nixon's domestic covert actions against the antiwar movement.

As Nixon's power decreased with each passing day of the Watergate hearings, his ability to intimidate the Communists in Vietnam also diminished. Nixon ended the draft and the troops had come home, so to most Americans the war was over. Matters got worse for the Nixon administration when Vice President Spiro T. Agnew was forced to resign, because of charges of tax evasion and taking bribes, on October 10, 1973. Congressman Gerald R. Ford was nominated and confirmed as vice president. Meanwhile, with negotiations ongoing in Vietnam, Nixon had made a secret pledge to South Vietnamese president Nguyen Van Thieu. If the Communists broke the cease-fire agreement, America would reenter the war in full force. But Nixon could not back up his promise. He was in serious trouble over Watergate and was on his way out of power. Facing almost certain impeachment, on August 8, 1974, Richard Nixon became the first US president to resign. Vice President Gerald R. Ford assumed the presidency, the only time America would have a president that no one elected.

President Gerald Ford, who was also on the Warren Commission, could do nothing to save South Vietnam. Congress would not allow any more funding for the South Vietnamese government and the US troops were out. It was only a matter of time. President Thieu, like many Vietnamese, could not believe the United States would abandon its enormous investment in Vietnam. They counted on a last-minute defense when the Communists reached Saigon. President Ford believed that America had a moral responsibility to South Vietnam, but there was little he could do. Funding had been cut off by Congress and the American people were done with Vietnam. On the morning of April 29, 1975, Tan Son Nhut airport in Saigon was under fire, preventing passenger planes from taking off. Americans and their South Vietnamese allies were ordered to evacuate, before being captured by the Communists. By late afternoon, most Americans and thousands of Vietnamese had reached the US carriers offshore. But many more thousands of Vietnamese were stuck in Saigon. Communist forces entered Saigon from six different directions. The Communists had attained their goal: they had removed the Saigon regime and reunified Vietnam. But the cost of victory was high. Nearly 1.5 million Vietnamese had been killed, and 3 million wounded, but the Americans were gone. America had lost over 58,000 in the war, and saw more than 300,000 wounded. It was America's first defeat.

Legacies of the Vietnam War

During the presidential campaign of 1976, former Georgia governor Jimmy Carter, Ford's principal rival, offered a strikingly different analysis of the Vietnam War's significance to the larger national story. Whereas Ford claimed that the Vietnam War was over and should not be a campaign issue in 1976, Carter would admit that sometimes governments can pursue policies contrary to the basic character of the people, and described the mood in the country after the collapse of South Vietnam as a "national malaise."

Reagan took a different approach from both Ford and Carter. He called Vietnam a noble cause. His rhetoric continues to inspire the neo-conservative movement today. George H. W. Bush and Bill Clinton each drew negative lessons from the Vietnam War. When Bush announced the successful completion of the Gulf War in 1991, he said that we had "kicked the Vietnam syndrome." Clinton often brought up the Vietnam experience to help explain why we did not intervene militarily on a large scale in Somalia, Haiti, Bosnia, Kosovo, and other problem areas around the world. Clinton announced the normalization of relations with Vietnam on July 11, 1995. To help stem the controversial nature of such a decision, he added that this was related to ongoing efforts to recover the remains of US servicemen missing in action, saying that we were honoring veterans while moving "beyond the haunting and painful past. ... The brave Americans who fought and died there had noble motives. They fought for the freedom and the independence of the Vietnamese people." It seems as though the greatest lesson of the Vietnam War came before it really began, when JFK said, "I don't think that unless a greater effort is made by the [South Vietnamese] Government to win popular support that the war can be won out there. In the final analysis, it is their war. They are the ones who have to win it or lose it."

Conclusion

When I started teaching my Vietnam War history course at Green River Community College I became friends with a Vietnam veteran named David Willson. David was the reference librarian who also taught a very popular Vietnam War and the Media course. He wrote the well known *REMF* (Rear Echelon Mother Fucker) series of novels [*REMF Diary*, *The REMF Returns*, and *In the Army Now*] based on his experiences as a clerk typist in Vietnam). David's encyclopedic knowledge of the war, war literature, and his own creative work inspired me to write *The Vietnam War Era: A Personal Journey* and my Kennedy Center American College Theatre Festival award-winning play *The Bronze Star*. The first time I visited David's office, I threw myself down in his 1950s-style TV chair and was surrounded by video films, books, papers, posters, old typewriters–like a used book store crammed into one small office. But the most prominent feature was a life-size cardboard John Wayne prominently displayed. David told me how important John Wayne was to American servicemen in Vietnam. He was the male ideal of a hero. If President Kennedy spurred that generation to war by saying " ask not what your country can do for you — ask what you can do for your country," it was John Wayne who taught those young men how to be a man.

I thank David for bringing the story of Joe Hooper to my attention. Joe had worked at Green River Community College after his tours of duty in the Army in Vietnam. Joe was also one of the most decorated veterans in American history. Staff Sergeant Hooper earned the Medal of Honor, two Silver Stars, six Bronze Stars, and eight Purple Heart medals. Joe had trouble adjusting to civilian life and was fired from his job at Green River. He died shortly thereafter at the age of 40. I asked David to give me something to say about Joe to all of my students, this is what he told me: "He was a casualty of war, and you can expect more of the same after Iraq and Afghanistan. Look at the history–this is a country made by war on the backs of vets who have never, ever been treated as promised. Hooper's story is a lesson on that failure. If we can't save our heroes, who can we save?"

It has always been fascinating to me how soldiers who have fought against each other in war, who have put every effort into killing each other, can many years later, after the war, have such respect and even love for one another. The comradeship of war, which we know bonds soldiers together in battle, transcends enemy lines as well. The question then becomes, how do we avoid putting ourselves into situations where we must kill other people that we do not know well enough to hate? Time after time I have heard combat veterans tell me that they went to war with certain convictions based on nationalism, patriotism, or even religious ideals, only to end up fighting merely to survive or to help their comrades survive, and then go home. One war leads to another in spite of our efforts to create peace. Why is this? I believe that nation-states, corporations, some religious groups, terrorist groups, and other entities do not have a vested interest in peace. In fact, to the contrary, they have a vested interest in war. The basic organizing principle behind the nation-state, corporations, and other entities, is for war or justification for war. The military-industrial complex that President Dwight D. Eisenhower warned us of is a reality. That being said, peace cannot be achieved by relying on governments or corporations or other entities, it must be achieved person to person. If individual people can think critically and not fall victim to propaganda, fear, vitriolic rhetoric, and jingoism, and realize that they are being used in a deadly game that profits only a few, then they can make advances toward peace in the world. The spontaneous truces that started with individual soldiers in World War I trenches are an example. I will end with a line from American poet Carl Sandburg's prose poem, *The People, Yes*. This line served as an inspiration for slogans used in the antiwar movement of the 1960s: "Sometime they'll give a war and nobody will come."

TIMELINE

1911

Ho Chi Minh (born as Nguyen Tat Tanh and then later Nguyen Ai Quoc) leaves Vietnam for a 30-year period of exile.

1919

January: Ho Chi Minh tries to petition President Woodrow Wilson for self-determination of Vietnam.

1920

December: Ho Chi Minh is one of the founding members of the French Communist Party.

1930

February: The Indochinese Communist Party is founded by Ho Chi Minh.

1940

September: Japan invades Vietnam.

1941

May: The Viet Minh is organized by Ho Chi Minh and Vo Nguyen Giap.

1944

September: Vo Nguyen Giap forms the Viet Minh army.

1945

August: The Japanese surrender.

September: Ho Chi Minh declares independence for Vietnam and Lieutenant Colonel Peter Dewey of the Office of Strategic Services (OSS, the forerunner of the Central Intelligence Agency or CIA) is the first American to die in Vietnam.

1946

March: Ho Chi Minh allows French troops into Vietnam in order to oust China.

December: The French–Viet Minh War begins.

1949

October: China turns to communism.

1950

January: China and the Soviet Union recognize Ho Chi Minh-led Vietnam.

February: The United States and Great Britain recognize Bao Dai-led Vietnam.

May: The United States begins its military aid to France in the war in Vietnam.

June: The Korean War begins.

1953

The United States is paying 80 percent of the costs for the French war effort in Vietnam.

July: Armistice is signed in Korea.

1954

March: The Battle of Dien Bien Phu begins.

April: The United States decides not to intervene in Dien Bien Phu.

May: The French are defeated at Dien Bien Phu.

June: Ngo Dinh Diem becomes prime minister of Vietnam.

July: The Geneva Conference ends with the Geneva Agreements, ending the French–Viet Minh War.

September: The Southeast Asia Treaty Organization is formed.

1955

January: The United States begins to give direct aid to the government of South Vietnam.

February: US military advisers start training South Vietnamese military.

July: The Chinese and the Soviets sign aid agreements with North Vietnam.

October: Diem defeats Bao Dai, founds the Republic of Vietnam, and becomes president.

1956

July: Diem refuses to have a reunification election.

1957

May: Diem tours the United States and gains Eisenhower's support.

1959

May: North Vietnam approves armed struggle in the South—men and supplies begin moving down the Ho Chi Minh trail.

1960

The National Liberation Front, or Viet Cong (VC), is established.

November: John F. Kennedy defeats Richard M. Nixon for the presidency.

December: There is an increasing crisis in Laos; the US has 900 US military advisers in Vietnam.

1961

January: Eisenhower warns of a military–industrial complex in his farewell speech.

April: The Bay of Pigs invasion of Cuba fails.

May: Vice President Johnson visits Vietnam, urges more US aid; the Laotian crisis ends.

October: Kennedy aides Walt Rostow and Maxwell Taylor visit Vietnam and urge increased US aid.

December: Kennedy increases the number of US military advisers in Vietnam to 3,200.

1962

February: The US Military Assistance Command-Vietnam (MACV) is established.

October: The Cuban Missile Crisis takes place.

December: Nearly 12,000 US military advisers are now in Vietnam.

1963

January: The VC defeat the South Vietnamese Army (ARVN) at Ap Bac.

May: The Buddhist uprisings in South Vietnam begin.

August: The ARVN attack Buddhist temples.

October: The United States supports a military coup against South Vietnamese president Diem and his brother.

November: Diem is assassinated; generals take over Vietnam. JFK is assassinated; Lyndon B. Johnson (LBJ) becomes president.

December: There are 16,000 US advisers in Vietnam; the VC steps up its attacks.

1964

April: General William Westmoreland is named MACV commander.

August: In the Gulf of Tonkin incident, a North Vietnamese patrol boat attacks the USS *Maddox*. The Tonkin Gulf Resolution is passed by Congress, giving LBJ war powers.

November: The VC attack Bien Hoa airbase and LBJ wins the presidential election.

December: The VC bomb Brinks Hotel in Saigon; US military advisers in Vietnam now number 23,200.

1965

February: The VC attack the US base at Pleiku and then LBJ orders airstrikes against the North Vietnamese.

March: The first US combat troops arrive in South Vietnam and the continuous bombing of North Vietnam (Operation Rolling Thunder) begins.

April: LBJ approves Westmoreland's request for 40,000 ground troops.

June: Air Marshall Nguyen Cao Ky becomes prime minister of South Vietnam.

November: In the Battle of the Ia Drang Valley, American troops fight the North Vietnamese Army (NVA) for the first time.

December: Bombing stops for Christmas; US troop strength is at 200,000.

1966

January: Bombing resumes.

October: Operation Attleboro involves attacking Communist bases near Cambodian border.

December: US troop strength reaches 400,000.

1967

January: North Vietnam say they will not negotiate until bombing stops; Operation Cedar Falls takes place in the Iron Triangle.

February: Operation Junction City takes place near the Cambodian border.

April: Anti-war protests begin in New York and San Francisco.

June: The Summer of Love begins in the Haight-Ashbury neighborhood of San Francisco.

July: Race riots break out in many US cities.

September: The South Vietnamese elect Nguyen Van Thieu as president, Nguyen Cao Ky as vice president.

October: Anti-war demonstrators march on the Pentagon.

December: US troop strength reaches nearly 500,000.

1968

January: The VC launch the Tet Offensive.

February: Famous US newsman Walter Cronkite admits that it does not look like we are winning in Vietnam. US and ARVN forces regain cities; Westmoreland requests 206,000 additional troops.

March: Creighton Abrams replaces Westmoreland as MACV commander; LBJ decides not to seek an additional term; the bombing of North Vietnam is suspended (except near the Demilitarized Zone (DMZ); the My Lai massacre takes place.

April: Dr. Martin Luther King, Jr. is assassinated.

June: Robert F. Kennedy is assassinated.

August: Violence breaks out at the Chicago Democratic National Convention.

October: Black Power demonstrations are organized at the Mexico City Olympics; Johnson ends all bombing in North Vietnam.

November: Richard Nixon beats Hubert Humphrey in the presidential election.

December: US troop strength is at 535,000.

1969

January: Paris negotiations are expanded to include the South Vietnamese and NLF.

March: The US begins its secret bombing of Cambodia.

June: Nixon announces the beginning of a phased withdrawal of US troops.

August: The Woodstock music festival takes place.

September: Ho Chi Minh dies at age 79.

October: The Vietnam moratorium, a series of nationwide peace demonstrations, takes place.

November: The My Lai massacre is revealed.

December: US troop strength is down to 475,000.

1970

February: Henry Kissinger and Le Duc Tho begin secret talks in Paris.

April: US and ARVN forces invade Cambodia.

May: Four students are killed at Kent State University and two students killed at Jackson State University.

December: US troop strength drops down to 334,000.

1971

February: Operation Lam Son 719 begins; the ARVN invade Laos.

March: Lt. William Calley is convicted of murder in the My Lai massacre.

April: 500,000 people protest in Washington, D.C.

June: The *New York Times* begins publishing the *Pentagon Papers*.

December: US troop strength is at 140,000.

1972

February: Nixon visits Red China.

March: The NVA assault the northern provinces of South Vietnam.

May: Nixon orders the mining of Haiphong Harbor, intensifies bombing of the North.

June: A break-in occurs at the Democratic National Headquarters in the Watergate Hotel/Office complex.

November: Nixon defeats George McGovern in the presidential election.

1973

January 22: LBJ dies.

January 27: The Paris Peace Accords are reached; America is out of the war.

March: The last US combat troops leave South Vietnam.

May: Congressional hearings on Watergate begin.

1974

August: Nixon resigns; Gerald Ford becomes president.

1975

April 30: Communists take Saigon; the Vietnam War over.

CREDITS

1. Fig. 10.1. Louis Meurisse / Agence de presse Meurisse, "Nguyen Ai Quoc (Ho Chi Minh)," http://commons.wikimedia.org/wiki/File:Nguyen_A%C3%AFn_Nu%C3%A4%27C_(Ho-Chi-Minh),_d%C3%A9l%C3%A9gu%C3%A9_indochinois,_Congr%C3%A8s_communiste_de_Marseille,_1921,_Meurisse,_BNF_Gallica.jpg. Copyright in the Public Domain.

2. Fig. 10.2. "Dwight D. Eisenhower, John Foster Dulles, and Ngo Dinh Diem," Department of Defense, U.S. Air Force, http://commons.wikimedia.org/wiki/File:Ngo_Dinh_Diem_at_Washington_-_ARC_542189.gif. Copyright in the Public Domain.

3. Fig. 10.3. "President John F. Kennedy," http://www.loc.gov/pictures/item/96523447/. Copyright in the Public Domain.

4. Fig. 10.4. Ira Jefferson "Jack" Beers Jr. "Lee Harvey Oswald being shot by Jack Ruby," Dallas Morning News, http://www.history-matters.com/archive/jfk/wc/wcvols/wh21/html/WH_Vol21_0022a.htm. Copyright in the Public Domain.

5. Fig. 10.5. Yoichi R. Okamoto "Lyndon B. Johnson," White House Press Office, http://commons.wikimedia.org/wiki/File:Lyndon_B._Johnson_photo_portrait-Black%27n_white.jpg. Copyright in the Public Domain.

6. Fig. 10.6. "Wounded US soldier during the Tet Offensive," U.S. Army, http://commons.wikimedia.org/wiki/File:Woundedsoldiervietnamwar1968.jpg. Copyright in the Public Domain.

7. Fig. 10.7. "Hugh Thompson," U.S. Military, http://commons.wikimedia.org/wiki/File:Hugh_Tompson_Jr.jpg. Copyright in the Public Domain.

8. Fig. 10.8. "Richard M. Nixon," http://www.loc.gov/pictures/item/96522669/. Copyright in the Public Domain.

9. Fig. 10.9. "South Vietnamese Refugees," U.S. Marines, http://commons.wikimedia.org/wiki/File:Vietnamese_refugees_on_US_carrier,_Operation_Frequent_Wind.jpg. Copyright in the Public Domain.

TEDDY TAKES ON THE PROTESTERS

BY DR. BRUCE OLAV SOLHEIM WITH ART BY GARY DUMM

 IN 1980 WE RENTED AN APARTMENT ABOVE A GASTHAUS IN MANNHEIM, WEST GERMANY WHERE I WAS STATIONED AS A U.S. ARMY JAIL GUARD.

ONE DAY THERE WAS AN ANTI-AMERICAN AND ANTI-NUCLEAR DEMONSTRATION ON THE STREET RIGHT BELOW OUR APARTMENT.

THE ARMY ORDERED US TO STAY INSIDE AND NOT CONFRONT THE PROTESTERS. I UNDERSTOOD THE ISSUES AND WAS EVEN SYMPATHETIC TO SOME OF THEIR CONCERNS, BUT IT WAS HARD FOR ME TO REMAIN QUIET AND NOT TAKE IT PERSONALLY WHEN THEY WERE BURNING THE AMERICAN FLAG.

Raus aus NATO!

FINALLY, I CAME UP WITH MY OWN PEACEFUL PROTEST IDEA. I TAPED A U.S. FLAG TO MY SON'S TEDDY BEAR AND WAVED THE FLAG AT THE PROTESTERS WHILE REMAINING HIDDEN BENEATH THE WINDOW SILL. THEY WENT CRAZY AND THE PARADE STOPPED FOR A WHILE SO THE PROTESTORS COULD HURL INSULTS AT MY SON'S TEDDY BEAR.

Kampf der Nato-Kriegspoliti

THE LOUDER THEY PROTESTED, THE MORE VIGOROUSLY I HAD THE TEDDY BEAR WAVE THE FLAG.

CHAPTER ELEVEN

THE CONSERVATIVE REVOLUTION

Objectives

1. Discover what led to the Conservative Revolution.
2. Compare Franklin Roosevelt and Ronald Reagan's presidencies.
3. Understand Reaganomics.
4. Examine the impact of the Reagan defense buildup.
5. Examine the legacies of the Reagan era and the end of the Cold War.

Personal History

The biggest controversy I could remember from high school was the rock versus disco music debate. I had a T-shirt that read "Disco Sucks!" By 1977 punk rock music was sweeping the country, and I went to a Ramones concert at an old hotel in Seattle. I was only six feet away from Johnny Ramone. I am still deaf from that concert. The energy was beyond belief and a little bit scary. Jimmy Carter was president, the Vietnam War was over, my brother had come home alive, and there was no draft. The Watergate hearings, Nixon's resignation, and the loss in Vietnam all created a feeling of hopelessness and depression. We did whatever we could to lift our spirits. I started at the University of Washington in fall quarter 1976. By winter quarter I was done, dropped out, on academic probation, lost—but I had become a very good at pinball and pool. I worked for my father as a carpenter, but he kept firing me. Then my mom would make him hire me back. This pattern persisted until I made the bold decision to break up this cycle of failure. I joined the US Army on Halloween 1978.

The military was not a popular option for young people in 1978. The country was still reeling from the loss in Vietnam, memories of protests, and the draft. When I told my best friend's dad that I had joined the Army he told me that I had just thrown my life away. Because I was basically clueless at age 20, I was shocked when my girlfriend was not happy that I had joined the Army and not told her. My parents were more understanding. After basic training and advanced individual training at Ft. McClellan, Alabama, I came home for leave and then it was off to West Germany for the biggest adventure of my life up to that time.

I was assigned to the 77th Military Police Detachment in Mannheim, West Germany, as a correctional specialist. I guarded military prisoners who had committed crimes ranging from drug possession to murder, rape, and selling weapons to terrorists (i.e., Baader-Meinhof Gang, Red Army Faction). It was hard to believe that American soldiers were committing such horrible crimes. I even guarded one guy who was facing the death penalty. We lived in an apartment next to Coleman Barracks, where I worked at the Mannheim Military Confinement Facility. Below our apartment was a Gasthaus (German inn with restaurant and hotel rooms). Every night I heard Pink Floyd's "The Wall" thumping over their huge speakers. My first son Bjørn was born when we were living there.

There were terrorists in Germany who targeted Americans. The Baader-Meinhof Gang and the Red Army Faction were two of the most notorious. We were always on alert. When I was in the guard tower at night I would stare at the fence line, my job being to keep prisoners from escaping. I was just as worried about prisoners escaping from inside the fence as I was terrorists killing me from behind, outside of the fence. One day the Red Army Faction fired a Soviet RPG (rocket-propelled grenade) at USAREUR (US Army Europe) Commander General Frederick Kroesen's car as he was on his way to work in Heidelberg. He survived and told reporters that if it had been an American weapon, instead of an inferior Russian one, he would be dead. My two older sons were born in Germany, and then we returned to the United States after having been gone for almost three years. A lot had changed. Music Television (MTV) had started. I felt like a stranger in my homeland.

I tried going to engineering school in Butte at Montana Tech, but I was not an engineer. I spent most of my time drawing a cartoon strip for the school newspaper and managing a rock band. I applied for Army flight school and was accepted in 1983. The Warrant Officer Flight Training program was difficult. They had a 50 percent washout rate. Somehow I made it through and in 1984 was sent to my duty station at Ft. Bragg, North Carolina, just as the troops were coming back from Operation Urgent Fury. Things did not work out for me. I started to doubt my mission and why I was in the Army. One day I met with the chaplain and told him that I was having trouble dealing with the fact that I have been training to kill and would probably get that opportunity before long. He put his arm around my shoulder and told me,

"Son, you have to remember, you would be killing Godless Communists." His response was not comforting and I was eventually discharged honorably in 1986.

Not long after I left the Army for good, I got a job with the Boeing Company in Seattle, Washington. I worked in the military part of Boeing on the B-1B bomber project. I liked my job, and the military structure of Boeing was something I was used to. When I was in the Army during the 1980s we got pay raises all the time. Those were good years for the military—no major wars, good pay. Then at Boeing I also benefited from the Reagan arms buildup of the 1980s, lucrative government contracts, and big money. I got raises at Boeing, too. One day the boss brought in a TV set and VHS video tape player to the office bay where I worked. He told everyone to gather around because he had a special video from General John T. Chain, Jr. He was the head of the Strategic Air Command (SAC). In the video he told us that our mission was vital and just as important as the mission performed by the active military. He reminded us of operation security and warned us of the enemy's intent to kill us all. "We stand ready to destroy the commies at the command of the president. We will not shirk in our sacred commitment and neither shall you," he said. Anti-nuclear demonstrations were everywhere in those days as part of the nuclear freeze movement. I began to question the whole arms race, nuclear deterrence, and the concept of mutually assured destruction (MAD).

THE CARTER YEARS

Jimmy Carter (James Earl Carter, Jr.) was born on October 1, 1924, in Plains, Georgia. He earned his Bachelor of Science degree from the US Naval Academy in 1946 and was chosen for the nuclear submarine program. In 1953 Carter left the Navy and took over his father's farm and business back in Plains. In 1962 he was elected to the Georgia Senate and then was elected governor of Georgia in 1971. Jimmy Carter came out of nowhere and was selected as the Democratic nominee in 1976 and then was elected president.

In 1982 President Carter founded the Carter Center—a nonpartisan and nonprofit organization that addresses national and international public policy. The Carter Center is dedicated to resolve conflict, promote democracy, protect human rights, and prevent disease. Jimmy and Rosalynn Carter volunteer one week a year for Habitat for Humanity, a nonprofit organization that helps economically disadvantaged people in the United States and other countries to renovate and build homes for themselves. He teaches Sunday school in Plains. In 2002, Carter won the Nobel Peace Prize "for his decades of untiring effort to find peaceful solutions to international conflicts, to advance democracy and human rights, and to promote economic and social development."

ASSESSMENT OF THE CARTER PRESIDENCY

Jimmy Carter got elected 1976 because of a backlash to Watergate, the resignation of Richard Nixon, and the loss in the Vietnam War. Americans wanted to elect someone who was outside of, and untainted by, Washington politics. Carter was relatively unknown outside of Georgia.

FIGURE 11.1. President Jimmy Carter

The problem was that he did not have insider connections and found it difficult to get anything done in the face of bureaucratic resistance. The conundrum for average American citizens is that, if you elect someone who is not part of the Washington political scene, they will not be encumbered by shady connections or owe any favors in Washington, but they will also not be able to get the machinery of government moving in any significant way.

Another difficulty that Carter had was his management style. Unlike Ronald Reagan or even Franklin D. Roosevelt, who were delegators, Carter was a micromanager. A president cannot afford to micromanage anything. There are simply too many things to manage. President Carter would micromanage one issue or problem, and meanwhile other issues or problems were left unmanaged and grew without any direction from the president. Part of this tendency toward micromanagement may have come from his engineering background. Engineers are required to be detail oriented. Roosevelt and Reagan, being delegators, simply gave their subordinates a general idea or direction and left it to them to come up with the detailed plans.

President Carter was also very unlucky. In an almost unbelievable incident in 1979, Carter was attacked by a rabbit while on a fishing trip. It was not just any rabbit, it was a big splay-footed swamp rabbit. The rabbit was distressed, or maybe had gone berserk, as it approached President Carter's boat. The rabbit made strange hissing noises and gnashed its teeth, and seemed to be intent upon climbing into the president's boat. Carter was able to scare it away with his oars. A more substantial threat was the situation in Iran.

THE RISE OF RADICAL ISLAM IN IRAN

In the Iranian Revolution of 1979, the Ayatollah Khomeini installed an anti-Western Islamic theocracy, replacing the pro-Western monarchy of the Shah of Iran (Mohammad Reza Shah Pahlavi). The CIA had helped overthrow the democratically elected prime minister Mohammad Mossadegh in 1953. Mossadegh had instituted social reforms and nationalized the Iranian oil industry, which prompted his overthrow. The Khomeini government referred to the United States as "the Great Satan" and suspected that the CIA would conspire to return the Shah to power. The decision was made to take American hostages when President Carter allowed the Shah of Iran to seek medical treatment in the United States. Iran claimed that it treated the hostages with respect, but that was not true. Some were treated well and others were tortured and subjected to mock executions. The hostages were not released until Reagan was sworn in as president in 1981. The Iranians did this on purpose to embarrass President Carter. The embassy in Tehran today is a museum and a symbol of the Iranian revolution. Every year on the anniversary of the hostage taking, Iranians hold rallies and yell "Death to America." President Carter may have had his difficulties as president, but he was and is an honorable man. By 1980 Americans were ready for a different style of leadership and a sense of renewed pride.

FIGURE 11.2. Ayatollah Ruhollah Khomeini

RONALD REAGAN AND THE CONSERVATIVE REVOLUTION

On February 6, 1911, Ronald Wilson Reagan was born in Tampico, Illinois. He studied economics and sociology, played football, and participated in theater at Eureka College. After his graduation, Reagan became a radio sports announcer. After a screen test in 1937 he earned a contract in Hollywood and appeared in 53 films over the next 20 years.

Reagan was later elected president of the Screen Actors Guild, where he got involved in the issue of communism in the film industry, and shifted his political views from liberal to conservative. In 1966 he was elected governor of California and in 1980 he beat incumbent Jimmy Carter and became president of the United States.

When Ronald Reagan took office in 1981, the United States had suffered through a decade of economic stagflation—high inflation, high unemployment, and low monetary growth. President Reagan felt he had a mandate to change the course America had taken, and to reinvigorate the American people and reduce their reliance on the government to solve their problems. It is somewhat ironic that Reagan, a former New Deal Democrat, basically began the process of dismantling the social welfare system that Franklin D. Roosevelt had built with the New Deal. President Reagan was shot by John Hinckley only 69 days after his inauguration, but he recovered quickly and returned to duty, causing his popularity to rise even higher. He worked with Congress to obtain legislation to stimulate economic growth, curb inflation, increase employment, and strengthen national defense. This program became known as Reaganomics.

FIGURE 11.3. President Ronald Reagan

REAGANOMICS

President Reagan called his plan "a second American Revolution for hope and opportunity." The media called it Reaganomics. The essence of Reaganomics was a reduction in taxes; a reduction in welfare and other entitlement programs; a reduction in government regulations on business, including environmental regulations; a reduction in the power of labor unions; control of the money supply; and a dramatic rise in defense spending.

Reagan initially called for a phased 30 percent tax cut, but Congress would only accept a 25 percent cut. During the presidential campaign Reagan had sold many people on the idea that the nation's economic troubles were owing to high taxes, excessive government regulation, and social welfare programs that stifled the growth of the economy. The tax cut was the key piece of the plan, and the bulk of the cut would be concentrated in the higher income levels. This economic theory came to be known as supply-side or trickle-down economics. Tax relief for the rich would enable them to spend and invest more, thereby stimulating the economy and creating new jobs. Reagan also believed that a tax cut would ultimately generate more revenue for the federal government, as businesses increased and flourished. The Reagan tax cut gave rise to inflation and the Federal Reserve was forced to raise interest rates, ultimately leading to a recession in 1981 and 1982. Internationally, high interest rates inflated the dollar and caused an imbalance in trade, with the United States exporting less and importing more. By 1983 the economy had stabilized and showed growth throughout the rest of the 1980s.

CUTS IN SOCIAL WELFARE

When Ronald Reagan was running for the Republican presidential nomination in 1976, he was laying the groundwork for his new economic plan for America. One way that he did this was by telling a story, and he was a great storyteller. He would talk about a woman in Chicago who had 80 names, 30 addresses, 12 social security cards, received Medicaid, received food stamps, and collected welfare checks under each of her names. She drove to the welfare office in her brand new Cadillac and her tax-free income was over $150,000 per year. The story was based on a real person from Chicago, but Reagan obviously exaggerated the details. Whether it was completely true or not, the impact on the American political system was real. The American public began to believe that some Americans were taking advantage of the system and that something had to be done.

As Reagan and Congress began to downsize and cut the budgets of social welfare programs, education, environmental protection, and others, the impact was almost immediate. The homeless population increased in the 1980s, as housing and social service budget cuts increased and the economy took a downturn. In 1980 federal funds accounted for 22 percent of big-city budgets, but by 1989 the federal government funding composed only 6 percent of urban revenue (part of a larger 60 percent decrease in federal spending to support local governments). It was largely (although not exclusively) in these urban areas that homelessness became widespread and most apparent. Directly tied to the rise in homelessness were cuts to federal low-income housing programs. One advocacy group claimed that Congress cut the budget in half for public housing and Section 8 (the government's housing voucher subsidization program), and that between the years 1980 and 1989 HUD's budget allocation declined from $74 billion to $19 billion. These types of cuts could have directly resulted in an inadequate supply of affordable housing to meet the growing demand of low-income families. In 1970 there were 6.5 million low-cost rental units and 6.2 million low-income households using the housing. By 1985, one homeless advocacy group claimed that the number of low-cost units had fallen to 5.6 million, and the number of low-income renter households had grown to 8.9 million. If true, this would have put more than 3 million low-income families at risk for homelessness. The 1980s also saw a continuing trend of deinstitutionalizing mental health treatment, based on cuts in federal funding for mental health. Americans who had been institutionalized in in-patient programs were released and provided with outpatient services. It stands to reason that people who have been institutionalized for any period of time would have great difficulty making it on their own, and would not be likely to keep up with outpatient medication schedules and follow-up appointments. A large percentage of these released patients ended up in the homeless system.

Many existing shelters and soup kitchens had to expand their facilities to accommodate the larger numbers of homeless people. Media coverage of the sharp increase in homelessness in America led to concerned citizens across the country demanding that the federal government provide assistance. After many years of advocacy and numerous revisions, President Reagan signed into law the McKinney-Vento Homeless Assistance Act in 1987—federal legislation that allocates funding to the direct service of homeless people. Many of the homeless were runaway children from broken homes, and veterans in ever-increasing numbers. The first signs of America's decline were emerging.

THE STRATEGIC DEFENSE INITIATIVE

The defense industry prospered under the Reagan administration. Massive government contracts were awarded to defense firms to upgrade the nation's military, and both conventional and nuclear weapons. Reagan proposed a space-based missile defense system called the Strategic Defense Initiative (SDI). Scientists were skeptical about the idea and critics called the plan Star Wars. SDI was initiated on March 23, 1983, with a speech by President Reagan. The intent was to build a complex anti-ballistic missile defense system that could prevent missile attacks. Although on the surface it seemed like a good plan, SDI was thought to violate the Anti-Ballistic Missile Treaty (ABM Treaty). Both the United States and the Soviet Union had offensive nuclear forces with massive retaliatory capabilities that basically cancelled each other out. This balance came to be known as mutually assured destruction. Any ABM system would upset the balance. For this reason, and because of the tremendous costs associated with SDI, the program was ultimately set aside. Critics made fun of SDI, or Star Wars, since it required the

FIGURE 11.4. President Reagan and Lt. Gen. Abrahamson at a Strategic Defense Initiative lab

development of space- and ground-based nuclear X-ray lasers, subatomic particle beams, and computer-guided projectiles fired by electromagnetic rail guns—all under the central control of a supercomputer system. These networked systems would destroy any incoming intercontinental ballistic missiles. The power requirements for such a massive and comprehensive ABM system would have to be reliant on nuclear power. At the end of the Strategic Defense Initiative, $30 billion had been invested in the program, with no results. The bigger significance of SDI was that it provided a defensive smokescreen for the massive arms buildup in the 1980s, which had a profound impact on the US economy and was in reality a missed opportunity to phase out all nuclear missiles in conjunction with a reasonable Mikhail Gorbachev.

ASSESSMENT OF THE REAGAN PRESIDENCY

Ronald Reagan and Franklin D. Roosevelt are very interesting in comparison. They both had congenial personalities and were great communicators. They both had an uncanny ability to communicate difficult concepts and make them easy for anyone to understand. They both tended to instill confidence and optimism in dark times. Both worked well with Congress and were skillful dealmakers. Reagan and Roosevelt each had great senses of humor and used that to disarm and charm their opponents and supporters alike. Lastly, they both had a tremendous impact of the direction of US political economy and ideology. From there, the similarities fall away. Reagan and FDR stand at separate ideological poles and still influence political discourse today.

The Reagan presidency produced mixed results. His increased defense spending, coupled with tax cuts, resulted in dramatic budget deficits during the 1980s. On the positive side, between 1980 and 1988 the unemployment rate dropped 2 percent, down to 5.4 percent and the number of Americans making less than $10,000 per year reduced by 0.5 percent, while the number of Americans making more than $75,000 per year grew by 5.7 percent. Although many Republicans had once rejected Reaganomics, it is now considered the very foundation of conservatism. They point out that the growth and prosperity of the 1990s was proof that Reaganomics was effective. Opponents of Reaganomics contend that the tax breaks for the wealthy and deregulation from the Conservative Revolution ultimately led to the current recession that began in 2007, and give President Clinton and President George H. W. Bush credit for the prosperity of the 1990s. Whichever way a person looks at it, it cannot be denied that Reaganomics had a strong impact on the American political economy, and the arguments raging between Democrats and Republicans currently are based on the two most ideologically influential presidents of the twentieth century—Franklin D. Roosevelt and Ronald Reagan. Just as FDR moved the entire political system to the left of center, Reagan moved the entire political system to the right of center.

Budget cuts required because of the tax cut and reduction in government spending led to less money allocated for science, engineering, and math education. This fact, coupled with the defense buildup and government money pouring into weapons programs and the military, caused a brain drain from civilian technology sectors. The best and the brightest engineers, scientists, and technicians moved from civilian-based technology jobs to black box defense projects, where they could make much more money. Consequently, the United States fell behind in terms of civilian applications of science and technology, and our economy suffered as other nations surpassed us. When President Kennedy called for putting a man on the moon by the end of the 1960s, the US government responded by heavily subsidizing science, math, engineering, and technical education. The best and the brightest who went to NASA were replaced with the next generation of scientists and engineers who filled private technology industry jobs. The legacy of all these years of neglect for public education is apparent in the low math and science achievement scores for American students today, compared to students in other countries. Also, a quick look at any college or university's math, engineering, or science department would reveal that most professors are foreign born. America simply does not have enough scientists and engineers.

Congress approved Reagan's tax cuts and defense buildup, but did not cut Social Security or Medicare, as Reagan had wanted them to. The result was an increased budget deficit. The national debt tripled from one to three trillion dollars during the Reagan years. The growth that Americans enjoyed during the 1980s came at a huge price for future generations. Perhaps President Reagan's most enduring legacy is the divide between liberals and conservatives. Liberals trust the government to make key decisions on production and distribution, while conservatives trust the market. Reagan's careful framing of the debate is advantageous for the conservatives, since Americans tend to naturally be suspicious of big government. Also, by making credit and the money supply tight, an aspect of Reaganomics, the Federal Reserve and central banks can ensure that the wages of ordinary workers do not grow too rapidly. In other words, controlling inflation is about making sure that the wages of the working class do not rise relative to the wealth of the rich. This causes a rise in upper-income groups and a lowering in lower-income groups. The rich get richer; the poor get poorer.

Then there is the exchange rate, which has a negative impact on the relative wages of workers who have been hurt by international competition through trade policy. An overvalued dollar essentially gives subsidies to foreign producers. Doctors and lawyers know that this sort of competition will drive down their wages and incomes. They make sure that there are barriers in place to protect them from international competition unlike factory workers who have no such protection. Working-class people usually do not see the importance of exchange rate policy and it is never part of any political debates. Exchange rates account for much of the upward redistribution of income since the 1980s.

Similarly, patent and copyright policies mostly aid large corporations and wealthy individuals. The United States now spends more than 2 percent of its gross domestic product, $300 billion a year, on prescription drugs that would likely cost less than one tenth as much if they were sold in a competitive market. Instead, debates have raged over tax cuts for the rich. Tax policies have little impact compared to tight control of interest rates, the exchange rate, and patent and copyright law, which never seem to enter into the national debate.

END OF THE COLD WAR

President Reagan's slogan for his foreign policy was "peace through strength." He increased defense spending 35 percent during his two terms in office, and wanted to defeat the Soviet Union and win the Cold War. At the same time that he was taking a hard line against communism around the world, Reagan met with Soviet leader Mikhail Gorbachev and negotiated

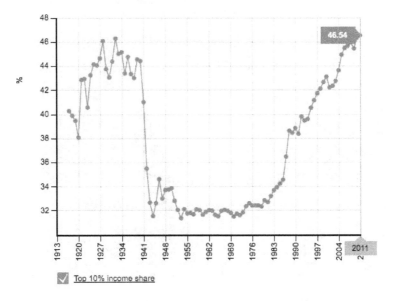

FIGURE 11.5. Top Income Share in the United States, 1913–2011

a treaty that eliminated intermediate-range nuclear missiles (IRBM). In addition to striking Libya in retaliation for an attack on US soldiers in West Berlin, and using the US Navy to escort oil tankers in the Persian Gulf during the Iran–Iraq War, President Reagan supported anti-Communist insurgencies in Central America, Asia, and Africa.

Many conservatives point out that Reagan won the Cold War with his defense buildup. Former Soviet officials have been asked if the Reagan military buildup had frightened the Soviet regime into collapse. Their answer was no. Of greater significance in terms of the collapse of the Soviet regime was the Russian invasion of Afghanistan. Soviet premier Leonid Brezhnev was convinced that the whole operation would be over in three to four weeks. Instead, the Soviet war in Afghanistan became like the American war in Vietnam. It lasted for years, led to massive casualities, pushed the Soviet economy to the brink of collapse, and ultimately was the graveyard of Soviet power.

Former Soviet officials recall Reagan's negotiation style and tactics. Reagan had a decent grasp on major issues (with the help of his famous 3 by 5 note cards) and, in an initial meeting with Mikhail Gorbachev, suggested that Moscow make a symbolic gesture by granting exit visas to some evangelical Christians who were sheltered in the US Embassy. Moscow agreed, and that led to a relaxation of tensions and further negotiations with Gorbachev. When the same Soviet officials were asked directly what brought down the Soviet Union, the answer was, "We did it to ourselves." Gorbachev's rise to power ushered in an era of perestroika (restructuring) and of glasnost (openness). US–Soviet relations improved during the mid-1980s. At a summit meeting in Reykjavik, Iceland, in October 1986, Gorbachev proposed cutting the nuclear arsenals of each side in half. Had it not been for disagreements over SDI, they would have reached an agreement. This summit did, however, lead to the December 1987 Intermediate Nuclear Forces (INF) Treaty. As the 1980s came to an end, much of the Eastern

FIGURE 11.6. President Reagan and General Secretary Gorbachev sign the Intermediate Nuclear Forces (INF) Treaty

bloc began to crumble, and on November 10, 1989, the Berlin Wall started to come down. In December 1991 the Soviet Union ceased to exist and the Cold War was over.

American conservatives claim that Reagan ended the Cold War. Putting aside for the moment the obvious point that the Soviet Union collapsed during George H. W. Bush's presidency, what validity does this claim have? Certainly, President Reagan's defense buildup played a role in the Soviet collapse. They could not keep up anymore with what Americans were doing. But equally important was the fact that communism just did not work as an economic system. As one observer called the Soviet era (referring to the time that had passed since the Russian Revolution), "seventy years on the road to nowhere." Another equally important factor was the leadership of Mikhail Gorbachev. Just as George Kennan had predicted in 1947, a new generation of Soviet leader had eventually emerged—one not personally tied to the 1917 Revolution, who was more willing to compromise and negotiate. A more important question is: Who won the Cold War? Americans assume that they did. But on careful examination one can see that a heavy price was paid. Other countries had surpassed the United States in many economic categories, not the least of which was per capita income. The American empire was in decline, hastened by the cost of waging the Cold War. One observer quipped ironically, "The Cold War is over, and Japan and Germany won."

According to International Monetary Fund (IMF) data, the United States currently ranks number 10 in the world in terms of gross domestic product (GDP) per capita income. In 1960 we ranked number 1, in 1970 number 3, in 1980 number 14, in 1990 number 10, and in 2000 number 4. These data suggest that the current recession has really hurt the United States.

CONCLUSION

The Conservative Revolution started by Reagan may last as long as the New Deal coalition, which finally collapsed around 1975 (more than 40 years). That would mean that around 2020 a new shift will take place. Will the center of the political spectrum in America shift to left of center again, more to the center, or farther right of center than it is now? The rise to power of Vladimir Putin has reminded many that the Russians are not moving toward democracy as many thought, they are moving back to a non-democratic, aggressive, Soviet style regime. The relationship between Russia and the United States today is not good. Heavy-handed moves by the Russians in Crimea and the rest of the Ukraine are not a good sign. The Norwegians, who share a border with Russia, have also noted a more aggressive nature. This is of great interest to me since my brother and I still own our family home in northern Norway. In 2014 Norway intercepted 74 Russian warplanes off its coast. No one expects the Russians to invade or interfere directly like in Crimea, Georgia, or the Ukraine, but the Russian rhetoric has returned to Cold War levels and they have plans to re-establish long idle arctic military facilities on the Kola Peninsula. The High North is of great strategic significance with all of its oil and gas. Still, Norway spends only a small percentage of its budget on defense. As a member of NATO (the North Atlantic Treaty Organization), it knows that the Russians would think twice about any serious moves in Norway. The United States would have to respond to any threats made to Norway. I believe the next American president will have to deal very seriously with the emerging power of Russia and its aggressive moves and potential threat to oil and gas resources in the High North. Back to the Future. Assuming that, the center of the American political spectrum may move farther to the right of center and we may not be able to look forward to peaceful times ahead or much of a chance for the middle class to get relief.

TIMELINE

1976

July 4: America celebrates its bicentennial.

November 2: Jimmy Carter is elected president.

1978

September 7: The Panama Canal treaties are signed.

September 17: The Camp David Accords signed by Egyptian president Anwar El Sadat and Israeli prime minister Menachem Begin. They both share the 1978 Nobel Peace Prize.

1979

January 1: The United States recognizes Communist China.

June 18: SALT II, the first nuclear arms treaty which assumed real reductions in strategic forces, is completed.

November 4: The American Embassy in Iran is occupied.

December 24: The Soviet Union invades Afghanistan.

1980

January 20: America boycotts the Moscow Olympics.

November 4: Ronald Reagan is elected president and Republicans capture the Senate for the first time since 1953.

1981

Reagan promotes "supply side economics," also known as Reaganomics.

January 20: The American hostages in Iran are released.

1982

January 4: The CIA organizes the Contra war against Nicaragua's Sandinista government.

June 8: President Reagan calls for a "crusade for freedom."

June 30: The Equal Rights Amendment dies.

1983

March 8: President Reagan denounces the Soviet Union as an "Evil Empire."

March 23: Reagan proposes the Strategic Defense Initiative (Star Wars).

October 23: A terrorist attack in Beirut kills 239 US Marines.

October 25: The United States invades Grenada (Operation Urgent Fury).

1984

July 12: Geraldine Ferraro is chosen as the vice presidential running mate on the Democratic ticket.

November 6: Reagan is reelected in a 49-state landslide victory over liberal Democrat Walter Mondale.

December: Congress bars military aid to the Contras.

1986

September 17: Associate Justice William Rehnquist is confirmed as Chief Justice of the Supreme Court.

September 26: Antonin Scalia joins the Supreme Court.

October 22: Congress enacts the Tax Reform Act of 1986, the second of the "Reagan Tax Cuts."

November: The Iran-Contra scandal draws national attention and threatens Reagan's presidency.

1987

June 12: In Berlin, President Reagan tells Soviet leader Mikhail Gorbachev to "Tear down this wall!"

August 4: The Federal Communications Commission (FCC) abolishes the Fairness Doctrine.

August 30: Pat Robertson, an Evangelical minister, founds the Christian Coalition.

December 8: Reagan signs Intermediate Nuclear Forces (INF) Treaty.

1988

February 18: Anthony Kennedy joins the Supreme Court.

March 16: Oliver North, John Poindexter, and other Iran Contra figures are indicted.

August 1: *The Rush Limbaugh Show* debuts on Premiere Radio Networks and will go on to become the highest-rated talk radio show in the United States.

November 8: George H. W. Bush is elected president.

1989

May 4: Oliver North is convicted for his role in the Iran Contra scandal.

March 24: The ship *Exxon Valdez* causes a massive oil spill in Alaska.

December 20: The United States invades Panama, leading to the overthrow of Manuel Noriega.

June 3: China's rulers crush a pro-democracy movement in Tiananmen Square.

November 10: The Berlin Wall falls as the satellite states free themselves from Soviet control.

1990

A recession begins in the United States.

Germany is reunited as Soviet troops start their withdrawal from Eastern Europe.

August 2: Iraq invades Kuwait.

October 9: David H. Souter joins the Supreme Court.

1991

January 16: The Gulf War begins.

October 15: Clarence Thomas, a black Republican, is confirmed as an associate justice of the Supreme Court after controversial hearings that focus on his relationship with one of his aides, Anita Hill, who accuses him of sexual harassment.

December 25: Communism collapses in Russia as the red flag is lowered for the last time. Reagan becomes a hero in Eastern Europe.

1992

November 3: George H. W. Bush is defeated by Bill Clinton in the presidential election.

Credits

1. Fig. 11.1. "President Jimmy Carter," http://commons.wikimedia.org/wiki/File:Jimmy_Carter.jpg. Copyright in the Public Domain.

2. Fig. 11.2. "Ayatollah Ruhollah Khomeini," http://commons.wikimedia.org/wiki/File:%D8%B9%DA%A9%D8%B3%DB%8C_%D8%A7%D8%B2_%D8%AE%D9%85%DB%8C%D9%86%DB%8C.JPG. Copyright in the Public Domain.

3. Fig. 11.3. "President Ronald Reagan," http://commons.wikimedia.org/wiki/File:President_Reagan_poses_at_the_White_House_1984.jpg. Copyright in the Public Domain.

4. Fig. 11.4. "President Reagan and Lt. Gen. Abrahamson at a Strategic Defense Initiative Lab," http://commons.wikimedia.org/wiki/File:Gen_Abe_%26_Reagan_(SDI).png. Copyright in the Public Domain.

5. Fig. 11.5. Source: Alvaredo, Facundo, Anthony B. Atkinson, Thomas Piketty and Emmanuel Saez, "Top Income Share in the United States, 1913-2011," http://topincomes.g-mond.parisschoolofeconomics.eu.

6. Fig. 11.6. "President Reagan and General Secretary Gorbachev sign the Intermediate Nuclear Forces (INF) Treaty," http://commons.wikimedia.org/wiki/File:Reagan_and_Gorbachev_signing.jpg. Copyright in the Public Domain.

TIMING IS EVERYTHING

BY DR. BRUCE OLAV SOLHEIM WITH ART BY GARY DUMM

I WOKE UP IN A COLD SWEAT FROM A NIGHTMARE EARLY ON THE MORNING OF SEPTEMBER 11, 2001. IN MY DREAM, THE WHOLE WORLD WAS CRUMBLING APART, AND THE EARTH WAS SHAKING VIOLENTLY.

LATER THAT MORNING I WAS ON A TOUR OF THE NAVAL STATION NORFOLK IN VIRGINIA WITH TWO OF MY COLLEAGUES WHEN, SUDDENLY, WE HEARD SIRENS, AND THEN ARMED MARINES ARRIVED TO CLOSE OFF THE GATE. THE TERRORISTS HAD STRUCK NEW YORK, AND NOTHING WOULD EVER BE THE SAME FOR ANY OF US.

WE WALKED TO THE BASE EDUCATION CENTER AND WATCHED ON THEIR TV. IT TOOK NEARLY FIVE HOURS BEFORE THE NAVY LET US LEAVE THE BASE. WE SAW MILITARY AIRCRAFT FLYING AND SHIPS GETTING READY.

AFTER SPENDING A FEW DAYS IN VIRGINIA BEACH, WE DECIDED TO RENT A CAR AND DRIVE TO NASHVILLE—
—ONE OF THE FEW OPERATIONAL AIRPORTS.

GATE 3

IN THE TERMINAL, I SAW A MAN IN ARAB GARB SURROUNDED BY MANY PASSENGERS. THEY WERE ALL STARING AT HIM. I FELT SORRY FOR HIM, BUT AT THE SAME TIME, I HOPED THAT HE WAS NOT ON OUR FLIGHT.

▲ Delta
SOLHEIM/BRUCE

BOARDING PASS
ELECTRONIC TICKET
2 012 1349658783 2

FLIGHT **DL77** DATE **12SEP** CLASS **B** ORIGIN **IAD**
COACH
OPERATED BY DESTINATIO **LAX**
DELTA AIRLINES INC.

DEPARTURE GATE **B26** ##SUBJECT TO CHANGE

WHILE WE WERE WAITING FOR OUR FLIGHT FROM NASHVILLE TO SAN DIEGO VIA NEW ORLEANS, I LOOKED AT MY ORIGINAL TICKET...

...IT WAS DELTA FLIGHT 77 FROM DULLES TO LAX, SEPTEMBER 12, 2001. THAT WAS THE VERY SAME FLIGHT THAT HIT THE PENTAGON ON SEPTEMBER 11, 2001. HAD THE TERRORISTS STRUCK ONE DAY LATER, I WOULDN'T BE HERE.

CHAPTER TWELVE

AMERICAN EMPIRE IN DECLINE

OBJECTIVES

1. Understand how 9/11 prompted a major shift in US foreign policy.
2. Compare the Bush Doctrine to containment.
3. Define the US foreign policy interests in Iraq and Afghanistan.
4. Understand what happened in the financial crisis of 2008.

PERSONAL HISTORY

The 1990s were eventful for me and for my country. I lost my mom on May 4, 1990, and my father on August 20, 1999. Those two terrible losses were the bookends for my 1990s. I also got divorced twice in the 1990s, so that is depressing. On the positive side, I earned my PhD in history in 1993, and my two youngest children were born in 1996 and 1999. The United States had tremendous growth early in the 1990s under Bill Clinton, but the tech bubble had burst by the end of the decade as George W. Bush became president. Our decline as a hegemonic power was accelerating.

I remember visiting Norway with my parents in 1972 and 1974, and all the talk was of oil, because massive oil and gas deposits had been discovered in the North Sea. Prior to this, Norway had been a very modest country, with its main export being fish. Relatives in Norway always told us how they wanted to come to America to make their fortunes and live like rich Americans. That was all about to change. Norway was about to transform itself into one of the world's richest countries (based on per capita income). My dad figured that hanging on to the old farm in northern Norway was not only nostalgic for him, but also a smart move financially.

My original goal of becoming a petroleum engineer and working in the North Sea oilfields never materialized, but I have maintained very close ties to Norway and to my relatives up North.

On September 11, 2001, when the terrorists hit New York, Pennsylvania, and Washington, D.C., I was on the largest naval base in the world in Norfolk, Virginia. I was working on a project to provide online college courses to sailors deployed on ships. Everything changed that day. Terrorism had existed prior to 9/11, of course, but the attack really brought it home for every American. As of this writing, it has been more than 15 years since the attack, and we are still fighting the global war on terror. That war has been going on since my youngest son was only two years old. The 9/11 attacks, which prompted the global war on terror, diverted attention and resources away from domestic problems in the United States. In 2007, the housing market collapsed in the United States, and I lost my house that I bought in 2001. I was not alone: millions of Americans lost their homes, including war veterans. I was not only teaching history, I was living it.

BILL CLINTON

President Bill Clinton may have been one of the smartest men to occupy the White House. He was born in Hope, Arkansas, and became the first baby boomer to reach the presidency. He did not serve in the military, because he was attending university in England and had a draft deferment. He served as governor of Arkansas for many years before getting the Democratic Party nomination in 1992. Clinton beat George H. W. Bush and was also lucky enough to have a Democrat-controlled House and Senate. Clinton defeated Bush by focusing on the sluggish economy and using the campaign slogan, "It's the economy, stupid." Clinton was also helped by the third-party campaign of billionaire Ross Perot, who took many Republican votes from incumbent president Bush.

Clinton was in office during the longest period of peacetime economic expansion in US history. He helped pass the North American Free Trade Agreement (NAFTA), but he failed to pass a national healthcare initiative, in spite of a full court press led by First Lady Hillary Clinton who headed the Presidential Task Force. In 1998, President Clinton was impeached for perjury and obstruction of justice related to a scandal involving White House intern Monica Lewinsky. He was acquitted by the Senate and most Americans put the scandal behind them because the US economy was good. In fact, while Clinton was in office, the nation enjoyed the lowest unemployment rates in recent history, the lowest inflation rate in decades, the highest homeownership rates in history, and improving economic equality. While his domestic policy achievements are impressive, Clinton was not as lucky with foreign policy. The disaster in Somalia is one example, and the genocide in Rwanda another. Brief US military intervention in Somalia was an attempt to provide humanitarian aid and secure the area so food and other supplies could reach the people. After fierce resistance from local war lords,

FIGURE 12.1. Bill Clinton

Clinton stepped up the military involvement, leading to a confrontation where 19 American soldiers were killed and, ultimately, the US forces pulled out. Clinton did not respond to the Rwandan genocide and nearly one million people were killed. He was also slow to deal with the rising terrorist threat posed by Osama bin Laden and al-Qaeda.

Clinton left office with the highest approval rating of any US president since World War II. Since then, he has been involved in public speaking and humanitarian work. Hillary Clinton has run for president, and served as secretary of state for President Obama, while Bill Clinton has remained active in charity work and campaigning for Democratic candidates, including Barack Obama.

THE AMERICAN CHARACTER

It is more difficult to write about recent history than events from the distant past. That is because we are more emotionally tied to recent events. Once you begin writing about events that no one alive today remembers, then it is easier. The old saying that "you can't see the forest for the trees" definitely applies. It might be a good idea to try to capture something about the character of the American people at this point. Although it would be a broad generalization, it can help sum up who the American people are, and will continue to be into the future. How do individual Americans form a collective character that can be examined?

The American people are very religious and although the US government is secular (in that there is a separation of church and state), the relationship between religion and government in America is uneasy. Compared to other countries around the world, the United States has more in common with the developing world than the modern industrialized world regarding religion. Americans also tend to be rather conservative and anti-revolutionary. This sounds rather odd because America was born of revolution. But a quick look at the nature of the American Revolution reveals, despite our romantic notions and myths, that it was not very revolutionary. In spite of their conservative nature, Americans do look for adventure, especially when defined as a frontier. In some ways, America is still very much like the Wild West, especially when compared to European countries. Americans like action in their lives, but they want their politics to be conservative.

Americans pride themselves as rugged individualists. In fact, most American legendary heroes could be classified as rugged individualists, who were not afraid to take risks and put their own lives on the line for what they believed in. At the same time, Americans also tend to be very nationalistic, even to the point of being jingoistic. It is not surprising that Americans are also very entrepreneurial. No one in America blames anyone else for wanting to get ahead financially, or flaunting their wealth, for that matter. In keeping with all of these characteristics, Americans also tend to be conflict- instead of consensus-oriented. Problems are solved through conflict, often with an accelerated time limit, since it can be said that Americans suffer from a national case of attention deficit disorder. Americans are very emotional and tend to jump right into the middle of something, without much hesitation or contemplation beforehand. Winston Churchill captured the American character perfectly: "You can always count on Americans to do the right thing, but only after they have tried everything else."

SHIFT FROM CONTAINMENT
TO THE BUSH DOCTRINE

In the run up to the American invasion of Iraq in 2003, President George W. Bush said, "It's a war in which we will hunt down those who hate America, one person at a time." Referring to the global War on Terror, President Bush set into motion the foreign policy and the direction for the United States in the new millennium. This global War on Terror may be a very long war, since there are a lot of people who do not like America, and those numbers seem to be increasing. The new foreign policy that emerged in the aftermath of 9/11 is known as the Bush Doctrine.

President Bush articulated the new Bush Doctrine in his National Security Strategy released September 17, 2002: "As a matter of common sense and self-defense, America will act against such emerging threats before they are fully formed. We cannot defend America while hoping for the best ... History will judge harshly those who saw this coming danger but failed to act. In the new world we have entered, the only path to peace and security is the path of action." Clearly, the Bush Doctrine is a departure from containment. It is much more aggressive and offensive in nature. The path of action President Bush spoke of is war. No longer will the United States contain the bad guys—they will take them out. The new threat was defined as rogue states, terrorist organizations, and states that support terrorism. The pre-emptive clause of the Bush Doctrine allows for first strike, based on imminent threat, and authorizes

FIGURE 12.2. George W. Bush

regime change. The Bush Doctrine is unilateral and does not require UN approval. The Bush Doctrine is considered a grand strategy, like containment, because it was precipitated by a crisis, it is comprehensive in scope, and it has both long- and short-term objectives.

As it turned out, 9/11 provided the opportunity to launch the doctrine. Containment had defined US foreign policy since 1947. The Bush Doctrine originated with the 1992 defense planning guidance drafted by Paul Wolfowitz, who was later President Bush's assistant secretary of defense. President Clinton did not like the plan, so it was shelved until after 9/11 and coincided with the rise of the neo-conservatives in the Bush administration. The basic premise of the Bush Doctrine is that American hegemony must be preserved, and that a lack of democracy creates terrorism. That being the case, the United States needs to create democracy in the Middle East. A dynamic tension developed between the neo-conservatives and the realists in the Bush administration. Colin Powell, being the lone realist, was the odd man out and did not survive the second Bush term.

TABLE 12.1. A comparison of US foreign policy before and after 9/11

	CONTAINMENT	BUSH DOCTRINE
DIPLOMATIC STYLE	Multilateralism	Unilateralism
INTERNATIONAL SYSTEM	Bipolar	Unipolar
THREAT	Communism	Terrorism
UNITED NATIONS	UN plays a role	UN not needed

The following table compares the policy shift from containment to the Bush Doctrine. One can see the dramatic difference. The Bush Doctrine is basically a go-it-alone type of policy, in addition to being more offensive in nature. Also, because US foreign policy, and American society in general, is conflict driven, a new enemy needed to be identified. The enemy shifted from communism to terrorism.

After World War II the United States realized the need for allies in dealing with an aggressive Soviet Union. Americans generally want to prevent wars instead of just fighting them. Containment, as originally conceived by George Kennan, was defensive in nature, but was realistic in terms of dealing with threat, specifically the threat from Russia. The United States helped create the United Nations in order to establish a peaceful world order. Although the United States had ventured down some militaristic roads since the end of World War II, and made plenty of mistakes, there was hope that US foreign policy would find a correct path. Containment became more militarized with National Security Council Document 68 (NSC 68) issued in 1950 just before the North Korea invaded South Korea. Even with the Vietnam War there was still some restraint provided by containment doctrine. The Bush Doctrine basically abandons any plans of a defensive strategy. It is pure aggression. The United States, having created the instruments of international law and formed alliances in order to keep the peace, has simply walked away from all that in order to pursue imperialistic aims and cling to hegemonic power at all costs. This is a recipe for disaster, as the events of the last 10 years have shown.

THE NATURE OF TERRORISM AND THE GLOBAL WAR ON TERROR

There is no international legal consensus for the definition of terrorism. The problem is that the term "terrorism" is politically, religiously, and emotionally charged. What is clear is that terrorism is a tactic of war, and not an enemy in and of itself. And terrorism, like war, is as old as humankind. The goal of terrorism is to strike fear into the hearts of one's enemies and cause a change in policy or behavior. The tactic of terrorism is depicted in the Bible. Genghis Khan employed terrorist tactics, as did Muslims during the Crusades. The term *terrorism* was not used until the Reign of Terror during the French Revolution in 1793–1794. Terrorists employ what is called an ancient "Eastern" style of warfare, with some modern twists. Eastern-style warfare targets everyone—military, civilian, men, women, and children. Eastern-style warfare has no rules. The challenge of dealing with terrorists is that they do not follow any rules, whereas Western society does, for the most part. Some people refer to Eastern-style warfare as fourth generation warfare. Since World War II, in Afghanistan, Iraq, Lebanon, Vietnam, and elsewhere, the United States has been faced with fourth generation warfare. The attack on the United States on 9/11 was a clear example of this old tactic. The question remains, what can the United States do to fight a fourth generation war?

Fourth generation warfare is conflict characterized by a blurring of the lines between war and politics, religion and civil society, soldier and civilian. The term was first used in 1989 to describe warfare's return to a decentralized form. In other words, fourth generation warfare has signaled the end of the nation-state's monopoly on warfare. Wars are now fought not strictly between nation-states, but between non-state actors and nation-states, or between non-national actors. This type of warfare is a return to the type of warfare common in premodern times. So, then, fourth generation warfare includes any war where one of the combatants is not a state, but rather a violent non-state actor. This type of warfare uses classical tactics that are considered unacceptable by traditional modern societies. The purpose, of course, is to weaken the nation-state's will to win by demoralizing the populace, taxing the economic system through endless warfare, and undermining the basic principles of decency, as the nation-state feels compelled to fight fire with fire.

First generation warfare was characterized by the use of massed manpower. Massed manpower describes warfare transitioning from roving bands of warriors attacking at random to the highly trained and disciplined Roman legions. Second generation warfare was characterized by the use of firepower. The Chinese invented gunpowder, which then came into use in warfare to hurl projectiles at an enemy. Guns and cannon changed the nature of warfare, moving opposing forces at a great standoff range. Killing in war became easier, with not as much hand-to-hand, face-to-face combat. Third generation warfare was characterized by firepower coupled with maneuver. The advent of tanks, airplanes, and other mechanized vehicles allowed opposing forces to attack from the ground and the air, in addition to waging naval battles. A good example is the German blitzkrieg in World War II, which featured fast-moving tank columns, Stuka dive bombers, and mechanized infantry, hitting civilian targets indiscriminately in order to cause maximum consternation and terror.

Finally, fourth generation warfare is characterized as an evolved form of insurgency that employs all available resources—often improvised or stolen from the enemy—to attack without mercy or regard for civilian lives, with the purpose of convincing an enemy that they will have to also fight with no rules, and causing them to realize that their strategic goals are either unachievable or too costly.

The US government has decided to fight a fourth generation war in its own way. Instead of strictly using regular US military units, US policymakers prefer private contractors, who are usually former US combat troops and special forces (mercenaries). These private contractors do not have to follow status of forces agreements and adhere to the Uniform Code of Military Justice. The US government can disavow their actions, should they be caught doing something illegal or immoral. When these contractors are killed, the Department of Defense does not have to report it publicly, so most Americans are unaware of what is going on. Such private contractor security personnel are provided by companies like Blackwater (now called Academi). Another method the US government has used is unmanned aerial vehicles (UAVs), or what the media calls drones. These aircraft can be used for observation or for offensive operations armed with missiles. There are thousands of UAVs between the US Air Force and the CIA and they are flying

FIGURE 12.3. American F-14 over burning Kuwaiti oil well, 1991

everywhere, all over the world. They cross international borders while the pilots of these drones are stationed half a world away, on bases in the southwestern United States. Missions are flown and the killing that takes place is far removed from the drone pilot, who sits in a comfortable chair watching video screens in an air-conditioned control room. If the UAV goes down, there are no casualties and POWs to worry about. It makes fighting a fourth generation war much easier. The problem, of course, is that if war is made easier, then it will continue. The horror of war is what makes people seek peace.

Gulf War/Persian Gulf War

The Iraq War did not start in 2003, as many Americans believe; it started in 1991. The Persian Gulf War (also known as the Gulf War) lasted a little over a month, with 258 Americans killed in action. The United States, Great Britain, France, Saudi Arabia, Egypt, Syria, and Italy went to war against Iraq on January 16, 1991, in response to Iraq's invasion and annexation of Kuwait on August 1, 1990. President George H. W. Bush sent 430,000 troops to Saudi Arabia to lead the UN-sponsored coalition and protect that country from an attack by Iraq. Congress gave President Bush approval for an air attack against military targets in Iraq and Kuwait. A brief ground offensive followed. American and coalition forces rolled over Iraqi president Saddam Hussein and his troops in just four days. In their rapid retreat, Iraqi forces set fire to more than 500 Kuwaiti oil wells. Eventually Iraq agreed to UN peace terms, including the imposition of both northern and southern no-fly zones. Saddam Hussein was allowed to remain in power.

WORLD TRADE CENTER BOMBING

The 9/11 attacks were not the first time terrorists targeted the Twin Towers in New York City. The World Trade Center bombing took place on February 26, 1993, when a truck bomb was detonated beneath the north tower. The bomb was supposed to knock the north tower (tower one) into the south tower (tower two), causing both towers to collapse and killing thousands of people. It failed to do so, but the blast did kill six people and injured more than a thousand. Omar Abdel Rahman (the Blind Sheikh) was the mastermind behind this attack.

OKLAHOMA CITY BOMBING

Gulf War veteran Timothy McVeigh detonated a truck bomb on April 19, 1995, outside the Alfred P. Murrah Federal Building in Oklahoma City, Oklahoma. The blast killed 168 people and injured hundreds more. Until 9/11, the Oklahoma City bombing was the worst terrorist attack to take place on American soil. Of the 168 who were killed in the powerful explosion, 19 were young children who were in the building's daycare center. More than 650 other people were injured in the bombing. McVeigh had earned the Bronze Star in combat operations in the Gulf War and became an anti-government militant after returning home. He became suspicious of the US government, especially President Bill Clinton. These suspicions were confirmed for McVeigh when the US government attacked survivalists in Idaho and Waco, Texas, in 1992 and 1993. He was put to death in 2001 and his co-conspirator, Terry Nichols, received a life sentence.

9/11 DETAILS

Early on the morning of September 11, 2001, 19 hijackers took over four commercial airliners (two Boeing 757s and two Boeing 767s) flying to San Francisco and Los Angeles after takeoffs from Boston, Newark, and Washington, DC. The hijackers chose large jets with long flights because they would be fully fueled. United Airlines Flight 93 left Newark International Airport at 0842 en route to San Francisco, with a crew of seven and 33 passengers, not including the four hijackers. After the passengers tried to seize control, the hijackers crashed the plane into the ground near Shanksville, Pennsylvania. American Airlines Flight 11 left Boston's Logan Airport at 0759 en route to Los Angeles, with a crew of 11 and 76 passengers, and the five hijackers. The hijackers flew the plane into the north tower of the World Trade Center. American Airlines Flight 77 left Washington Dulles International Airport in northern Virginia at 0820 en route to Los Angeles, with a crew of six and 53 passengers, and the five hijackers. The hijackers flew the plane into the Pentagon. United Airlines Flight 175 left Logan Airport at 0814 en route to Los Angeles, with a crew of nine and 51 passengers, and the five hijackers. The hijackers flew

FIGURE 12.4. September 11 in New York

the plane into the south tower of the World Trade Center. According to the 9/11 Commission Report, almost all of the hijackers had expired visas. The hijack pilots trained in US flight schools, where they paid in cash. The suicide pilots all only had a private pilot's license, but were paying to learn how to fly wide-body jets. This is a major red flag because one does not jump from a single-engine Cessna to a 767 in the normal progression of flight training. A few of them were even caught in flight simulator's learning how to fly into buildings. None of this information got through the tangled bureaucracy of law enforcement and government.

OSAMA BIN LADEN

Born in 1957, Osama bin Laden was the founder of al-Qaeda, the jihadist organization responsible for the 9/11 attacks on the United States, and many other attacks against civilian and military targets. He was a member of the wealthy Saudi bin Laden family. Osama bin Laden was at one time on the American side, during the Soviet war in Afghanistan in the 1980s, and his mujahideen (holy warrior) fighters were funded by the United States. After the Soviet Union withdrew from Afghanistan in February 1989, bin Laden returned to Saudi Arabia. Osama bin Laden and several others formed al-Qaeda in 1988. The Iraqi invasion of Kuwait in August 1990 prompted bin Laden to offer the services of his mujahideen to King Fahd in order to protect the holy cities of Saudi Arabia from the Iraqi army. The Saudi monarch refused bin Laden's offer, choosing instead to allow the United States and allied forces to deploy troops into Saudi territory. That deployment enraged bin Laden, who believed that the presence of foreign troops in Saudi Arabia was sacrilegious. After speaking publicly against the Saudi government for welcoming American troops, he was forced to leave in 1990 and went into exile in Sudan. He was eventually kicked out of Sudan and cut off from his family stipend of nearly $7 million per year.

Osama bin Laden returned to Afghanistan in 1996 and formed a relationship with Mullah Mohammed Omar and the Taliban. In August 1996, bin Laden declared war against the United States because of the continuing American presence in Saudi Arabia. From 2001 to

2011, the US government considered bin Laden to be a major target and had a $25 million bounty on his head. On May 2, 2011, bin Laden was shot and killed inside a private residential compound in Abbottabad, Pakistan, by US Navy SEALs and CIA operatives in a covert operation ordered by President Barack Obama. He was basically hiding in plain sight, which has made many people wonder how long the US government knew of his whereabouts.

Captured al-Qaeda documents, according to Abdel Bari Atwan in his book the *Secret History of Al Qaeda*, provide an important glimpse into their strategy:

1. Provoke the United States into invading a Muslim country.
2. Incite local resistance to occupying forces.
3. Expand the conflict to other countries, and force the United States to fight a long war of attrition.
4. Convert al-Qaeda into an franchised ideology that does not require direct control.
5. Cause an economic collapse of the US-dominated world economy, which would lead to political chaos and the rise of global jihad led by al-Qaeda.

Reading through these objectives, one can see how successful al-Qaeda has been.

LEGAL BASIS FOR GLOBAL WAR ON TERROR

The authorization for use of military force in the global War on Terror came in the form of a joint resolution passed by Congress on September 14, 2001. The authorization granted the president the authority to use all "necessary and appropriate force" against those whom he determined "planned, authorized, committed, or aided" the September 11th attacks, or who harbored said persons or groups. This resolution shared a lot in common with the Tonkin Gulf Resolution that gave President Johnson authorization for war in Vietnam. The two major components of the global War on Terror are the war in Afghanistan (also known as Operation Enduring Freedom, or OEF), and the war in Iraq (also known as Operation Iraqi Freedom, or OIF). There have been many other smaller operations, not as well known, under the umbrella of the global War on Terror.

THE WAR IN AFGHANISTAN (OPERATION ENDURING FREEDOM)

On October 7, 2001, Operation Enduring Freedom began with a mixture of strikes from land-based aircraft and cruise missiles launched from both US and British ships and submarines. The initial military objectives of OEF included the destruction of terrorist training camps and infrastructure within Afghanistan, the capture of al-Qaeda leaders including Osama bin Laden, and termination of terrorist activities in Afghanistan. The operation was originally called Operation Infinite Justice, but that name was later changed because it was likely to offend Muslims in Afghanistan. President George W. Bush also slipped in a remark he made about the operation, saying, "This crusade, this war on terrorism, is going to take a while." This remark prompted widespread criticism from the Islamic world and likely contributed to the renaming of the operation as well.

In the first phase of OEF, ground forces of the Afghan United Front working with US and British Special Forces, aided by US air support, removed the Taliban regime from power in Kabul and most of the rest of Afghanistan in a matter of weeks. Most of the senior Taliban leadership escaped across the border to Pakistan, along with Osama bin Laden. The democratic Islamic Republic of Afghanistan with an interim government under President Hamid Karzai was created. In 2004 the Afghan people held general elections and reaffirmed the government and president. The International Security Assistance Force (ISAF) was established by the UN Security Council in December 2001 to secure Kabul and the surrounding areas. NATO assumed control of ISAF in 2003. ISAF includes troops from 42 countries (including Norway), with NATO members at the core.

Comparisons have been drawn between OEF and the Vietnam War. For one thing, both wars were authorized by similar resolutions, not a declaration of war. In both cases the US government was trying to create a nation built from fragments. No one power has ever been able to rule Afghanistan for very long. That is why it is known as the graveyard of empires. In Vietnam, the remnants of French colonialism tainted US efforts at nation-building, as most of the people cared little for which government was in charge as long as they had their plot of land and could worship their ancestors. In Afghanistan, the terrain and climate are inhospitable and society is decentralized and tribal. The United States has never had sufficient troop

FIGURE 12.5. US Special Forces and Northern Alliance

strength and logistics to support and eradicate all Taliban insurgents. The same was true in Vietnam—the United States could never cut off all support to the Viet Cong in the South or stop the infiltration of regular North Vietnamese combat troops. Just like in Vietnam, US forces in Afghanistan operated from large forward operating bases, where they searched out the enemy to destroy them. US and NATO forces hit hot spots of insurgency, what the troops called "whack a mole." In both cases the countries were underdeveloped and had a largely illiterate population with a long tradition of successful resistance against foreign powers. The populations in both Vietnam and Afghanistan protected insurgent enclaves. US forces who fought in both Iraq and Afghanistan say that fighting in Afghanistan was harder because of the terrain and the battle-hardened fighters who were older and more experienced than those fighting in Iraq. And lastly, both the Afghan government and the government of South Vietnam were not respected by the majority of their own people and were kept in power primarily with US aid.

THE IRAQ WAR (OPERATION IRAQI FREEDOM)

In his state of the union address on January 29, 2002, President George W. Bush first used the term Axis of Evil. The term referred to governments who support terrorism and seek weapons of mass destruction. Bush labeled Iran, Iraq, and North Korea as the axis of evil. So it is not all together surprising that President Bush ordered the invasion of Iraq.

The Iraq War (also referred to as the Occupation of Iraq, the Second Gulf War, or Operation Iraqi Freedom by the United States military) was a conflict that occurred in Iraq from March 20, 2003, to December 15, 2011. The United States and Great Britain claimed that Iraq had weapons of mass destruction (WMD) and posed a threat to the region. Additionally, the US government claimed that Saddam Hussein was part of the 9/11 conspiracy, thereby further justifying military action against him. In 2002 the United Nations Security Council passed Resolution 1441, which called for Iraq to cooperate with UN weapon inspectors to verify that Iraq did not have WMD and cruise missiles. They found no evidence of WMD, but could not verify what weapons Saddam did have. President Bush did not want to wait any longer for verification and ordered the invasion of Iraq on March 20, 2003.

The American attack began with a decapitation strike to topple the Iraqi leadership. This is what Defense Secretary Donald Rumsfeld called "shock and awe." In April 2003, US, British, and other coalition forces quickly rolled over the Iraqi Army, though some forces loyal to Saddam Hussein, who would later form the core of a postwar insurgency, continued to fight. On May 1, 2003, President Bush declared the end of major combat operations in Iraq from the deck of the aircraft carrier USS *Abraham Lincoln*. Continued minor conflict throughout the country were dismissed as the desperate acts of "dead-enders" by Defense Secretary Donald Rumsfeld. In May 2003, the Iraqi Army and intelligence services were disbanded, which sent hundreds of thousands of well-armed men into the streets. This order, along with an earlier

FIGURE 12.6. Capture of Saddam Hussein

decision to purge Baathists (those loyal to Saddam's former political party) from the government, would have long-lasting negative effects.

US troops finally found Saddam Hussein hiding in a one-man hole near his hometown of Tikrit in December 2003. One month later, the Bush administration conceded that there were no WMD in Iraq. Sectarian violence began to rise in March 2004, as al-Qaeda in Iraq set off a series of suicide bombs, striking Shiite holy sites in Baghdad and Karbala. In Fallujah, four American contractors were killed, burned, and hanged from a bridge after photographs of the treatment of Iraqi prisoners at Abu Ghraib were made public. In September 2004, in the runup to Iraq's national elections, 15,000 US and Iraqi forces assaulted the insurgent stronghold of Fallujah in central Iraq. The urban fighting was successful, but 38 US troops died in the operation. In early 2006, Sunni extremists destroyed the gilded Shiite shrine in Samarra. The attack set off another wave of sectarian violence. Elections in 2006 brought the Shiite United Iraqi Alliance into power. They named Nouri al-Maliki prime minister. Maliki had close ties to Iran.

Saddam Hussein was condemned to death in his trial in November 2006. In January 2007 President Bush announced a "new way forward" in Iraq, promising an additional 20,000 troops to bring stability in and around Baghdad. In June 2007, US forces began recruiting Sunni tribe members, many former insurgents, to take up arms against militants working with al-Qaeda in Iraq. The so-called awakening tactic was credited to General David H. Petraeus, and it reduced insurgent violence in the second half of 2007. The US–Iraq Status of Forces Agreement was signed in 2008, which stated that all US troops would be out of Iraq by the end of 2011. In December 2009 only four American troops were killed, the lowest figure since the war began. On August 18, 2010, formal American combat operations in Iraq ended as the last combat brigade departed for Kuwait.

An opinion poll taken in Iraq revealed that 87 percent of the Iraqi people prefer a dictator to democracy. As of this writing, sectarian violence continues in Iraq, with many casualties every day. Many of the bases and cities secured and built up by the US military effort in Iraq have now fallen to Islamic State (ISIL) forces. President Obama has dramatically increased the number of military advisers in Iraq, and secured billions in funding to fight Islamic State. This is in addition to the CIA and private contractors who never left. Nearly 4,500 American troops have been killed in Iraq, and more than 2,300 have been killed in Afghanistan. Because emergency medical care is so much better now than it had been in previous wars, the number of killed in action is lower than would be expected based on the tempo of combat operations, but the number of severely wounded has risen dramatically. More than 52,000 US servicemen and women have been injured in Iraq and Afghanistan, and those two countries are no closer to peace and democracy than they were when the global War on Terror started.

THE GREAT RECESSION

How did the American Dream become the American Nightmare? The late George Carlin, who was not only a fine comedian but also a genius at political commentary and satire in the spirit of H. L. Mencken, said that "they call it the American Dream because you have to be asleep to believe it." New studies reveal that the social divide between rich and poor in the United States has grown much larger in the current economic crisis, and the United States is now one the most unequal of all of the modern industrialized economies.

President Barack Obama, supported by a coalition of moderate and progressive liberals, was initially elected not only to end the wars in Iraq and Afghanistan, but also to reverse decades of wage stagnation, mounting poverty, and attacks on the social welfare system. However, President Obama, like President Bush, responded to the financial crisis of 2008 by supporting the bailout of the finance industry, not the people. This demonstrated a fundamental political reality: no reform that benefits the working class can come from a government and two-party system that is subservient to the economic elite. One problem is that the official US government statistics on unemployment are not painting an accurate picture.

Northeastern University analyzed unemployment in 2009 and found that, for those in the bottom 10 percent of household earnings, unemployment was at the Great Depression level of 31 percent. According to the Economic Policy Institute, middle-class families have lost jobs, homes, and retirement savings during the recession, but that is just part of a trend going back to the early 1980s. Since 1980, nearly 35 percent of total income growth in the United States was grabbed by the top one-tenth of 1 percent of income earners. The bottom 90 percent shared only 15.9 percent of income growth in the same period. According to a United Nations measurement of the national distribution of family income, the United States had the highest level of economic inequality of the highly industrialized countries in 2008. It was ranked below Sri Lanka and similar to Ghana and Turkmenistan.

Yet working-class Americans do little to change this situation. Part of the problem is perception. Most Americans believe that anyone can go "from rags to riches" by working harder. The reality of the US economy is not what most people perceive to be true, especially when it comes to economic inequality. Statistics show that whatever economic class one is born into in America is the one they will die in. There are exceptions, of course, but that is the norm. The banks were given billions of dollars in bailouts in a crisis they themselves caused, and then turned around and gave their executives huge bonuses while working-class Americans were not able to get simple loans. A *New York Times* report revealed that John G. Stumpf, the head of Wells Fargo Bank, took home $18.7 million in 2009. Jamie Dimon of J.P. Morgan was number two, with $17.6 million in compensation. Lloyd Blankfein, whose company Goldman Sachs took tremendous profits in the financial collapse, was awarded $10 million.

THE HOUSE OF CARDS

The financial crisis, which began in 2007, is linked to reckless lending practices by financial institutions, and the growing trend of pooling home mortgages and selling and trading them as securities. US mortgage-backed securities, which had risks that were difficult to determine, were marketed around the world. The Federal Reserve lowered the federal funds rate to 1 percent for more than a year, which allowed huge amounts of credit-based money to be thrown into the financial system, thereby creating an unsustainable economic boom based on credit.

This was especially true with the global speculative rise in real estate and equities that reinforced the risky lending practices. This unstable financial situation was made more fragile by a sharp increase in oil and food prices. The emergence of sub-prime loan (sub-prime loans are loans made to high risk borrowers) losses in 2007 started the crisis, and exposed other risky loans and over-inflated asset prices. With loan losses stacking up, and the fall of financial services firm Lehman Brothers on September 15, 2008, a major panic broke out on the inter-bank loan market. As share and housing prices declined, many large and well-established investment and commercial banks in the United States and Europe were hit with huge losses and faced bankruptcy. The US government presented this situation as a crisis that required a public bailout. The media and the government portrayed the crisis in apocalyptic terms and said that it was something that would bring down the United States. The American public bought in to the hysteria.

Ultimately, the amount of debt in the US economy can be traced to economic inequality. Middle-class wages remained stagnant while wealth concentrated at the top. Middle-class homeowners, facing a rising cost of living, took equity from their homes and piled up the debt hoping that the housing values would continue to rise so they could pay off their debt. The mortgage-backed security (stocks tied to sub-prime loans) triggered the economic crisis of 2008. The cause of the financial crisis was a shadow banking system that was supported by like-minded members of Congress (Democrats and Republicans) who never regulated the banking industry properly, as they took money from bankers to finance their campaigns.

THE GREAT RECESSION HITS HOME

It would be worthwhile to look at the financial crisis in a microcosm. In Glendora, California, one could buy a modest 3-bedroom house in 2001 for about $225,000. That house would be unimproved—no pool, nothing fancy. By 2007, that same house was worth over $600,000. What many people did was to take out home equity loans to keep step with rising consumer prices, gas prices, food prices, and the general cost of living. People also used their homes as cash machines to take vacations, put in swimming pools, buy new cars and RVs, and basically live above their means because housing prices kept going up and people had confidence that they could easily sell at a tremendous profit, even after they took out such risky home equity loans. Well, when the perceived value collapsed, it was time to pay the piper. So, if a person bought the home for $225,000 in 2001 and took out another $225,000 in home equity loans, they would owe about $450,000. But when the housing bubble burst, their house went back to its natural value, real value if you will, of around $250,000. Consequently, the home owner owed $450,000 on a home worth $250,000. And because hours were cut, wages were flat, and some lost their jobs entirely because the whole economy was based on artificially high home values and easy credit, the homeowner could not keep up with the payments and had to walk away. This created a glut of bank foreclosures around the country. The old saying is very true: "If you owe the bank a little money and you can't pay it, you are in trouble. But if you owe the bank a lot of money and can't pay it, the bank is in trouble." The banking collapse dried up credit, and businesses failed all over the country in a ripple effect. Some cities and states were harder hit than others. Nowhere was the damage more severe than in Detroit, Michigan.

FIGURE 12.7. Unions and Shared Prosperity

DECLINING POWER OF UNIONS

In the first 30 years after World War II, labor unions were able to raise wages and living standards for members and non-members alike. Into the early 1970s, both average compensation and labor productivity doubled. Labor unions sustained and shared prosperity. There was a wage premium for union workers that also benefited non-union workers. Unions also had tremendous political power that translated into favorable legislation for the working class (minimum wage increase, job-based health benefits, Social Security, high marginal tax rates on the rich). The more union members there are, the less the upper 10 percent of the economic strata controls the national income (see graph above). In other words, higher union membership equates to a fairer distribution of income.

With the Conservative Revolution and the Reagan administration's determination to beat labor into submission, labor's bargaining power collapsed. The consequences have been disastrous for the working class. Early in the twentieth century, only 10 percent of the American workforce belonged to a union. At the same time, inequality was a harsh reality, with more than 40 percent of the national income going to the richest 10 percent of Americans. This gap widened in the 1920s. But in 1935, with the implementation of the New Deal, workers gained basic collective bargaining rights and over the next decade, union membership grew dramatically. As a result, there was a decline in percentage of national income controlled by the upper 10 percent. This continued until the early 1980s when unions came under attack—in the workplace, in the courts, and in public policy. As a result, union membership has fallen and income inequality has worsened to levels not seen since the 1920s.

THE RESULTS

US manufacturers have chosen to move their manufacturing overseas, especially to Asia, because labor is cheap and environmental regulations are more relaxed than in America. The impact on the United States is profound: a decline in union jobs, trade imbalance, and negative ripple effects to all other industries. A trip to the Port of Long Beach, California, is all it takes to understand the problem. Huge container ships come in from Asia fully loaded with all of the consumer items Americans buy. When the same ships go out they are loaded with garbage, the largest US export out of Long Beach. The Asian countries use that garbage to remanufacture new items and packaging and sell it right back to Americans. Garbage is just raw material and does not stimulate an economy, not unlike the old British colonial system where Great Britain would extract raw materials from their colonies and manufacture goods in England, then sell those manufactured goods back to the colonies at a tremendous profit. The value lies in production, not in harvesting raw materials.

A quick look at almost any American city reveals a crumbling infrastructure: broken roadways, old water systems leaking, bridges collapsing, factories abandoned and rusting, storefronts boarded up, and car lots empty. Because the US government has focused on defense and has not invested in infrastructure, education, and keeping American jobs at home, the country is in decline. Public schools no longer provide the education once promised to all American children. Most elementary school teachers have to spend their own money to provide their students with the basic things they need in the classroom. Sadly, students are not faring well on national assessments. Less than one-third of US fourth graders are proficient in reading, mathematics, science, and American history. More than half of low-income students cannot even demonstrate basic knowledge of science, reading, and history.

US 8th graders ranked 19 out of 38 countries on mathematic assessments and 18th in science. US 12th graders ranked 18 out of 21 countries in combined mathematics and science assessments. The No Child Left Behind Act, with its emphasis on testing and punishment of poor-performing schools, has done more harm than good. Low-income schools get punished for low test scores and get less funding, creating even more problems.

DIVIDE AND CONQUER

Part of the problem for average Americans trying to make sense of the decline of the United States is that the American media is dominated by just a handful of powerful corporations. One example is what has happened to grassroots political movements like the Tea Party and Occupy Wall Street. The American corporate media portrays the two groups as polar opposites, which on the surface seems to be true. Tea Party activists are generally 45 and older, with many in their 60s. What began as simple protests and rallies moved on to become a more organized effort to influence local and national electoral politics, establish local chapters, and maintain a hierarchical administrative structure. By contrast, the Occupy movement has mostly younger activists who ignored traditional politics and have resisted bureaucratic organization. Instead, they focused on protests and rallies. Once those rallies and protests were dispersed by police, there was no organization to sustain the movement. A *Time* magazine poll in October 2011

FIGURE 12.8. Occupy Wall Street

found that 54 percent of those polled had a favorable opinion of Occupy Wall Street, while 86 percent believed Wall Street itself and lobbyists had too much influence in Washington. But, by April 2012, an *NBC News/Wall Street Journal* poll found that 71 percent of respondents said they did not support Occupy Wall Street. The government and the corporate media had successfully changed public opinion.

Occupy Wall Street began on September 17, 2011, in Zuccotti Park, located in New York City's Wall Street financial district. The movement focused on social and economic inequality worldwide. Their slogan, "We are the 99 percent," referred to income inequality and wealth distribution in the United States between the wealthiest 1 percent and the rest of the population. Apparently the US government took them very seriously. On December 29, 2012, the *Guardian* newspaper provided US government documents revealing that the FBI and the Department of Homeland Security had monitored Occupy Wall Street through its Joint Terrorism Task Force, despite the fact that it was a peaceful movement and not in any way connected to terrorism. The *New York Times* reported in May 2014 that declassified documents showed extensive surveillance and infiltration of groups related to the Occupy movement across the country.

The Tea Party movement is supposedly on the other end of the political spectrum. The Tea Party is an American political movement known for its conservative positions. The movement has been described as a combination of libertarian, populist, and conservative activists. The Tea Party has organized multiple protests and supported various political candidates since 2009. Polls have found that slightly over 10 percent of Americans identify as a member. The name refers to the Boston Tea Party of December 16, 1773. The origins of the current Tea Party movement can be traced back to 2007 and Republican congressman Dr. Ron Paul. His presidential campaign directly contributed to creating a libertarian revival and a divide in the Republican Party. Ron Paul continues to be a prominent force in the Tea Party movement by endorsing Tea Party candidates, and also giving talks and speeches alongside prominent Tea Party activist, and 2008 vice presidential candidate, Sarah Palin.

The interesting thing is that the two movements have some core interests in common. Here is a list of what they have in common:

1. Special interests are too powerful.
2. End bailouts.
3. Return power to the people.
4. Keep American jobs.
5. Neither political party adequately represents average Americans.

So, in spite of the corporate media and US government's efforts, the truth is revealed. The two movements have much in common. The best way to make sure none of these grassroots organizations ever succeed is to divide and conquer—an ancient and still effective strategy.

The recession caused a giant drop in consumer demand, but also stagnating or declining wages for most workers. Real median wages fell by about 2.8 percent between 2009 and 2012. The most recent census data show that while a small group of rich people are getting richer, the middle class is getting poorer. US median income fell to $50,054 in 2011, down 8.1 percent since 2007. The economy is losing good jobs, which are increasingly replaced with low-wage, often part-time jobs. Workers' wages as a percentage of the economy are the lowest they have ever been.

The official 7.6 percent unemployment rate is bad enough, but the real number is actually about twice that. In alarming numbers, more Americans are working part time, but not because they want to. These involuntary part-timers now number more than 8.2 million. In 2012, the median salary for a unionized worker was about $49,000, as opposed to about $39,000 for their non-union counterparts. Thirty years ago, 1 in 5 US workers were union members; now it is about 1 in 10. Higher education in the United States is becoming an unaffordable luxury. By conservative estimates, the cost of a college education is now 50 percent higher than it was 30 years ago. Public colleges and universities are cheaper than private schools, but they are not cheap enough. As states cut funding, the cost of attending a four-year public institution has risen by 5.2 percent each year of the last decade. Student loan debt in this country now exceeds $1 trillion. Working-class families simply can no longer afford to send their children to college.

President Obama Is Mr. Spock

The American people elected President Barack Obama as an anti-war candidate who said that he would end the wars in Iraq and Afghanistan. He even accepted the Nobel Peace Prize in Oslo, Norway, in 2009 based on these promises. President Obama had been at war longer than any other American president. US armed forces are involved in at least 80 countries in an ongoing War on Terror. Although fewer actual American soldiers are in harm's way, the war continues by other means (i.e., drone strikes). The global War on Terror was certainly an inherited war, to be sure, but how will President Obama be judged in history? In his Nobel Peace Prize speech, Obama said that humanity must reconcile "two seemingly irreconcilable truths—that war is sometimes necessary, and war at some level is an expression of human folly." President Obama had a dilemma that is not yet solved and, perhaps, unsolvable. Military historian John Keegan has said that war is a bankruptcy of policy. Maybe there is no solution that even the best and brightest in Washington can ascertain. It may be time to look to popular culture for an answer.

It has become apparent that President Obama is like Mr. Spock from the original *Star Trek* TV series and movies. Spock had a human mother and a Vulcan father and was always struggling to control his human emotions to be more Vulcan. Spock was almost always logical in all of his duties, even under stress. Several times during the series, Captain Kirk and others

FIGURE 12.9. Barack Obama

would call Spock a "half-breed." Spock was often ridiculed for being seemingly emotionless and logical. Those same folks would then turn around and tease him for showing emotion, even though he did so only on rare occasions. Obama had a black African father and was raised by his white American mother. President Obama has said that tribalism had destroyed his father. In other words, emotionally charged, narrow-minded self-interest drove Obama's father instead of logic and cool-headed rationality. Obama's mother moved around a lot, and as a result, the president desired stability in his life and for his family. A person's upbringing often impacts their worldview.

Many people voted for Barack Obama in 2008 because they believed he would end the global War on Terror. Instead, he, in some respects, intensified the war, although not with traditional combat forces. President Obama did pull regular US troops out of Iraq in 2011, but the war continues in Afghanistan, and now some forces have gone back into Iraq to battle the Islamic State (ISIS). The Obama administration (SEAL Team 6) was able to kill Osama bin Laden in May 2011, something the Bush administration was either incapable of or unwilling to do. President Obama, in the role of terrorist hunter, also dramatically increased the use of military drones and seemed to prefer using special forces instead of regular combat troops.

President Obama's 2010 national security strategy was very similar to President George W. Bush's in 2006. Both emphasized American leadership, the most important theme of Bush's national security strategy. But was Obama just following the Washington playbook? In other words, was he carrying out what the defense establishment or the Military Industrial Complex wanted him to do? President Obama dropped the "global War on Terror" label but proceeded with the same legal reasoning, including expanding presidential power and detention policies, unilateral drone strikes wherever terrorists are found, and the use of special forces raids. Obama's surge in Afghanistan was similar to Bush's surge in Iraq in 2007. President Obama did not truly end the war in Iraq or end the war in Afghanistan. Both of those countries remain destabilized and under threat. Critics on both sides of the aisle have been harsh in reviewing his policies. During his first term, critics called Obama's style "Bush-Lite." However, President Obama proved to be more accommodating with both Russia and China than the Bush administration had been. Obama wanted a growing and economically prosperous China as a partner to maintain world order. If China fails, it could fall back on nationalism and choose a path of conflict. Obama believed that we have more to fear from a China under threat than a strong, confident China.

President Obama and President Bush had two very different ideologies, styles, and temperaments. Maybe these differences are not quite like Captain Kirk and Mr. Spock, but President Bush was more emotional, more religious in a sense, whereas President Obama had a more laid-back style, "No Drama Obama," as the pundits say. Bush preferred to make it known what his direction was; Obama played things closer to the vest. The key is, however, that President Obama did not deviate that much from President Bush in terms of foreign policy until after his reelection in 2012. President Obama was given no easy task, inheriting from his predecessor a global War on Terror on two major battlefronts and the home front, a financial crisis, a health care crisis, an education crisis, and an immigration crisis. Obama would like to be remembered for reducing US military presence overseas, having no troops

FIGURE 12.10. Leonard Nimoy as Mr. Spock

in harm's way, and creating a strong and vibrant economy with full employment. The years 2015–2016 showed President Obama breaking somewhat from the Bush Doctrine and Washington playbook and forming his own Obama Doctrine.

THE OBAMA DOCTRINE

President Obama was often criticized by Republicans and others for being too cautious and leading from behind when it came to foreign policy. His philosophy, according to reporters who talked to the president during a trip to Asia in 2014, was simple: "Don't do stupid shit." He acknowledged that the Iraq invasion in 2003 was a mistake. Obama believed that only three threats warranted direct US military intervention in the Middle East:

1. Threat posed by al-Qaeda
2. Threats to Israel
3. A nuclear Iran

Faced with the problems he inherited and trying to fulfill his campaign promises, President Obama pulled US troops out of Iraq in 2011. That decision may have been premature as he then sent in special forces to help battle ISIS who filled the vacuum in Iraq. Although Obama's Afghanistan surge from 2009 to 2012 was like the surge Bush ordered in Iraq, Obama explained this by saying that he was "jammed" by the Defense Department to execute the surge. Then, in 2011, President Obama was presented with a crisis in Libya.

The Arab Spring, manifested in violent and non-violent protests and rebellions in the Arab world, began in December 2010 in Tunisia. By February 2012, many former leaders had been removed from power in Tunisia, Libya, Egypt, and Yemen. An even more dangerous civil war broke out in Syria in 2011. US involvement in Libya began with a UN mission to remove Muammar Gadhafi in 2011. The US and UN–backed effort to topple the Gadhafi regime has led to chaos as several armed factions vie for power, and the people of Libya have suffered. Under Gadhafi, although it was a repressive regime, Libyans enjoyed the highest standard of living in Africa. President Obama later admitted that the Libyan intervention was a mistake and even called the mess in Libya a "shit show." He believed that the price of direct US action is much higher than the price of inaction and has learned that America's friends in the Middle East act only in their own interests, which are not always consistent with American interests. The Libya mess convinced him to pivot toward Asia and Latin America and focus less on the Middle East.

Some of Obama's critics felt that his reticence was making things worse. These critics said that President Obama had no doctrine and simply followed the advice of a few close advisors, especially Valerie Jarrett, and reacted to situations as they occured. Obama's style was similar to Franklin D. Roosevelt, who preferred close advisors and envoys to cabinet members. As far as Russia went, Obama believed that President Vladimir Putin led a second-rate world power desperate for respect at home and recognition abroad. Obama felt that we should let Russia intervene and make terrible mistakes in the Middle East, not the United States. He pointed out that they were hemorrhaging financially with a bad economy and suffered also from demographic problems. President Obama did not feel a need to counter Putin's moves in Syria or make too much of it. Many Americans called for a stronger US response in the Ukraine, but Obama believed that the Ukraine was a core interest for Russia, not for America, and we have to be very clear what our core interests were.

Republicans often invoke the Reagan legacy in foreign policy, but much of his legacy is overblown. The Iranian hostage release during Reagan's inauguration was a slap in the face to President Jimmy Carter, not due to fear of President Reagan. The collapse of the Soviet Union was due as much to Mikhail Gorbachev and communism simply not working as an economic system as it was to Reagan's arms buildup. In Central America, we see that Reagan's arch-nemesis, Daniel Ortega, is still in power. The real achievement of the Reagan years was the arms control deals and the relationship with Gorbachev. President Obama noted several of his own administration's accomplishments:

1. The U.S. economy growing stronger
2. More Americans having health care due to his Affordable Care Act (Obamacare)
3. Global leadership on climate change
4. An opening to Cuba
5. The Iran nuclear deal to delay the Iranian bomb
6. Continuing the fight against terrorism worldwide and the killing of Osama bin Laden
7. The Trans-Pacific Partnership
8. The legalization of same-sex marriage

Critics of Obama could counter each of his self-stated accomplishments, but such is the nature of US politics today, totally polarized with little or no bipartisanship. The truth probably lies somewhere in between. As my mother used to say, "our friends are never as good as we think they are, and our enemies are never as bad as we believe they are." President Obama wanted to be remembered for his wise decision not to intervene in Syria. He wanted to be remembered for eliminating chemical weapons from Syria and preventing another Iraq-like war for the United States. In his fight against terrorism, Obama insisted that ISIS was not an existential threat and argued that climate change was. Climate change worried him, because it made current problems worse. Obama did not believe that terrorism posed as great a threat to the United States as the public believed and feared. ISIS was a wild card in an already messy Middle East. The complicated relationship with Saudi Arabia and close ties to Israel have always made US foreign policy in the Middle East rather tricky and no less so during the Obama administration. American policy planners found themselves trapped in the Sunni-Shiite divide without understanding its origins or full implications. Some US allies like Pakistan seemed more like enemies than friends. The root of the problem was what Obama called tribalism, or narrowly defined self-interest that keeps nations locked in conflict.

President Obama has spoken about what he called resilience in foreign policy. He noted that some European countries push the United States to take military action, but then fail to follow through and do their part. This type of inaction amounts to free-ridership with the United States taking all the risks and doing the heavy lifting. Obama wanted to pivot to Asia and Latin America, where he believed the United States would be better rewarded for its efforts. He was trying to break free from the Washington playbook and the Bush Doctrine, and his refusal to invade Syria pointed this out. The Obama Doctrine was like Eisenhower's moderation where the United States minimizes risks, cuts spending, strategically retreats, and shifts military and defense burdens to allied nations. The Obama Doctrine also took on seemingly sacred cow policy positions on Cuba, Iran, and Pakistan. The opening to Cuba was part of Obama's Latin American pivot, the Iran deal was designed to make a scary and dangerous nation less scary and dangerous, and dealing honestly with Pakistan and Israel was part of a larger disengagement from the Middle East. Could the Iran deal, which angered the Saudis, have been Obama's version of the China card? The Iran card would have been a counter to the influence of Saudi Arabia in the region and would have cleverly played the Sunni-Shiite divide to a US advantage. Saudi Arabia is the home of Wahhabism, which has fueled radical Islamic groups around the world. Saudi Arabia even funded these groups until recently when they became targets. We cannot abandon our relationship with Saudi Arabia, because they can be powerful allies. As we learned in the *Godfather* movies, "keep your friends close and your enemies closer." Obama felt that Islam needed to go through a religious reformation to make US policy in the Middle East work. He also was consistently frustrated with Israeli president Benjamin Netanyahu. Once again, the tribalism issue.

According to President Obama, diplomacy, technocrats, and bureaucrats help keep America safe and secure. Obama said that he would have liked to deal with smart autocrats and technocrats in the Middle East who were emotionally contained. He wished the leaders in the Middle East were more like the Scandinavians, whom he admired. He was strongly against theatricality and playing for the 24-hour news cycle. He believed that we should be careful not to make our enemies a bigger threat than they actually were and insisted that we needed to build resilience, be smart, and stay focused on reality in forming our foreign policy. Obama had to pull back the reins on Secretary of State Hillary Clinton and John Kerry, who both demanded more intervention than Obama.

Was the Obama Doctrine effective? Maybe it is too early to tell. Critics have pointed out that terrorism is growing, and we are not winning. Some have called it the "drip, drip, drip policy." They call for a military ground strategy to defeat the terrorists and a plan to defeat them ideologically as well. Most of these critics point to the Iran deal as an example of the failed Obama Doctrine. Obama said that he was not bluffing with the Iran nuclear deal. If Iran did not sign, he was going to take out their capability. He wanted to believe that his greatest achievement would be keeping us out of intractable problems, especially in the Middle East. He was, however, willing to act swiftly when it came to technology-driven drone warfare. One of his main goals was to take out the caliph of ISIS, Abu Bakr al-Baghdadi. But at the same time, he knew that trying to fix the problems in the Middle East would only deplete our resources, put Americans in harm's way, and damage our global credibility. Most Americans and many people in Europe misunderstood ISIS as a religious group with fanatical beliefs. In actuality, ISIS is simply a militant group seeking power, resources, and territory using religious fervor as a catalyst and rationale. Many of the captured ISIS fighters have little understanding of Islam. Obama believed that we should redouble our connection to areas of the world that hold a better chance for success of US policy (i.e., Asia and Latin America) and limit our investment and exposure in areas of the world that are not likely to produce positive outcomes. In a few years, we will see whether Obama's approach was successful.

In an article in the May 5, 2016, edition of *The New York Times Magazine*, David Samuels interviewed Ben Rhodes, deputy national security adviser for strategic communications in the Obama administration. Rhodes is a novelist and does not have a national security background. Even though Rhodes has a Master of Fine Arts in Creative Writing, he became "the single most influential voice shaping American foreign policy," except for President Obama himself. Rhodes saw foreign policy as a literary exercise that required the creation of plotlines, heroes, villains, and story arcs. No one understood the president's thinking on foreign policy more than Rhodes. Rhodes described this as a "mind meld" with President Obama. Of course, one of Mr. Spock's talents was his ability to conduct Vulcan mind melds with other beings and even intelligent machines. In an episode of the original *Star Trek* series called "A Taste of Armageddon," Spock blasted an alien planet's disintegration chambers to end their endless cycle of computer warfare. When confronted, Spock said that he was simply "exercising a peculiar variety of diplomacy." At the same time, Spock also held a deep reverence for logic in all interactions and a peaceful ethos. This was revealed in another episode called "Is There in Truth, No Beauty?" Spock wore an Infinite Diversity Through Infinite Combinations (IDIC) pin on his uniform. The dialogue revealed that this ethos was at the foundation of his Vulcan culture. Spock went on to say, "The glory of creation is in its infinite diversity. And the ways our differences combine to create meaning and beauty."

I believe that President Barack Obama exhibited these Vulcan characteristics of logic and seeking peaceful solutions to complex problems, but he also exhibited, like Spock, his other half, determined to take whatever action was necessary at that moment to achieve the desired result. When Leonard Nimoy, who played Spock in the *Star Trek* series, died in 2015, President Obama eulogized him. "Long before being nerdy was cool, there was Leonard Nimoy. Leonard was a lifelong lover of the arts and humanities, a supporter of the sciences, generous with his talent and his time. And of course, Leonard was Spock. Cool, logical, big-eared and level-headed, the center of *Star Trek*'s optimistic, inclusive vision of humanity's future." He went on to say, "I loved Spock." When Obama met Leonard Nimoy in 2007, he greeted him with the well-known Vulcan salute and greeting, "Live long and prosper." Life imitated art once again.

THE YEAR **2016** AND BEYOND

BLACK LIVES MATTER

A recent social movement has taken root and expanded in the past few years. The Black Lives Matter movement began with the shooting death of Trayvon Martin in 2013 by George Zimmerman, who was a neighborhood watch volunteer. After Zimmerman was acquitted, the movement started and focused on the shooting of other African Americans by the police.

As of this writing, many professional athletes and others take a knee or remain seated during the playing of the national anthem in order to protest the killing of black people by the police and continuing racial injustice in America. I have read many different statements, heard different speeches, and have tried to come up with my take on the situation. As a historian, I thought that maybe past events and people from the past could help us understand what is going on today. Last summer, I imagined speaking to President Abraham Lincoln, my favorite president. I do this every now and then, speak to historical figures that is. It might seem strange, but it is a helpful way to use history to inform and advise us about the current problems we face. I asked President Lincoln what he thought about Black Lives Matter. He said, "Of course black lives matter. I gave my life for that very same cause. I want to remind everyone of something important. Please permit me to quote myself, 'We are not enemies, but friends. We must not be enemies. Though passion may have strained it must not break our bonds of affection' … we must appeal to 'the better angels of our nature.' And let me add, my heart is heavy for the loss of all American lives, but we must take this opportunity to complete our journey we began so long ago. We should be 'dedicated to the great task remaining before

FIGURE 12.11. Black Lives Matter protest in New York City, NY

us ... that from these honored dead, we take increased devotion to that cause for which they gave the last full measure of devotion ... that we here highly resolve that these dead shall not have died in vain ... that this nation, under God, shall have a new birth of freedom ... and that government of the people ... by the people ... for the people ... shall not perish from the earth.'" And with that he doffed his stovepipe hat and turned to go.

If you look at percentages provided by various law enforcement agencies and the news media, 26 percent of people killed by the police in 2015 were African American, 50 percent were white, and 17 percent were Hispanic. According to the Census Bureau, we know that African Americans make up only 12 percent of the US population, whites 64 percent, and Hispanics 16 percent. So, based on these statistics, it can be said that African Americans are being killed by the police disproportionately. That is very clear. Of the police who are shooting, 10 percent are black officers. Focusing just on police shootings ignores the overall problem of violence in America. In 2016 in the city of Chicago alone, 762 people were murdered according to Chicago newspapers. Of those murdered in Chicago, 620 were black. Police killed 11 people in Chicago in 2016. Nationwide, more than 16,000 people are murdered each year, with black people making up more than half of the homicide victims. So, the question remains, what can we do and where do we go from here?

How can we still have such problems when, for the last seven years, we have had a mixed-race (white and black) president? Dr. Cornel West who is a former Princeton professor of philosophy, says the Black Lives Matter movement is a "marvelous new militancy" that should focus "on love and justice," he told CBS News. West thinks that we are in bad shape in terms of race in America. He believes that President Obama kept the race problems at arm's length and did not hit them directly. West even called him "a black puppet of Wall Street." The result of this lack of direct action, West said, is Black Lives Matter.

2016 PRESIDENTIAL ELECTION

A paradigm shift may be occurring in both the Democratic and the Republican Parties. Few could have predicted that a businessman and reality TV star like Donald Trump would win the Republican nomination, much less the presidency. Hillary Clinton was a more obvious candidate, but Senator Bernie Sanders put up a good fight, and eventually Clinton prevailed with possibly some assistance from a corrupt Democratic Party nomination system. It is perhaps an odd comparison, but Trump's rise is somewhat like the rise of Jimmy Carter in the 1976 election. A vote for Jimmy Carter was a vote against the Washington establishment. The Republican convention in Cleveland was a grandiose tribute to Trump's impossible mission as a billionaire populist. His rise confounded the Republican party establishment and splintered it into several pieces. The Democratic convention in Philadelphia was more of a neo-liberal coronation of Hillary Clinton with Senator Sanders officially giving his blessing, much to the chagrin of his fervent supporters.

WHAT HAPPENED TO HILLARY CLINTON?

Many people are asking how Hillary Clinton could have lost the election. A simple answer is that she did not generate the enthusiasm needed to get Democrats to vote. If you dig deeper, this lack of enthusiasm could be that the Clintons are Gilded Age politicians in progressive clothing. They are part of the Conservative Revolution that Reagan started in 1980. In fact, even though he is branded as a left-wing liberal and even a socialist, President Obama was rather conservative. Women who have become prime ministers and presidents around the world usually come to office if they are martyrs, mother figures, or conservative enough to not pose a threat to the establishment. Hillary Clinton knew that the more conservative she became, the more mainstream voters she would attract. Her foreign policy inclinations were more like Bush administration policies than President Obama's. Clinton has very conservative roots, as she was a Goldwater Republican early in her adult life. Clinton seems to be pushing the idea that she is not a doctrinaire cultural liberal and that she has consistently favored working toward conservative goals (preservation of the family, protection of children) by using activist government means. Ronald Reagan used to be a New Deal Democrat. He was fond of saying that he did not leave the Democratic Party, the party left him. Clinton might eventually say the same thing about the Republican Party. The bottom line is that traditional liberalism is dead. Ted Kennedy was probably the last of the old-line liberals. Powerful corporations have influenced politics and both political parties.

Are we returning to the Gilded Age of cronyism? What can we make of this 2016 presidential election cycle? We know that more than half of the money pouring into super political action committees come from just 50 mega-rich donors (both liberals and conservatives). The last time wealth factored into politics this directly was in 1896 when corporations and banks helped put Republican William McKinley in the White House. This was all made possible today, because the Supreme Court decided in *Citizens United v. Federal Election Commission* that the government could not restrict independent political expenditures by a nonprofit corporation. Where does that leave the average citizen looking for responsive government representation? We need to look back for an answer.

The original Gilded Age came to an end when both parties supported organized labor, income tax, antitrust enforcement, and financial regulation. Now, Republicans and Democrats have worked together to cement the two-party system and dismantle the remnants of the New Deal social welfare state. Both parties court populist grassroots causes and issues that divide liberals and conservatives, but the parties are more alike than different. This is false populism. As distasteful as Donald Trump is to many folks, he has pointed out something very ugly in our political system. People are easily distracted, manipulated, and divided while the wealthiest retain their power and control. Bernie Sanders generated enthusiasm, especially among Millennials. I believe he could have beaten Donald Trump, because Sanders represented change, and Clinton did not.

THE RISE OF DONALD TRUMP

Donald Trump was able to run against both parties in his campaign. He ran against the Republican Party and Democratic Party establishments. He also cleverly condemned the press and used them to promote his campaign. He set himself up as an outsider, which appealed to the voters who felt disenfranchised by the establishment. Donald Trump may have done the Republican Party a favor by shaking it by the roots and transforming it into some type of post-modern, populist, progressive amalgam. Much of Trump's support is channeled from disdain for the extremely erudite and professorial Barack Obama. There is a strain of anti-intellectualism in American politics, and Obama personifies the cool-headed intellectual. Often Trump has been compared to Hitler and other dictators. He reminded me, sometimes, of Italian fascist dictator Benito Mussolini in his mannerisms, but neither of those characterizations is correct. I believe he is more like P.T. Barnum, Buffalo Bill Cody, or any of the men responsible for the construction of the transcontinental railroad. All of them were truly American iconic figures, visionary, creative, driven, financially successful, and rather shady.

The 2016 presidential election season featured a classic neo-liberal in Hillary Clinton, an autocratic narcissist with a populist twist in Donald Trump, and a self-proclaimed democratic socialist in Senator Bernie Sanders. None of the three candidates totally excited the folks in the Black Lives Matter movement. Although Sanders should have excited them due to his more left-wing populism leaning toward Dr. Martin Luther King, Jr.'s social democracy, more African Americans have favored the old neo-liberalism of Clinton. Donald Trump was not very successful in gathering minority voters, but as it turned out, it did not matter. When you look at the exit polls from Cable News Network, 58 percent of white people voted for Trump, 8 percent of African Americans, 29 percent of Latinos, and 29 percent of Asians. Regarding gender, 53 percent of men voted for Trump and 42 percent of women. Pew Research Center data show that African Americans and young people did not come out and vote in the numbers that the Clinton campaign anticipated. In fact, fewer Democrats turned out to vote than in recent elections. Nearly 70 million Democrats voted in 2008, 60 million in 2012, and around 59 million in 2016. Republican voting remained constant the last three elections. Only 46 percent of Millennials (age 18–35) voted compared to 61 percent of Generation X (age 36–51), 69 percent of Baby Boomers (age 52–70), and 72 percent of the Silent Generation (age 71 and over). Had all Millennials voted, Clinton would have won in a landslide. When you look at how each county voted in 2016, you see that Trump took rural areas, and Clinton secured the urban areas. The Democratic Party inefficiently concentrated its support in urban centers while the Republicans under Trump spread out their support across vast rural areas. The Democrats were tone-deaf when it came to the voice of rural America, and they failed to read the subtext. Rural America wanted change.

Donald Trump's victory will probably not provide the social change that Black Lives Matter supporters or liberals want, but neither would have a Hillary Clinton presidency. Trump will definitely be friendlier to business than President Obama was, but at the same

FIGURE 12.12. Donald Trump and Hillary Rodham Clinton

time, he will probably get the United States out of trade deals that he feels take away American jobs. Will the economy improve? No one is certain. Will he actually institute mass deportations? Probably not. Will he ban all Muslims from entering the United States? Probably not. Will he set back advances for ethnic minorities in the United States? Probably not. Will he try to overturn *Roe v. Wade*? Probably not. Will he try to reverse the rights that gay and lesbian people have won? Probably not. In spite of all of the rhetoric, Trump will have to move a giant government bureaucracy, and that is not easy. Also, most Americans would not support any of those measures outside of the heat of a political campaign season. César Chávez once said, "Once social change begins; it cannot be reversed." We cannot go back. It is hard to predict what a President Trump will do militarily. People assume he will improve relations with Russia, pressure North Atlantic Treaty Organization countries to pay their fair share, and get the United States out of the Iran nuclear deal. Time will tell. As of this writing, it is pretty clear that Russian hackers tried to interfere in our election. I believe their main goal is to spread fear and anger and divide our nation. It is important to keep in mind that the Russians cannot defeat America, only we can do that if we allow differences and divisions to tear us apart. America needs to remain strong and united to handle the challenges that lie ahead. Intelligence experts warn that at least 90 nations are either already unstable or will be shortly; the next four years will be difficult ones for President Trump and America.

We continue to be a nation that is constantly at war (either with ourselves at home or enemies abroad) never healing from the last war until we are in a new one. The wars come home with us and permeate our society. This has fed into our already conflict-driven society and goes a long way toward explaining gun violence in the United States. Our culture is a culture of violence, just like the old westerns I used to watch when I was a kid. Richard Slotkin wrote a book about America called *Gun Fighter Nation*. The premise is that US national identity is derived from the violent conquest of the indigenous people of the western frontier.

FIGURE 12.13. William F. "Buffalo Bill" Cody

Springing forth from this are continuing problems of racism, imperialism, war, and even anti-intellectualism. Slotkin attributes gun violence in the United States to the pervasive western myth. That is a good take on our culture, I am afraid. This can change, but we have to free ourselves from the military industrial complex President Eisenhower warned us of in 1961. As he said, "The potential for the disastrous rise of misplaced power exists and will persist." There are no easy solutions, but I believe that a lasting peace can only come when everyone decides to put aside the old myths, change the paradigm of violence, sober up, put away our six-shooters, and deal with each other respectfully, honestly, openly, and non-violently. As Dr. Martin Luther King, Jr. said after the murder of Malcolm X in 1965, "I believe firmly in non-violence. I think we have got to learn to disagree without being violently disagreeable and this whole philosophy of expressing dissent through murder must be vigorously condemned."

CONCLUSION

I have been helping young veterans at Citrus College return to civilian life and acclimate to college since 2000. In 2007, Manuel Martinez, Ginger De Villa-Rose, and I started our Boots to Books transition course. Boots to Books was the first college credit transition course for return-ing veterans in the nation. I have noticed that these young veterans, like my brother and his gen-eration of Vietnam veterans, and every generation of war veterans since the Revolutionary War, fight for what they believe to be right, for their country, their families, their friends, and their buddies in the trenches. These brave young men and women join the military to get their lives together and to take the burden off their families and provide for their own college education through the GI Bill. These reasons are noble and good. However, their bravery is often used by others for a more sinister purpose. Wars are often started by greedy, money hungry, and power hungry leaders and politicians. Colonel William V. Wenger, US Army (retired), often tells his students, "Old men make decisions that more of the young must die."

Colonel Wenger, who has taught at the US Army War College, served in Iraq with General Petraeus, served in Afghanistan in high-level positions, and is privy to the inner workings of the Pentagon and Washington politics, has become very disillusioned with the wars in Iraq and Afghanistan:

> We never implemented a realistic, informed, resourced national strategy for either fight. We did not understand the dynamics of the cultures, the region, the religion, the needs of the people and their mindset. We also had no coherent vision of our national security strategy (and still do not). We just wanted to impose our version of democracy on a people and region that were and are not prepared, educated, conditioned, or desirous of what we thought they needed. . . . Until the public gets better involved in our national decision-making we will be led by unscrupulous politicians into wars of economic benefit for the elite few.

Many people believed that electing Barack Obama would reverse the gains made by conservatives since Reagan and reestablish a left-of-center liberal state. That simply has not worked out the way many people thought it would. The same will be true for President Donald Trump and his goals. I have come to the conclusion that people who get elected president often find that once they are in the oval office, they do not have as much control as they thought they would have. Maybe the key is to address the baseline socio-economic issues, as well as our predilection for violent conflict. I am reminded of the words of labor and civil rights leader César Chávez, "Non-violence really rests on the reservoir that you have to create in yourself of patience, not of being patient with the problems, but being patient with yourself to do the hard work."

It appears the decline of the United States began with the assassination of President John F. Kennedy. His assassination led to the Vietnam War and, ultimately, the end of the left-of-center New Deal coalition begun by Franklin D. Roosevelt. The conservative revolution that began with Reagan's election still has a firm grip on the lives of most Americans. To make matters worse, we no longer have privacy. National Security Agency (NSA) whistleblower Edward Snowden revealed a deep level of intrusion into our everyday lives. Our worst "Big Brother" nightmares have come true. We live in a national security state, but all of this can be reversed if people wake up and take back their lives and their country. As Theodore Roosevelt would have pointed out, we are out of balance. We have big business, big government, but we no longer have big labor unions to protect the working class. Economic power equates to political power. Until that situation is rectified, nothing will get better for most Americans. And we need not allow ourselves to be driven by fear, anger, and tribalism. We need to do the hard work and make history.

TIMELINE

1990

April 24: The Hubble Space Telescope is launched.

August 2: Iraq invades Kuwait.

1991

January 16: The Gulf War begins in order to remove Iraq from Kuwait.

August 6: The World Wide Web debuts.

October 15: Supreme Court candidate Clarence Thomas's confirmation hearings take place.

December 25: The Cold War ends as the Soviet Union dissolves.

1992

April 29: Los Angeles riots that erupted after the Rodney King verdict spread across the country.

May 7: The Twenty-Seventh Amendment is passed, prohibiting changes to Congress members' salaries from taking effect until after an election of representatives.

August 16: Hurricane Andrew, a Category 5 hurricane, kills 65 people and causes $26 billion in damage to Florida and other areas of the US Gulf Coast.

November 3: Bill Clinton defeats President George H. W. Bush.

1993

February 26: A truck bomb explodes in the parking garage under the World Trade Center in New York City, killing 6 people and injuring thousands.

February 28: The Branch Davidians engage in a standoff with law enforcement near Waco, Texas, that leads to the deaths of 76 people, including leader David Koresh.

March 12: The "storm of the century" strikes the Eastern seaboard.

April: Massive flooding along the Mississippi and Missouri Rivers kills 50 people and devastates the Midwest.

December 21: President Clinton signs "Don't ask, don't tell" into law.

1994

January 1: The North American Free Trade Agreement (NAFTA) goes into effect.

January 17: The Northridge earthquake kills 72 and injures 9,000 in the Los Angeles area and causes $20 billion in damage.

November 8: Republicans gain control of both the House and the Senate for the first time since 1955.

1995

April 19: The Oklahoma City bombing kills 168 and wounds 800.

July 12–15: A heat wave kills 750 urban poor and elderly in Chicago.

October 3: Retired professional football player O. J. Simpson is acquitted of two charges of first-degree murder in the 1994 slayings of his ex-wife and her friend.

November 14: A budget crisis forces the federal government to shut down for several weeks.

1996

June 25: The Khobar Towers bombing kills 19 US servicemen in Saudi Arabia.

July 17: TWA Flight 800 explodes off Long Island, killing all 230 aboard.

July 27: The Centennial Olympic Park bombing at the summer Olympics in Atlanta kills 1 and injures 111.

1997

October 27: The Dow Jones Industrial Average follows world markets and drops 7 percent in one day.

1998

January 21: President Clinton is accused of having a sexual relationship with 22-year-old White House intern Monica Lewinsky.

August 7: US Embassy bombings in Tanzania and Kenya kill 224.

October 12: Gay college student Matthew Shepard is brutally murdered near the University of Wyoming.

November 13: Former Arkansas state employee Paula Jones, who had accused President Clinton of sexual harassment, settles out of court.

1 9 9 9

March 29: The Dow Jones Industrial Average closes above the 10,000 mark for the first time.

April 20: Two teenage students murder 13 other students and teachers at Columbine High School.

October 31: The first officer deliberately crashes Egypt Air Flight 990 south of Nantucket, Massachusetts, killing 217.

December: Everyone fears the Y2K bug will cause computers to crash worldwide.

2 0 0 0

October 12: The destroyer USS *Cole* is bombed in Yemeni waters, killing 17 US Navy sailors.

November 7: George W. Bush loses the popular vote to Al Gore, but wins the electoral vote after a Supreme Court decision.

2 0 0 1

September 11: 19 terrorists hijack four planes and crash them into the World Trade Center, the Pentagon, and a field in Shanksville, Pennsylvania.

September 18: Anthrax attacks kill 5 and infect a further 17 through the US postal system.

October 7: The United States launches the invasion of Afghanistan, marking the start of Operation Enduring Freedom (OEF).

October 26: The Patriot Act passes.

November 12: American Airlines Flight 587 crashes in Queens, New York, killing 265.

2 0 0 2

January 8: The No Child Left Behind education reform bill is signed.

October 2: Ten people are killed and three are injured in the Beltway sniper attacks around the Washington, DC, area.

November 25: The Department of Homeland Security is created.

2 0 0 3

February 1: Space shuttle *Columbia* disintegrates upon re-entry into the Earth's atmosphere, killing all seven astronauts.

March 19: The invasion of Iraq (Operation Iraqi Freedom or OIF) begins.

December 13: Saddam Hussein is captured.

2004

February 4: The social networking website Facebook is launched.

May 17: Massachusetts becomes the first state to legalize same-sex marriage.

June 5: Former US president Ronald Reagan dies from complications resulting from Alzheimer's disease.

November 2: George W. Bush is re-elected.

2005

August 23: Hurricane Katrina devastates the Louisiana, Mississippi, and Alabama coastlines, killing at least 1,836 people and causing $81 billion in damage, making it the costliest natural disaster in US history.

2006

November 7: The Democratic Party retakes control of both houses of Congress.

2007

January 4: Democrat Nancy Pelosi becomes the first female speaker of the US House of Representatives.

January 10: George W. Bush orders a troop surge that increases the number of US troops in Iraq and ultimately leads to major victories for coalition and Iraqi forces against the insurgency.

April 16: A South Korean student shoots and kills 32 other students and professors in the Virginia Tech massacre before killing himself.

August 1: The I-35W Mississippi River bridge in Minneapolis, Minnesota, collapses, killing 13 people.

December: The Great Recession officially begins in December.

2008

July: US oil prices hit a record $147 per barrel.

September 20: The global financial crisis begins as the stock market crashes.

November 4: Barack Obama is elected 44th president of the United States, becoming the first African American to hold the office.

2009

February 27: The first of a series of Tea Party protests are conducted across the United States.

February 17: President Barack Obama obtains congressional approval for a $787 billion stimulus package, the largest since the Eisenhower administration.

June 25: Pop icon Michael Jackson dies.

October 28: The Matthew Shepard Act passes, criminalizing discrimination based on sexual orientation, gender identity, sex, or disability.

November 5: Nidal Malik Hasan kills 12 servicemen and injures 31 in the Fort Hood shooting.

2010

April 20: The Deepwater Horizon oil rig in the Gulf of Mexico explodes, spilling millions of gallons of oil into the sea.

November 7: The controversial Patient Protection and Affordable Care Act (Obama Care) is passed by thin margins in Congress.

2011

March 19: The launch of Operation Odyssey Dawn begins, part of a United Nations military intervention in the Libyan civil war.

May 2: Osama bin Laden, leader of al-Qaeda and mastermind of the 9/11 attacks, is killed.

May 22: A tornado strikes Joplin, Missouri, killing 154 and injuring 1,000, making it the deadliest single US tornado ever reported.

July 21: The space shuttle *Atlantis* touches down, ending the 30-year shuttle program.

September 17: The populist Occupy Wall Street protest movement begins when activists camp themselves in New York City.

September 20: With the repeal of the "Don't ask, don't tell" policy, gays and lesbians can serve openly in the military.

2012

July 20: A gunman kills 12 and injures 58 at a movie theater in Aurora, Colorado.

October 22: Hurricane Sandy devastates the Northeast coast, killing over 100 people.

November 6: President Barack Obama is re-elected.

December 14: A gunman kills 26, including 20 children, at the Sandy Hook Elementary School in Newtown, Connecticut.

2013

February 3: Former police officer Christopher Dorner murders three people in Southern California, starting the largest manhunt in Los Angeles history.

April 15: Terrorists attack the Boston Marathon.

June 5: Edward Snowden, former NSA analyst, releases top secret documents about internal surveillance of American citizens.

June 7: Six are killed in a mass shooting in Santa Monica.

June 26: The Supreme Court strikes down the Defense of Marriage Act.

2014

May 27: A student at University of California, Santa Barbara, stabs and shoots six students to death.

August–December: Grand jury decisions in Ferguson, Missouri, and New York City, involving police killings of black men leads to violence and riots and the killing of two police officers.

November 3: One World Trade Center opens in New York City.

November 4: Republicans take control of the US Senate and maintain control of the House.

December 17: President Obama announces diplomatic relations with Cuba.

2015

January 7: The ISIS shooting attacks occur at Charlie Hebdo (a satirical magazine) in Paris.

January 26–27: A blizzard hits the East Coast, and more than 60 million people are affected.

February 1: The New England Patriots beat the Seattle Seahawks in the Super Bowl amid accusations of cheating.

February 11: The American Cancer Society publishes research that shows cigarette smoking mortality is greater than previously thought.

February 16: A federal judge in Texas halts President Obama's executive order on immigration allowing states to file suit.

February 26: Federal Communications Commission rules in favor of net neutrality.

March 3: Israeli prime minister Benjamin Netanyahu speaks before Congress, attempting to deter the Iran nuclear deal.

March 9: President Obama issues an executive order declaring Venezuela a national security threat.

March 11: A gunman shoots two police officers in Ferguson, Missouri.

March 19: Scientists urge a worldwide moratorium on gene editing methods to genetically engineer the human genome in a way that can be inherited.

April 1: California governor Jerry Brown signs an executive order mandating a 25 percent reduction in water use, because of continuing severe drought.

April 11: President Obama and Cuban president Raul Castro discuss normalizing relations in Panama City, Panama.

April 25: Major rioting and protests occur in Baltimore.

April 27: Protests and rioting occur in Baltimore after the death of Freddie Gray in police custody.

May 3: Islamist gunmen are shot dead by police in Garland, Texas, at an exhibition of drawings of the prophet Muhammad.

June 9: Former Gold Medal Olympic athlete Bruce Jenner comes out as a transgender woman.

June 17: A white gunman kills nine African Americans in Charleston, South Carolina.

June 23: The United States announces that tanks and heavy weapons are to be positioned in Eastern Europe to counter Russian aggression in the Ukraine.

June 26: Gay marriage is fully legalized in all 50 states by the Supreme Court.

July 10: The Confederate battle flag is removed from the South Carolina State House.

July 16: A gunman shoots and kills five people at a US Military Recruiting Center in Chattanooga, Tennessee.

July 20: The United States reopens the embassy in Havana, Cuba.

September 3: Rowan County, Kentucky, clerk Kim Davis is sentenced to prison for refusing to issue marriage licenses to same-sex couples.

September 18: Volkswagen is caught cheating on emissions standards.

September 22–27: Pope Francis visits the United States.

September 28: The National Aeronautics and Space Administration (NASA) announces that liquid water flows on Mars.

October 1: Nine people killed at Umpqua Community College in Roseburg, Oregon.

October 9: President Obama decides to suspend the training of Syrian rebels.

October 15: President Obama announces that the American presence in Afghanistan will continue through 2017.

October 30: President Obama orders 50 US special operations ground troops to Syria.

November 12: NASA scientists report that carbon dioxide levels continue to rise.

November 13: ISIS attacks occur in Paris.

December 2: A mass shooting by ISIS supporters occurs in San Bernardino, California, killing 14 people.

December 3: The Defense Department announces that all combat roles will be open to women by April 1, 2016.

December 7: Republican presidential candidate Donald Trump calls for complete ban on Muslims entering the United States.

2016

January 2–26: An armed militia takes over a government building in Oregon. The occupation ends with one militiaman being shot dead and five others being arrested, including Ammon Bundy.

January 5: President Obama issues executive orders to further enforce gun laws.

January 6: North Korea claims to have successfully tested a thermonuclear weapon.

January 9: The Powerball lottery exceeds $1 billion for the first time.

January 14: The Academy Award nominations do not reflect diversity, creating a controversy.

January 18: Oxfam publishes a report stating that world's 62 richest people are as wealthy as half the world's population.

February 1: The World Health Organization declares a global public health emergency over the rapid spread of Zika-linked conditions.

February 2: The first case of Zika contracted on the US mainland (Texas) occurs, and the second known sexually transmitted case is confirmed in Texas.

February 13: Supreme Court Justice Antonin Scalia passes away.

March 1: Donald Trump and Hillary Clinton are the big winners in the Super Tuesday primary elections.

March 11: Violence at a Donald Trump campaign rally causes four injuries and leads to the cancellation of the rally.

March 14: NASA releases data showing that February 2016 was the warmest month ever recorded globally to date.

March 20: President Obama and his family visit Cuba—the first American president to do so since Calvin Coolidge in 1928.

March 22: ISIS attacks occur in Brussels, Belgium.

April 12: Scientists and Internet entrepreneurs, including Yuri Milner, Stephen Hawking, and Mark Zuckerburg, announce an interstellar project to send a robot spacecraft to Alpha Centauri.

May 22: US president Barack Obama arrives in Vietnam for a three-day tour.

May 28: Harambe, a gorilla form Cincinnati Zoo, is shot after dragging a boy who fell into his enclosure.

June 12: A gunman claiming allegiance to ISIS kills 49 and wounds 53 at a gay nightclub in Orlando, Florida.

June 23: The United Kingdom (UK) votes to leave the European Union (EU) in its "Brexit" referendum.

June 24: British prime minister David Cameron resigns after the UK votes to leave the EU.

June 26: Iraqi forces retake the city of Falluja from ISIS.

June 27: The US Supreme Court strikes down a Texas law restricting abortion.

June 29: US Defense Secretary Ashton B. Carter lifts the Pentagon's ban on transgendered people serving in the US armed forces.

July 5: NASA's Juno spacecraft successfully enters Jupiter's orbit.

July 5: The Federal Bureau of Investigation (FBI) releases a report stating Hillary Clinton was "extremely careless" in handling classified emails.

July 6: African American Alton Sterling is shot by Louisiana police in Baton Rouge while being restrained.

July 6: African American Philando Castile is shot by police in St. Paul, Minnesota, after being pulled over for a broken tail light.

July 9: A lone gunman shoots and kills five police officers in Dallas, Texas. This happened during a protest march against fatal police shootings of African Americans.

July 15: An attempted military coup in Turkey fails, with nearly 300 killed and 6,000 arrested.

July 29: Hillary Clinton accepts the Democratic nomination for US president at the Democratic convention in Philadelphia—the first woman so nominated by a major US party.

September 17: A terror bomb in Chelsea, New York, injures 29.

September 20: African American Keith Lamont Scott is shot dead by a black police officer in Charlotte, North Carolina, provoking violent protests in the city.

October 7: The *Washington Post* releases videotape of Donald Trump boasting of groping and kissing women without consent.

October 13: American singer-songwriter Bob Dylan is awarded the Nobel Prize for Literature.

October 28: FBI director James Comey announces that the FBI will be restarting the investigation into Hillary Clinton's emails. This causes Clinton's lead to drop heavily within days.

November 6: James Comey tells Congress there is no evidence in emails that Clinton should face charges over the handling of classified information.

November 8: Donald J. Trump is elected the 45th president of the United States.

November 12: Anti-Trump protests continue in many big cities in America.

November 26: Communist revolutionary and former Cuban president Fidel Castro dies.

December 23: In a diplomatic rebuke of Israel, the United States abstains on a UN Security Council resolution, demanding an end to Israeli settlements.

December 26: In Chicago, 53 people are shot and 13 killed over the Christmas holiday weekend. More than 700 people have been murdered in Chicago in 2016.

December 29: President Obama announces sanctions against Russia for election hacking and expels 35 Russian diplomats.

2017

January 12: Russian hacking scandal escalates with unconfirmed reports of Trump campaign connections to the Russians coming out in the midst of Trump cabinet confirmation hearings.

January 20: Donald J. Trump is inaugurated as the 45th president of the United States.

CREDITS

1. Fig. 12.1. "Bill Clinton," http://commons.wikimedia.org/wiki/File:Bill_Clinton_1995_im_Parlament_in_London.jpg. Copyright in the Public Domain.

2. Fig. 12.2. Eric Draper, "George W. Bush," http://commons.wikimedia.org/wiki/File:GeorgeWBush.jpg. Copyright in the Public Domain.

3. Fig. 12.3. Lt. Steve Gozzo "American F-14 Over Burning Kuwaiti Oil Well, 1991," U.S. Navy, http://commons.wikimedia.org/wiki/File:F-14A_VF-114_over_burning_Kuwaiti_oil_well_1991.JPEG. Copyright in the Public Domain.

4. Fig. 12.4. "September 11 in New York," U.S. National Park Service, http://commons.wikimedia.org/wiki/File:National_Park_Service_9-11_Statue_of_Liberty_and_WTC.jpg. Copyright in the Public Domain.

5. Fig. 12.5. "US Special Forces and Northern Alliance," U.S. Army, http://commons.wikimedia.org/wiki/File:SF_Sgt_Mario_Vigil_with_SF_and_NA_forces_west_of_Konduz_in_November_2001.jpg. Copyright in the Public Domain.

6. Fig. 12.6. "Capture of Saddam Hussein," U.S. Military, http://commons.wikimedia.org/wiki/File:SaddamSpiderHole.jpg. Copyright in the Public Domain.

7. Fig. 12.7. Copyright © Transplanted Mountaineer (CC by 2.0) at https://www.flickr.com/photos/33524327@N00/1218476612/.

8. Fig. 12.8. Source: Colin Gordon "Unions and shared prosperity," Economic Policy Institute, http://www.epi.org/publication/unions-decline-inequality-rises/.

9. Fig. 12.9. Copyright © David Shankbone (CC by 3.0) at http://commons.wikimedia.org/wiki/File:Day_47_Occupy_Wall_Street_November_2_2011_Shankbone_2.JPG.

10. Fig. 12.10. Copyright © transplanted mountaineer (CC by 2.0) at https://commons.wikimedia.org/wiki/File:ObamaSouthCarolina.jpg.

11. Fig. 12.11. NBC Television, "Leonard Nimoy as Mr. Spock," https://en.wikipedia.org/wiki/File:Leonard_Nimoy_as_Spock_1967.jpg. Copyright in the Public Domain.

12. Fig. 12.12. Copyright © The All-Nite Images (CC BY-SA 2.0) at https://commons.wikimedia.org/wiki/File:-BlackLivesMatter_Boycott_Fox_News_and_The_NY_Post_(15992259398).jpg.

13. Fig. 12.13. Copyright © Krassotkin (CC BY-SA 3.0) at https://commons.wikimedia.org/wiki/File:Donald_Trump_and_Hillary_Clinton_during_United_States_presidential_election_2016.jpg.

14. Fig. 12.13a. Copyright © Gage Skidmore (CC BY-SA 3.0) at https://commons.wikimedia.org/wiki/File:Donald_Trump_by_Gage_Skidmore_3.jpg.

15. Fig. 12.13b. Copyright © Gage Skidmore (CC BY-SA 2.0) at https://commons.wikimedia.org/wiki/File:Hillary_Clinton_(24037852830).jpg.

16. Fig. 12.14. "William F. 'Buffalo Bill' Cody," https://commons.wikimedia.org/wiki/File:Buffalo_Bill_Cody_by_Sarony,_c1880.jpg. Copyright in the Public Domain.

EPILOGUE

So we have come to the end of the book, but not the end of the story. I hope you have enjoyed this new approach to history; I know I have. I think it is important to offer some suggestions, since I have spent much of this book pointing out things that have gone wrong in our society. I see a connection between peace and prosperity for all. If we spend all of our time, effort, and money fighting wars, as we have especially since World War II, then we will not fully enjoy freedom and the fruits of our labors. I offer something I call Peaceful Security. My assumption is that everyone would like to live in peace, enjoy prosperity, and secure a wonderful future for their children and grandchildren, and beyond. Here are my six steps to Peaceful Security:

1. Low-voltage politics
2. Incrementalism
3. Common objectives
4. Soft power
5. Balanced security interests
6. Common development

The first step toward Peaceful Security is to tone down the harsh rhetoric. No one can think if they are too busy being angry with other people. Simply listen to the quiet voice of reason in your head and speak kindly to one another. Next, find small things to agree on. Do not waste your time initially trying to hammer out agreements on the most difficult points, get a bunch of smaller things agreed to first. Next, identify common objectives, the things you all want. You will probably find out they are the same. Fourth, use soft power. An example of this is how popular American movies are around the world. Even in countries that hate America, they love American movies. Same goes for music. The arts can cut through prejudice, hatred, and many other differences. There are other examples of soft power. The key is to rely not simply on force and intimidation. I have often found that if I simply listen and do not react to people, I learn a lot and can solve problems without conflict. Fifth, make sure everyone feels secure. If your neighbors built a 20-foot barbed wire fence around their property with minefields and machine guns and attack dogs, they might feel secure—but you will not. The last step is common development. The main source of conflict in the world is the lack of prosperity and hope. Where you have poverty, you have conflict. Hatred grows in impoverished soil. If people have their basic needs met, then they can move beyond survival mode and appreciate and love life. It seems so simple, but that is what makes it hard. Justice and peace come from rational people working very hard. Bad things happen automatically. It is not fair, but it is nevertheless true.

The former manager of the Los Angeles Dodgers said that there are three kinds of people in the world—There are those people who make things happen, those who watch things happen, and those who ask what happened? My history teaching mentor Dr. Sidney T. Mathews always said that there are two ways to go in life: the way of boredom and the way of adventure. I encourage each of you to be the person who makes things happen as you choose the path of adventure.

Joseph Stiglitz, a Nobel Prize–winning economist, has said that it is increasingly difficult for Americans to climb up the economic ladder. The United States has one of the highest levels of income inequality among developed nations. He went on to say that "the American Dream is a myth." He believes that income inequality is the result of politics and policies influenced by big business during Reagan's Conservative Revolution. Average working-class wages have stagnated while executive salaries have risen exponentially. His recommendation is to reduce the power of monopolistic big business that leads to low wages. This will take a lot of hard work from the American people to fix a system that is essentially broken.

A student of mine from West Africa shared something with me recently. He told me that in the Republic of Benin in West Africa, oral history has a very important place in society. Storytellers who carry on this oral history tradition are known as *griot*. When a *griot* from the Baatonu culture in the Republic of Benin begins to tell a story he starts with this phrase: "people make history." It is a way to thank his ancestors and to teach and inspire the people. This is a good lesson for all of us and fits nicely with how this book began.

In closing, I would like to return to the late comedian George Carlin and his sharp social and political commentary. George said, "You have owners, the big, wealthy business interests own this place. Forget the politicians; they are put there to make you think you have a choice. You don't have a choice, you have owners … and what they don't want is a population that is well informed and capable of critical thinking." He is correct in the sense that good people have to work hard to make things right. Well, that is the part where you come in, my dear reader. Even though "the table is tilted and the game is rigged," as George said, I do think you have this choice. The choice for you young Americans is simple—either continue to let the 1 percent control and dominate the political, cultural, social, spiritual, and economic life of this country, or wake up and take back your country. It is time to make history.

CPSIA information can be obtained
at www.ICGtesting.com
Printed in the USA
LVHW061911120319
610392LV00006B/7/P